clinical teaching:

methods of instruction
for the retarded

clinical teaching:
methods of instruction for the retarded

ROBERT M. SMITH
The Pennsylvania State University

McGraw-Hill Book Company
New York, St. Louis, San Francisco, Toronto, London, Sydney

clinical teaching:

methods of instruction
for the retarded

Library of Congress Catalog Card Number 68–14761
58905

1 2 3 4 5 6 7 8 9 0   M A M M   7 5 4 3 2 1 0 6 9 8

preface

In many schools, mentally retarded children are receiving an inadequate education because their teachers have failed to understand the scientific basis for educational methods. The antiquated notion which suggests that teaching is solely an art has been dispelled. An increasing body of empirical and theoretical literature has described procedures for reliably altering the behavior of children. Two threads seem particularly predominant in this literature. First, there is a clear need for teachers of the retarded to provide a highly stimulating and structured environment if skills are to be taught effectively and efficiently. Second, the components of instruction at all levels of the special-education program require clear identification and proper sequencing so that the retarded are not forced to make conceptual leaps.

v

This book, which is directed to teachers of the mentally retarded, attempts to employ a systematic theoretical position throughout so that teachers will have a stable yardstick against which behavior, development, techniques of instruction, and the course of study can be measured. In addition, effort has been made to translate and use that empirical literature which is clearly applicable to problems in teaching the mentally retarded.

The notion of clinical teaching, which is focused upon in this text, requires that teachers gain an increased sophistication in testing for and identifying those specific areas in which each child is relatively weak and strong. The child's educational program, then, is formulated on the basis of evidence, with the frequently predominant influence of the teacher minimized. This reorientation toward teaching the mentally retarded is based on **1** the clear indication that "homogeneous classes" no longer exist and that wide variation between and within children can be readily identified, **2** increased sophistication in measurement techniques which has led to the development of new and more powerful diagnostic tools, **3** the manifest need for components of subject matter to be identified and appropriately sequenced, **4** the direct applicability and relevance of the results of psychological studies to the processes of teaching and learning, and **5** the encouraging results from educational research which has demonstrated the efficacy of employing various remedial techniques with those children who manifest learning disabilities.

It is the author's hope that the material presented in this book will help the special-education teacher become a more skillful "artist" because of an increased sensitivity to those components of teaching and learning which have a clear scientific basis. The ultimate goal is that the mentally retarded become more astute problem solvers and well integrated into the community.

It is with gratitude that I acknowledge the interest, dedication, and continued assistance of those who have helped in the preparation of this document. Many of the ideas presented here are not solely the author's; they reflect an association with the excellent program at the University of Illinois, the experiences of the many special-education teachers with whom the author has had the pleasure of interacting, and the capable reactions of many colleagues, particularly Professors Stanley Deno, John Neisworth, Grayson Wheatley, and William Moody. Vita Sembiante and Cindy Yoquelet carefully and skillfully devoted a great deal of time and effort in typing various drafts of the manuscript. The author is especially grateful for the encouragement and patience of his wife, Bette, and children, David and Andrew, throughout the process.

ROBERT M. SMITH

contents

preface   *v*

one   **status of professional awareness**
in the education of the mentally retarded   *1*
The Extent of Professional Involvement   *2*
Nature of the Research Effort   *4*
The Attention of Educators to Problems
    of Mental Retardation   *7*
The Preparation of Teachers: Some Crucial
    Needs and Issues   *11*
Selected References   *12*

two   **the nature of cognitive development**   *14*
Dimensions of Intelligence   *14*
The Openness of Human Ability   *17*
Assessing Intellectual Ability   *28*
Selected References   *30*

three   **assessing individual differences**   *32*
Rationale for Concern about Individual Differences   *33*
The Significance of Inter-individual Variability   *34*
The Significance of Intra-individual Variability   *36*
Diagnosing Strengths and Weaknesses   *37*
Generalized Learning Characteristics   *40*
Selected References   *47*

four   **primary methodological concerns**   *50*
Scope and Sequence   *51*
Educational Objectives for the Retarded   *52*
Fundamental Principles of Instruction   *54*
Teaching Considerations in Areas of Frequent Weakness   *61*
Selected References   *70*

five   **perceptual-motor development:**
the foundation for subsequent learning   *71*
Sequence of Perceptual-Motor Development   *72*
Rationale for Emphasizing Perceptual-Motor Development   *74*
Hebbian Relationships   *76*
Perceptual-Motor Development of the Retarded   *79*
Assessment of Perceptual-Motor Competence   *80*
Developing Perceptual-Motor Skills   *84*
Selected References   *91*

six	**developing areas of communication**	**92**
	The Significance of Speech for Effective Verbal Communication	93
	Stages of Speech Development	96
	Speech Characteristics of the Retarded	96
	Assessment of Speech Difficulties	100
	Procedures for Correcting Speech Difficulties	103
	Language: The Primary Means for Communicating Ideas	108
	Language Characteristics of the Retarded	109
	Assessing Language Difficulties	112
	Procedures for Developing Language Skills	114
	Developing Skills in Written Communication	121
	Selected References	126
seven	**instructing in reading**	**128**
	Basic Reading Objectives	130
	Evaluating Reading Skills	130
	Procedures for Reading Instruction	142
	Selected References	160
eight	**instructing in arithmetic**	**163**
	Basic Arithmetic Objectives	164
	Evaluating Arithmetic Skills	165
	Procedures for Arithmetic Instruction	174
	Selected References	197
nine	**developing personal and social skills**	**199**
	Dimensions of Personal, Emotional, and Social Growth	201
	Methods for Teaching Social, Personal, and Emotional Skills	211
	Selected References	224
ten	**preparation for gainful employment**	**225**
	Pragmatic Considerations for Occupational Education	226
	Basis for a Successful Work-Study Program	230
	Teaching Considerations	233
	Selected References	245
eleven	**adult education for the mentally retarded and their parents**	**247**
	Dimensions of the Postschool Program	248
	Adult Education for Parents of the Mentally Retarded	253
	Selected References	259
twelve	**elements of organization and administration**	**263**
	Considerations within Classroom Units	264
	Considerations between Classroom Units	274
index		**279**

clinical teaching:

methods of instruction
for the retarded

status of professional awareness
in the education
of the mentally retarded

The decade of the 1960s has evidenced an escalation of professional involvement among disciplines concerned with problems of mental retardation. This increased interest and activity has been precipitated by (1) greater emphasis on elevating the social order and enhancing the station of those less well endowed within our society, (2) encouraging medical breakthroughs related to the condition, (3) the demonstrated cause-and-effect relationship between the nature of one's environment and the incidence of mental retardation in society, and (4) the great amount of Federal, state, and agency support in financing the research and training programs of disciplines concerned about the condition. The role of the Federal government in coordinating efforts among the various fields interested in problems of mental retardation has been substantial and has resulted in the publication of the Report of the President's Panel on Mental Retardation entitled "National Plan to Combat Mental Retardation" (1962). This report has proved to be a major stimulus for increasing professional activity in areas related to mental retardation.

THE EXTENT OF PROFESSIONAL INVOLVEMENT

Various disciplines are concerned with the problems of mental retardation. Medical specialists, including pediatricians, obstetricians, physiologists, biochemists, teratologists, and geneticists, are interested primarily with cause, or etiology, and in those aspects of the prenatal environment which are related to and perhaps causative of intellectual retardation. These specialists focus their attention on determining causes which, it is to be hoped, will lead to the control of all those mechanisms which result in an intellectually retarded individual.

In like manner, psychologists have a history of interest in working with the retarded. These specialists are concerned, basically, with assessing behavioral dimensions specific to the retarded and with comparing their behavior against other populations of individuals. Even within the general area of psychology, specialists have emerged by concentrating efforts on specific areas related to behavior such as learning, motivation, personality characteristics, and social competencies of the retarded.

Educators have focused effort on manipulating the environmental situations of retarded persons in order to foster more effective and efficient learning by them. Primary attention has been focused on altering the physical environment, considering methodological procedures, and developing curricula. Although dimensions such as etiology and psychological techniques for assessing factors of strength or particular weakness of the retarded may be of academic interest, these should not be areas of primary concern to the teacher.

Sociologists, anthropologists, lawyers, and other professionals have examined problems related to mental retardation from their own perspectives.

The accelerated interest in the study of this condition and the intense activity of professionals representing various fields has been bought at a price. Difficulty exists in the intercommunication of ideas among interested disciplines. Because of the precise and restricted nature of professional interest, scientists have been forced, by necessity, to employ definitions and use esoteric language peculiar to their own perspective. This has resulted in effective within-discipline but poor interdiscipline communication.

A major cause of poor communication among fields of interest is the relatively minimal effort exerted by investigators in translating findings from research and interpreting these results for scientists from other fields. Some effort has been made by Federal agencies and professional organizations to facilitate communication through support of interdisciplinary conferences and large research and development centers, wherein, for example, a medical school and college of education look at mutual problems with a team approach.

Finally, difficulty in the communication of ideas among specialists is due, in large measure, to the lack of a generally accepted, systematic theoretical position. For example, to explain mental retardation from a psychological or physiological frame of reference is often theoretically incompatible with the views of educators or sociologists.

Although these communication difficulties exist among the different fields, it should be emphasized that their basic scientific goals are quite compatible and, in fact, are similar. Three basic objectives characterize any scientific inquiry—including those fields concerned with mental retardation. The first level objective is to *describe* phenomena and to relate other variables which may exert significant influence on their manifestation. The second scientific objective is to *predict* the occurrence of the phenomena. Admittedly, some overlap exists between these two stages of inquiry; however, accurate prediction is dependent on adequate description. The final goal of scientific investigation is to *control*. In order to effectively control a condition (etiology from the perspective of medicine and behavior from the point of view of educators), the condition must be describable and its occurrence accurately predictable.

Each stage of scientific inquiry can be viewed either in a global or in a specific manner. For example, a teacher can be concerned with describing, predicting, and controlling the total environmental situation of educable retarded children in her class in order to effect adequate social, personal, and intellectual development. This would involve a global attack on areas of concern. Simultaneously, the teacher may be concerned with describing, predicting, and controlling a very specific type of atypical classroom behavior of one child which occurs under certain, rather specific, circumstances. This behavior may be antagonistic to the general goals of the educational program and to effective learning on the part of the child.

Disciplines concerned with the study of mental retardation attack problems similarly, in the same relatively sequential fashion, and with the same goal in mind—control of the phenomena. When characteristics of conditions such as retardation are stable and occur under the same circumstances, in the same fashion, and to the same degree on each occurrence, the goals of describing, predicting, and controlling the condition can be realized relatively quickly. Mental retardation is not a unitary entity; it is characterized by many variations and nuances. For example, certain behavior may be related to intellectual retardation with one group of subjects and not with another. Substantial variation exists among the retarded in the degree of subnormality, primary etiological factors, appropriate habilitation practices, and prognosis for success as adults.

Because of the multifaceted and heterogeneous nature of the condition, it must be realized that no *one* population of mentally retarded individuals exists. In fact, retardation is represented by a number of unique populations each of which may differ in characteristics which in themselves are of different magnitudes of significance to each discipline. Because of this heterogeneity, scientists have had great difficulty proceeding beyond the level of description. A group of characteristics typical of a particular population of retarded persons may not be descriptive of other retarded populations, although the same degree of intellectual subnormality could be exhibited. There is great difficulty, therefore, in generalizing results of scientific observation. Moreover, scientific work in disciplines investigating mental retardation is proceeding at different speeds through the three levels of scientific inquiry.

NATURE OF THE RESEARCH EFFORT

Heretofore, research activity related to mental retardation can be characterized as being more basic than applied. Research dealing with biochemical correlates of the condition, specific psychological characteristics of the retarded, and the type and degree of anatomical deviations from the normal illustrates the past focus of study. Less interest has been shown in conducting *in situ* types of experimentations most of which have direct and obvious applicability to management of the retarded.

Moreover, the traditional research emphasis in this field has been molecular rather than molar in character. Investigators have chosen to study small, well-defined problems and not large, general areas of concern. For example, substantial effort has been given to investigating discrimination learning or other specific factors of cognition. Fewer studies have considered more global concerns, such as the efficacy in placing certain groups of retarded persons in an unique environment which theoretically should influence behavior and performance in specified areas of functioning. The laboratory approach characterizes the former technique; an *in situ* strategy describes the latter.

Aside from the fact that much of the research has come from medicine and allied fields such as physiology, biochemistry, and psychology, there are specific reasons why past research efforts are molecular and basic. Fundamentally, these are the result of certain research methodological considerations.

Scientists have been concerned about the heterogeneous nature of the retarded. To generalize findings from a specific sample of subjects to all groups of mentally retarded is, indeed, hazardous. Fortunately, in the early stages of research, investigators have exercised caution by identifying research problems which could be finely delineated and by using subjects whose characteristics are readily descriptive and who represented a large population of the retarded. The collection of a substantial number of studies on specific topics allows for their synthesis and the observation of common threads. This provides movement toward a more global or molar attack characteristic of *in situ* research.

A word should be said concerning sampling difficulties. Locating an adequate sample of subjects for study is a particularly difficult problem because of the relatively small incidence of mentally retarded subjects in the population and the variability in their characteristics. Sampling bias may occur frequently because of nonrepresentation. For example, in a study designed to assess a specific reading characteristic, such as comprehension, among environmentally deprived retarded children, it may be desirable to exclude children with minimal neurological involvement since comprehension could be related to the variable being studied for that group and not for non-organically involved children. To include subjects from both groups might obliterate significant findings that would have been evident if the groups had been studied independently. Researchers, therefore, must identify homogeneous groups for study and identify other variables which could actively influence factors being studied.

To further complicate the research effort, in addition to cognition, other dimensions influence the performance and behavior of the mentally retarded. For example, the social milieu in which individuals are reared influences patterns of behavior and styles of living. The retarded are no less influenced by the dynamic nature of social expectations and pressures. Indeed, one might speculate that they are more vulnerable to social pressures and at the same time less adept at effectively responding to such demands. The consequences of this inadequacy are likely to be felt in other areas of life, such as emotional development and mental health. Moreover, the range of characteristics of the various social situations among retarded children makes it difficult to control these potentially important variables. The researcher, therefore, must give careful consideration to such dimensions.

Because research with the mentally retarded offers opportunities for exploring new aspects of the condition, there have been relatively few attempts at replicating other studies. This presents a problem for those interested in making use of research findings. A basic requirement of research is that findings be reliable. One would hesitate to alter an existing program on the basis of a single, circumscribed research report, irrespective of how dramatic the findings. The safe strategy is to adhere to the status quo. Because of this legitimate hesitation of educators to change programs without adequate documentation and because of the minimal effort exerted by researchers to interpret and translate findings into practical considerations, much of the research in mental retardation has not become part of the general habilitative program.

The history of research in mental retardation, moreover, has shown a hesitancy on the part of investigators to explore areas potentially unfruitful. If an investigator reports findings which are not significant, few would be inclined to replicate the experiment unless there were obvious gross errors committed. This is an unfortunate fact of life since chance alone could account for nonsignificant findings when, in fact, a significant difference may exist.

To illustrate, assume that a certain theory suggests that technique A will foster more rapid learning than technique B with educable mentally retarded children. When tested, this difference was not observed. Typically, this research is duly reported, filed, and most often lost in the archives. Even assuming an appropriate research method and design, chance alone could result in treatment A not being significantly superior to treatment B. Such studies are rarely replicated because investigators are hesitant to study areas which have been relatively unproductive in the past. Therefore, the possibility of a research breakthrough could be stymied. This situation is not peculiar to research efforts in mental retardation; indeed, it is characteristic of other large unexplored territories.

Studies in the behavioral sciences are often characterized by relating many variables to one another. Correlational analysis is the statistical technique most frequently used. This approach makes possible the study of the degree of relationship which exists between variables and is often employed in research with the mentally retarded. An investigator who wishes to correlate social class with mental retardation may observe a moderately high relationship between these two variables, perhaps on the order of .60 to .75. It is possible to relate any number of variables. For example, hair color, number of push-ups, size of the right foot, and intellectual ability could be correlated. We cannot assume that one variable causes the occurrence of another simply because a high relationship among variables was observed. Obviously, the color of one's hair or the size of a right foot does not cause intellectual subnormality. Factors characteristic of one's social class, however, may influence to some extent the intellectual ability of an individual. The fact that *correlation does not necessarily mean causation* is important and should be kept in mind in reviewing results of research.

It was stated earlier that research in mental retardation has been primarily basic. Increased financial support has not only escalated basic research in mental retardation, but it has caused a definite trend toward more applied research. Research and development centers are being established to study the educational problems of retarded children in a more global fashion. Dissemination of research results is another major objective of these centers. These trends will result in more attention being given to the interpretation and translation of research for those working directly with the mentally retarded. Findings from studies will be applied to classroom problems much more rapidly. This, then, will lead to an increase in applied *in situ* studies which test out habilitation procedures under existing conditions.

THE ATTENTION OF EDUCATORS
TO PROBLEMS OF MENTAL RETARDATION

Historical overview

The first systematic attempts at training and educating the mentally retarded began during the late 1700s and were primarily the result of · attention by physicians. The focus of their educational procedures dealt with techniques for training the senses. Training of the retarded began initially in France with the early attempts to provide systematic instruction located in institutions for the blind and in institutions for the deaf.

Itard is considered to have conducted the first systematic training program by attempting to educate Victor, the wild boy of Averyon.[1] Although Victor had been diagnosed as an "incurable idiot," Itard provided him with a program which was designed to:

1 *Create an interest in the social life as opposed to the nomadic, vagabond existence to which he was accustomed*
2 *Produce refinement in understanding the significance of sensory experiences by exciting those organs concerned with sensation*
3 *Encourage speech development through imitation by making vocal communication necessary*
4 *Expand his world of social experiences and create a breadth of desires and wants*
5 *Encourage Victor to use simple mental operations to satisfy his physical needs*

For more than five years Itard worked with Victor, systematically and continually, attempting to lead the boy from the life of a savage to that of a civilized person. The program terminated when Victor left in a rage. Itard perceived his efforts as being in vain and reported his

[1] For a description of Victor's characteristics and Itard's report of the educational program, see Itard, 1962, as translated.

findings in general publications and in a report addressed to the Minister of Interior.

The French Academy of Science, however, acknowledged the effort Itard had made in training Victor by recognizing the substantial contributions he had made to education. Perhaps one of the most educationally significant points made by the Academy was to remind Itard that it was most appropriate that Victor be compared only with himself by measuring his degree of growth. This may have been the first instance in which the educational value of intra-individual assessment was emphasized.

Itard's influence in the education of retarded children, and the subsequent statement by the French Academy of Science, was quickly felt elsewhere. Itard was Séguin's teacher and influenced many others, including Madame Montessori, who developed self-instructional teaching devices,

Based primarily on the work of Itard, Séguin viewed the possibility of educating the mentally retarded in a more optimistic light than was characteristic of many during the middle 1800s. At the age of twenty-five, Séguin endeavored to train an idiot boy to use his senses more effectively. After eighteen months of training, the child had made substantial progress in cognitive and communication activities. The significance of the event was acknowledged by professional and lay people interested in the retarded, and Séguin began using his training procedures with a larger number of retarded children. His classic book, published in 1866, described his procedures. Doll has characterized these methods as involving ". . . orderly sequences from passive to active, from sensation to perception, from gross to the refined, from known to the unknown, from observation to comparison, from attention to imitation, and from patterned activity to spontaneity." [2]

Paralleling present-day thinking, Séguin emphasized the need to teach in context, utilizing actual life situations as the basis for instruction. These, it was hoped, would assist the retarded child to develop a conceptual understanding instead of rote. The need to vary the mode of presentation and to help the children associate perceptions from various sense modalities was emphasized in his program. Although Séguin stressed sensation, he was conscious of the need to provide the retarded with opportunities to develop social skills through group play and for the teacher to exhibit concern for moral development of the child.

The similarity between the basic tenets of Séguin's method and contemporary thinking by educators is striking. Without empirical

---

[2] Eugene E. Doll, "A Historical Survey of Research and Management of Mental Retardation in the United States," in Trapp and Himelstein (eds.), *Readings on the Exceptional Child*, Appleton-Century-Crofts, Inc., New York, 1962, p. 27 (used with permission).

data to support his techniques, Séguin was aware of the need for the teacher to use fundamental principles of learning in the instructional program. For example, he suggested actively involving the child, assisting him in observing relationships and associating incoming stimuli with the existing repertoire, helping him to develop skills related to socialization, and teaching for a conceptual instead of rote understanding. All these suggestions, although consistent with contemporary thinking, originated with Séguin. There is no doubt that his work has had substantial impact on education generally, although his notoriety outside of special education circles has not been consistent with his contributions.

The training procedures developed by Séguin were elaborated upon by Maria Montessori, an Italian physician. Her techniques, emphasizing self-teaching on the part of the child through the manipulation of materials, were developed primarily for children in residential schools. European schools have employed her techniques and materials much more than have American schools. Basic to her procedures was the feeling that children should (1) proceed at their own rates, (2) be exposed to a flexible program which capitalized on the spontaneous interest inherent in young children, (3) be provided with a learning situation and environment which was fun and pleasurable, (4) be given opportunities for repetition to the extent desired by the individual child, and (5) make use of the environment for self-improvement. There has been a recent revival of interest in the Montessori procedures in America. Montessori schools have been established to train teachers and to provide preschool instruction, in most instances, to children who show potential as being intellectually bright.

Various points of view concerning the education and training of the mentally retarded were expressed during the early and middle 1900s. During this time there had been a gradual shifting from a physiological orientation to a more psychosocial emphasis. Descoeudres (1928) emphasized the Dewey concept of "learning by doing"; Duncan (1943) encouraged enhancing relative weaknesses in verbal areas by assisting children to relate nonverbal (manual) abilities to academic areas using a project technique; and Inskeep (1926) suggested modifying the regular school program by teaching retarded children fewer skills, presenting them with less complicated materials of instruction, and gauging instruction at a lower level.

Contemporary educational trends

Beyond the middle 1950s, educational practices employed with the retarded have been based primarily on evidence from fields other than education. Psychology, for example, because of the basic nature of the research, has provided direction for educational practices.

Unfortunately, as stated earlier, most of the basic research applicable to education has not been interpreted or translated into procedures relevant to effective classroom instruction. Many of the specific methodological procedures employed in classes for the educable retarded, therefore, have been based on broad generalizations appropriate to almost all school children and on a commonsense interpretation of their potential educational significance. There has been a trend, however, toward more applied educational research with the retarded.

Research effort by special educators has been devoted largely to studying administrative plans and curricular considerations for the retarded. The pros and cons of including special classes in regular schools versus having comprehensive special schools have been the subject of frequent discussions at professional meetings and in the literature, although empirical resolution has not been forthcoming. Some people have suggested that a systematic investigation of curricular problems of the retarded would be a more fruitful area for study.

The course of study, indeed, is an extremely vital dimension to be considered. The need for the systematic sequencing of instruction and the identification of reasonable program scope is basic to achieving the goals of education. The development of curriculum guides has been based on two considerations, (1) the unique characteristics the children exhibit and (2) their predicted level of accomplishment in social, personal, and occupational areas.

Although the curriculum and administrative plans are important concerns, most educators would agree that methods of instruction, or what the teacher does in the classroom, are basic to effective and efficient teaching and learning. The inherent difficulties in studying the teaching and learning processes and the slowness in interpreting and translating basic research into clear and manageable educational constructs have resulted in little research attention being given to investigating methodological considerations. It is clear, however, that a single "cookbook" approach for teaching the retarded will not work.

Concern among educators for clearer direction in appropriate teaching strategies from research has resulted in more effort being given to defining significant idiosyncratic characteristics of the various groups of retarded children. Essentially, this effort is caused by the variety of populations represented and the high incidence of multiple disability among retarded children. Attention to individual differences among the retarded with learning difficulties is needed if effective educational practices are to be provided. This belief among educators has led to the development of new, more sensitive diagnostic instruments.

THE PREPARATION OF TEACHERS:
SOME CRUCIAL NEEDS AND ISSUES

Because of the unique learning characteristics of the retarded and the substantial alteration required in the basic objectives of the school program, it is necessary for a teacher to receive special clinical and remedial preparation. Moreover, it would seem desirable that the special-education teacher exhibit certain personal traits. In addition to those traits desired of a good teacher of intellectually normal children which result in a classroom environment conducive to effective learning, a teacher of the mentally retarded must be satisfied with demonstrations of minimal change by the children. The retarded, obviously, will learn at a rate substantially slower than intellectually normal children. Not only will it take longer for them to learn a concept or fact, but a lesson will need to be repeated several times, in a variety of ways, and using many sense modalities. Children will forget quickly, and the teacher will need to review and repeat material. Many teachers find this situation difficult to tolerate, perhaps because of a personal need to see dramatic changes in behavior and intellectual growth on the part of the students. To press students for a performance beyond their present level of capabilities because of a desire to see more dramatic change is inconsistent with good teaching strategy for the retarded.

Flexibility is a second important characteristic for teachers of the retarded. Teachers must be able to switch quickly from one method of instruction to another when a child exhibits difficulty in learning a concept. Frequently, it is necessary to abandon a lesson plan and return to the student's earlier level of skill development when it is obvious that more work is needed in a necessary foundation area. Not to adapt instruction spontaneously will result in ineffective teaching and the development of negative feelings toward the total school program.

Universities and colleges are constantly faced with the problem of deciding what constitutes adequate preparation for teaching retarded children. Without listing specific courses, adequate preparation for teachers of the retarded might include the following types of experiences and understandings:

1 *A stable and comprehensive philosophical point of view should be developed which considers, among other things, individual variation, the value of the individual, the place of the retarded in society, reasonable goals and expectations in training and educating the retarded, and the relationship between conceptual and rote understanding by the child.*

2 *The teacher needs to have a firm understanding of appropriate ob-*

jectives and goals which are sensitive to the common characteristics of the various populations of retarded as well as to the unique characteristics of each retarded child. A sensitivity to and a concern for educationally significant individual differences should be focused upon in teacher-education programs.

3 Teachers of the retarded should have a complete understanding of some basic theoretical position against which classroom practices and techniques can be evaluated. The theory chosen should be sufficiently broad in scope to include areas in addition to cognitive development. Further, the theory should provide direction concerning appropriate sequencing of activities and those foundation skills basic to efficient and effective learning.

4 Teachers of the mentally retarded should have some sensitivity to and minimal skill in elementary and informal educational diagnostic procedures appropriate to the classroom. The teacher must constantly assess a child's performance and alter the mode of instruction, materials, and curriculum according to each child's pattern of strengths and weaknesses.

5 Since the teacher of the retarded is interested in manipulating a child's environment in order to provide the most propitious conditions for learning, there is needed, first, an awareness of what constitutes an ideal environment for learning and, second, an understanding of techniques available for effecting such environmental conditions. It is possible to view this manipulation of the child's environment from a general perspective (e.g., the total special-class environment) as well as in terms of a specific technique for organizing materials and the instructional strategy for teaching, for example, discrimination among shapes.

6 Teachers should be provided with an opportunity to develop basic skills in interpreting and translating research findings from various disciplines into practical classroom activities.

SELECTED REFERENCES

Descoeudres, Alice: The Education of Mentally Defective Children, D. C. Heath and Company, Boston, 1928.

Doll, Eugene E.: "A Historical Survey of Research and Management of Mental Retardation in the United States," in Trapp and Himelstein (eds.), Readings on the Exceptional Child, Appleton-Century-Crofts, Inc., New York, 1962, p. 27.

Duncan, John: Education of the Ordinary Child, The Ronald Press Company, New York, 1943.

Inskeep, Annie L.: Teaching Dull and Retarded Children, The Macmillan Company, New York, 1926.

Itard, Jean-Marc-Gaspard: *The Wild Boy of Aveyron,* translated by George and Muriel Humphrey, Appleton-Century-Crofts, Inc., New York, 1962.

President's Panel on Mental Retardation: *A Proposed Program for National Action to Combat Mental Retardation,* Government Printing Office, Washington, D.C., 1962.

the nature of cognitive development

This chapter surveys certain major factors related to cognitive development. This area is of special significance in the study of mental retardation. Irrespective of the definition of the condition to which one would subscribe or the degree of disability among subjects, all populations of the mentally retarded exhibit relative weakness in cognitive development. This is a primary characteristic of these people and exerts an influence on other areas of behavior. The student interested in education of the mentally retarded should understand the central concepts related to the development and assessment of cognitive abilities.

DIMENSIONS OF INTELLIGENCE

To study mankind, his society, feelings, motives, and achievements, one must be primarily concerned with investigating the nature of man's intellect. It is relatively simple to describe, predict, and control phenomena which are manifestations of the physical world. More difficult for man is the study of himself, particularly a basic aspect of his personality—the intellect. Only within the last sixty-five years has man described the factors of intellect in any scientific way. The other basic objectives of a science, to predict and to control, have not been scientifically considered to the same degree because of the major problems of identifying, measuring, and quantifying mental attributes.

Early schools of thought

Late in the 1890s investigations concerned with understanding the nature of intelligence moved from philosophical to empirical explanations. The scientific developments precipitating this change of strategy include the improvement of research methods and tools for explaining and measuring behavior. Of equal significance was the movement toward emphasizing individual differences.

One early approach to explaining intelligence, since repudiated, was called *faculty theory*. Intelligence was conceived as a number of abilities located in specific areas of the brain. It was thought that bumps on the head presented an external manifestation of intelligence and that mental abilities could be evaluated by a trained observer "reading" the bumps.

Binet, a French psychologist, devised one of the first intelligence scales in 1905. He believed that intelligence is expressed as a combined mental operation in which processes operate as a unified whole. Binet's idea of mental age evolved from his adoption of the concept of developmental tasks and levels and the idea that children of certain ages are capable of specific types of tasks increasing in complexity with advancing years. Binet collected a number of simple tasks, found the average at which a large group of children could accomplish each task, and placed them in order of difficulty according to age. The performance data collected on children at different age levels allowed Binet to develop reference points for purposes of comparing responses by other children to the various tasks. His scale emphasized verbal factors of intelligence.

The Binet Scale seemed to be appropriately useful with retarded children. Others have adapted this scale for specific purposes. In America, Terman revised the Binet Scale, and it was published in 1916 as the Stanford-Binet Intelligence Scale. Subsequent revisions were done in 1937 and 1960.

In the early 1900s Spearman (1923) devised a two-factor theory of intelligence. His belief was that intelligence is composed of a general ability and certain specific abilities. Thurstone (1926) expanded this two-factor theory by suggesting that a group of factors, termed *primary mental abilities*, more accurately described intelligence. The abilities he identified were number, spatial, memory, verbal, word fluency, and reasoning.

Structure of intellect model

Continued advances in testing theory and statistics allowed for the further development of models to explain the nature of intelligence. Guilford (1956) proposed a structure of intellect which is similar in concept to the periodic table of elements. He hypothesized 120 possible factors of intelligence, 80 of which have been identified with a specific test developed to evaluate each factor. Research activity soon began in an attempt to develop tests for the other factors postulated as elements of intelligence. One of these tests and the factors of intellect which it evaluates is given for illustrative purposes.

To measure the factor of ideational fluency, or the production of many ideas in which freedom of expression is encouraged and quality is of no concern, the Unusual Uses Test is often used. The subject is asked to list as many ways as he can think of to use a common object, e.g., a brick. After four minutes, the number of uses listed by the subject, without counting repeats, constitutes a fluency score.

Spontaneous flexibility is another factor which Guilford identified. This factor can also be evaluated with the Unusual Uses Test. Each response by the subject is assigned a category. For the "brick question," categories such as construction, paving, weapon, tool, recreation, and decoration are used. A tabulation is made of the number of "shifts" or category changes observed between adjacent responses as the scorer proceeds through the list in the same order as they were written by the subject. An illustration of the scoring of spontaneous flexibility is presented on page 16.

The links between category codes indicate the shifts. Subjects A and B had equal fluency scores, but subject B had a higher flexibility score than subject A.

This represents only one of many tests Guilford and his associates have developed to measure factors of intelligence. The tests, their scoring systems, and the dimensions which each evaluates have been described elsewhere.[1]

After this historic presentation, it soon became obvious that tests such as the revised Stanford-Binet Intelligence Scale and the Wechsler Intelligence Scale for Children (WISC) were sampling only a small group of intellectual abilities, perhaps as little as 25 percent of the factors postulated by Guilford. For example, factors such as

[1] For a comprehensive review of Guilford's model and the tests which have been designed to assess the various factors of intellect, the reader is referred to Guilford, Kettner, and Christensen (1954), or Guilford (1959).

SUBJECT A

Response number	Category code
1	4
	)
2	1
3	1
	)
4	2
5	2
6	2
7	2
Fluency	7
Flexibility	2

SUBJECT B

Response number	Category code
1	2
	)
2	1
	)
3	2
	)
4	1
	)
5	2
	)
6	4
	)
7	2
Fluency	7
Flexibility	6

verbal fluency, flexibility, originality, and elaboration are not evaluated using the standard intelligence tests.

Although some psychologists have criticized the Structure of Intellect Model proposed by Guilford, it has acted as a primary stimulus for new research ideas on the nature and development of cognition. The Structure of Intellect Model has resulted in scientists looking at intelligence as a multifaceted phenomenon.

THE OPENNESS OF HUMAN ABILITY

At the turn of the century a major controversy arose between those who considered intellect dependent on heredity and those who believed that the environment was the most significant determinant of one's intellectual status. This controversy paralleled the development of theories attempting to explain the nature of intelligence. The advocates of fixed intelligence through genetic transmission and the environmentalists justified their respective positions with evidence which often was biased or incompletely analyzed. For example, the hereditarians recalled that men of distinction in Great Britain came from a small group of families. They tended to overlook the fact that these gifted people lived in a peculiarly stimulating environment.

The report of the Kallikaks by Goddard (1913) was cited by this group as evidence of the predominant influence of the genes on intelligence. This study compared the descendants of an illicit union of

Martin Kallikak with those who were descendants of his lawful wife. More social degenerates and mentally deficient persons were found to be descendants of the illicit union than from the lawful marriage. The conclusion reached was that the difference was due to heredity. Again, Goddard did not indicate the inferior nature of the environment associated with the illegitimate family.

The environmentalists, too, had difficulty explaining their position concerning intellectual development. Studies that compared the performance of children who were given early practice on tasks with those who were unpracticed indicated that the latter group caught up after very little practice (Shirley, 1931). Observation suggested that behavioral development, like somatic development, seemed to follow a predetermined course (Coghill, 1929). The environmentalists attacked this dissonant evidence presented by the hereditarians by indicating the uncontrolled nature of the studies cited. They countered with other evidence which showed that deprivation of experience decreased the *rate* of behavioral development in *infant* organisms. Research by the environmentally oriented scientists emphasized that the age at which the organism was deprived was of significance.

Genetic and environmental interaction

Even now the specific influences of the environment and the genes are unknown, although studies using animals and human beings as subjects are providing results which are leading gradually to clarification of this issue. It is apparent that intellectual ability is not the result of genetic inheritance nor of the environment alone. The fact that some type of interaction occurs which leads to a certain level of cognitive development is no longer in dispute.

Dobzhansky (1955) has conceptualized the hypothesized relationship between an individual's inherited characteristics (genotype) and degree of environmental favorableness. Accordingly, a person's genetic endowment establishes a range within which behavior (in this instance, intelligence) develops. The specific pattern of behavior an individual develops within this hypothesized range is dependent on the degree of restrictiveness of the environment. The observable results from the interaction between a certain genotype and a specific environment is called *phenotype*.

Gottesman (1963) has schematized these hypothesized relationships according to Dobzhansky's conceptualization. Figure 2-1 presents the components of this schema. From this diagram it is apparent that those with poor genetic endowment (Genotype A) have the potential for effecting less reaction to environmental stimuli (whether favorable or deprived) than those who have been blessed with more ideal genetic components (Genotypes C and D).

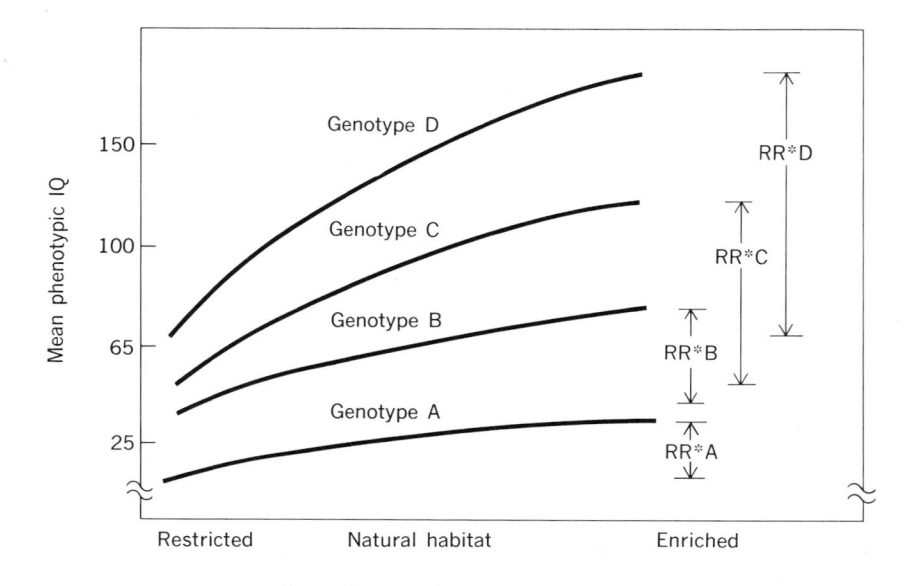

FIGURE 2-1 *Concept of reaction range; four hypothesized genotypes.* **(From:** Handbook of Mental Deficiency. **Edited by N. R. Ellis. Copyright © 1963 by McGraw-Hill Book Company. Reprinted by permission of McGraw-Hill Book Company.)**

Specifically, children represented by Genotype A might well be described as trainable-level children, such as those with phenylketonuria, whose etiology is genetic, as distinguished from some type of intrauterine environmental complication. The average IQ of children living in a normal environment could be expected to be approximately 25 or 30. In a restricted environment or in an enriched circumstance, a minimal amount of positive or negative deviation could be expected. The restricting nature of the genotype does not allow for dramatic differences in phenotypic expression, and thus, the range and standard deviation on intelligence tests for these subjects is typically small.

The components of inheritance for children represented by Genotype B are more favorable than for children with Genotype A in that the former group has the potential for more substantial change to occur, according to the favorableness of their environment. Not only is the phenotypic expression of intelligence greater for B than A, but the possible reaction range resulting from association with a highly deprived or enriched environment is wider for the more favorably endowed group.

The curve for Genotype C represents a group of persons whose average IQ under typical circumstances is 100. Notice that the possible range in the phenotypic expression of intelligence is approximately between 65 and 125, depending on the type of environment. Empirical evidence from preschool programs and the placement of children in an orphanage or foster home while siblings remain in a more deprived environment supports this hypothesized reaction range.

Finally, children with the most favorable genetic endowment (Genotype *D*) exhibit the widest possible range for reacting to various environmental situations.

The hypothesized cause-and-effect relationship which exists between inheritance and the type of environment with which an individual is associated is subtle and not completely understood. Although genetic transmission is important, with research beginning to point to the possibility of eventually controlling heredity by manipulating DNA and RNA molecules, it is essentially irrelevant to the major concerns of education. Thus, the teacher's concern should be with manipulating the child's environment to maximize genotypic potential.

Fewer children are retarded because of inadequate inheritance than are retarded because of some type of environmental difficulty, whether it occurs prenatally, at the time of birth, or during the postnatal period. Behavioral scientists have focused their research attention on the postnatal period. By attempting to control genetic components and manipulating the environment in various ways, researchers have provided evidence concerning the learning characteristics of organisms reared in different environments. For example, by employing animals from similar genetic stock, it is possible to investigate the influence of various types of environments on mental ability.

Hebb (1949) found by blinding rats at infancy and comparing their performance on an "intelligence test" with littermates who were blinded later that the latter group made fewer errors. This result suggested that the extra experience gained from being blinded later facilitated "mental" development. In another experiment (Hebb, 1949) some rats were raised as pets while their littermates were cage-reared. The rats reared as pets performed in a significantly superior manner to cage-reared rats on the Hebb-Williams Intelligence Test. Moreover, they profited more from continued training, which was concomitantly received by the cage-reared animals, suggesting that the richer early experiences of the pet group facilitated later learnings.

It is becoming clear from the results of such studies, that intelligence is plastic and that it is not totally fixed nor predetermined. Animals that are exposed to certain stimulating experiences at specific periods of life perform at a higher level on various intellectual and social dimensions than do their nonstimulated but genetically similar counterparts.

Physiological correlates of environmental manipulation

Not only does it appear that certain stimulation will elevate the rate of mental development in organisms, but there is evidence suggesting that an alteration in brain chemistry of stimulated or deprived animals will occur as a result of the environment. Rosenzweig, Krech, Bennett, and Diamond (1961) have reported results of an interesting series of experiments in which they have explored relationships between learning, environment, brain biochemistry, and heredity. Figure 2-2 describes the general design of these experiments.

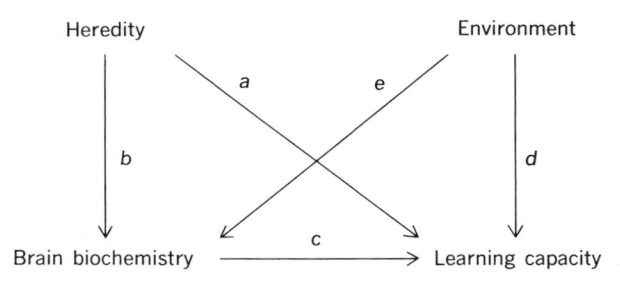

FIGURE 2-2 Schematic design of variables studied by Rosenzweig. (From: M. R. Rosenzweig, "Heredity, Environment, Brain Biochemistry, and Learning," in Current
Trends in Psychological Theory. Pittsburgh: The University of Pittsburgh Press, 1961. Reprinted by permission
of The University of Pittsburgh Press.)

Their experiments can be divided into two major groups: (1) those designed to study the relationships among heredity, brain biochemistry, and learning capacity, and (2) those concerned with the study of relationships among environment, brain biochemistry, and learning capacity. The results of their series of studies have implications for teaching the retarded.

In studying the genetic determinants of learning capacity, the scientists used two strains of rats. One group was selectively bred for their maze brightness and the other group for their maze dullness. Genetically smart and genetically dull rats were sacrificed and their neural structures examined. The genetically smart rats showed a significantly greater amount of activity in certain neural enzymes known to foster cortical transmission than did the genetically dull rats. In addition, the genetically smart rats performed more adequately on a series of maze tests than did the genetically dull strain. The conclusion reached was that heredity not only determines learning capacity but also is related to neurophysiological function.

The second series of experiments was concerned with environment, brain biochemistry, and learning capacity. Controlling genetic strains, a group of rats was placed in a stimulating environment. Their littermates were reared alone in small, bare cages. The stimulated group was raised in large cages with peers and had a different set of toys available for play each day. The stimulated rats proved superior at problem solving, and when their brains were analyzed, the cortex of these animals proved to be heavier than those of their isolated littermates. Moreover, a more optimum balance between neural enzymes was observed in the privileged than in the deprived rats. This is one of the first reports indicating that a propitious environment, which allows the organism to experience a variety of stimuli, will not only increase learning activity but also alter brain chemistry. The implications of these findings for education are worth considering.

Early intervention

Although physiological differences cannot be evaluated, there does appear to be significant variation between the intellectual levels of children who have experienced *early* stimulation experiences compared with their counterparts who have not received such stimulation. For example, Kirk (1958) studied children who were removed from a deprived environmental setting and given *preschool* experiences and/ or foster-home placement. Significant increases were observed in their rate of intellectual development when compared with sibling controls who had remained in the home and/or did not receive the preschool experience. In fact, this research reports that children who were left in the deprived environment remained at their initially tested level and in some cases, tended to decrease to lower levels of intellectual functioning. This study followed the earlier work of Skeels, Dye, Wellman, and Skodak and essentially supported their findings.[2]

In light of these considerations, it is of basic concern that psychology and education attempt to determine the type of environment(s) which will either facilitate or inhibit intellectual development. Similarly, educators and other behavioral scientists need to better understand the most opportune period in a child's life for stimulating this potential increase in mental ability. The research is not clear on either of these points; it appears, however, to be much more difficult to alter the path of mental functioning in children who have been placed in a stimulating situation after age eight or nine, than in preschool youngsters. It is not clear which of the many specific factors of intellect are being influenced by altering the child's environment, nor is it known whether specific physiological alterations are occurring in the child's neural structures.

In the absence of specific answers to these questions from

[2] For example, see Skeels and Dye (1939), and Wellman (1940).

research, the scientist must always depend on theoretical explanations for direction. Since the teacher is concerned with manipulating a child's environment to maximize intellectual potential, it is necessary that he understand some broad systematic explanation of mental development.

Hebb's theory of mental development

In explaining his position concerning cognitive development, Hebb (1949) differentiates between innate potential in the development of intellectual functioning (Intelligence A) and the functional or measurable level (Intelligence B). Intelligence A cannot be measured since it is a manifestation of dimensions such as the quality and robustness of brain functioning, one's genetic contributions, and other components quite apart from the experiential determinants of intellect. On the other hand, Intelligence B is more measurable and, although perhaps a rough estimate of Intelligence A, basically dependent on the nature of an individual's environment and the degree of variety of experiences the organism has encountered.

Hebb has suggested that the ratio between the amount of neural tissue concerned with the function of association and the amount concerned with sensory input and output determines the potential of an organism for learning. Presumably, organisms with a higher association/sensory ratio can develop more complex networks of association at maturity. Organisms lower on the phylogenetic scale, with lower ratios between the association and sensory areas, have progressively less ability and skill for more complex learning. For example, although an elephant has more neural weight than a man, the elephant's A/S ratio is substantially smaller.

Although more complex relationships can be learned by species with high A/S ratios, simple relationships can be learned as rapidly by lower as by higher species. For the more phylogenetically advanced organism, first learning is slower than in lower species. Consider, for example, the speed of motor learning in the newborn calf in contrast to that of higher species.

PERCEPTION OF EVENTS Basic to Hebb's theory is the notion that an organism experiences a variety of perceptions related to an event. As this myriad of perceptual experiences associated with an event is repeated, a network of neural cells fires as a unit. Eventually, as the organism experiences this event on repeated occasions, and the associated combination of perceptions related thereto, the stimulated neural cells begin to establish a closed system in which firing continues after the stimuli have ceased. Cell assemblies of single stimulated neurons become established in the course of repeated excitation.

As these perceptual acts are repeated, the intercellular bonds become strengthened and lead the assembly to function as a unit. The assumption is made that whenever an impulse crosses a synapse, subsequent transmission between these neurons is easier. If this synapse cross occurs frequently enough, a physiological alteration at the synapse is effected either as an anatomical growth (*synaptic knob* in Hebb's terms) or as a metabolic change.

Presumably a given cell assembly consists of numerous neurons widely dispersed over a large portion of the brain. This apparently accounts for the finding that lesions in adults, resulting from some type of trauma, often do not destroy abilities; whereas, in young children who have not developed these complex associational networks, cortical lesions are much more permanently damaging.

As experience proceeds in time and sequence, cell assemblies become associated with each other and form an exceedingly more complex associational pattern, which Hebb labels as *phase sequences*. Thus, a large and extensive associational network becomes established around several related events, each of which has idiosyncratic as well as similar and shared perceptions.

To illustrate, suppose you were involved in the event of cooking a steak over a charcoal fire in your backyard. Associated with this event are a variety of perceptions of an auditory, visual, tactual, and olfactory nature. In each of these areas a variety of rather discrete perceptual events can be experienced. For example, you would not only hear the fire, but also receive the auditory perceptions of steak sizzling, the metal of the burner expanding and contracting, and the admonishments of your guests to be sure that their steak is either rare or well done. Similarly, a variety of rather discrete perceptions in the other areas would be evidenced.

As these perceptual experiences occur over and over every time you charcoal steaks, they tend to become associated with one another. These perceptions are transmitted to various neurons resulting in an associational network eventually being established. Following the establishment of this cell assembly, the reception of one or more of the perceptual experiences, such as *smelling* a sizzling steak, immediately results in the total cell assembly firing. Simply smelling a steak, without having received other associated percepts, will result immediately in an image being established around the event of cooking a steak. Figure 2-3 diagrams the hypothetical interaction among such perceptions.

Cell assemblies become associated with one another and form phase sequences. For example, the event of cooking a steak could become associated with a birthday, anniversary, inviting the boss for dinner, receiving a raise, or some other type of event. Perceptions associated with each of the cell assemblies become related to perceptions from other assemblies. When you smell a steak cooking, the

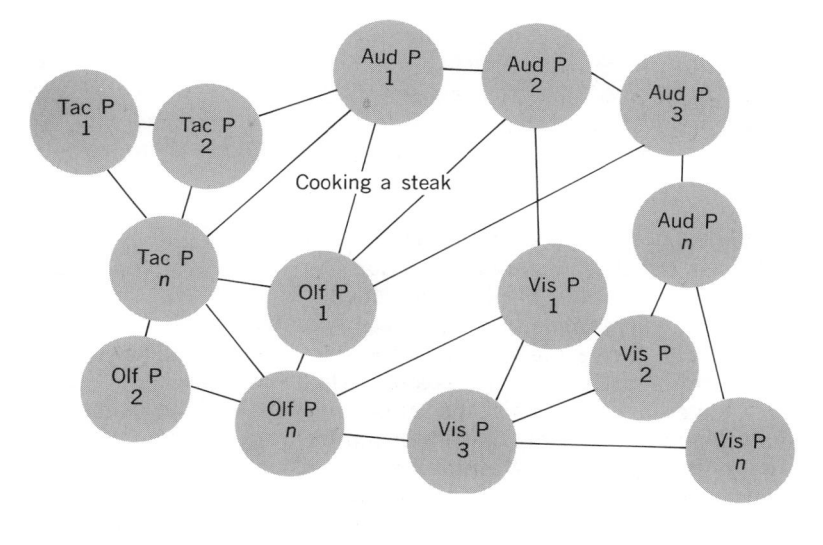

FIGURE 2-3 *Interrelationship of perceptual experiences concerned with a specific event (infinite number of possible associational bonds).*

appropriate cell assemblies immediately become active and in turn, stimulate networks related to other events. Close temporal and spatial contiguity must be present for cell assemblies to become associated and form phase sequences. These higher-level associational structures will develop only after a certain amount of interassembly facilitation has been established through repeated excitation.

According to Hebb, intelligence develops as the organism forms these complex and diffuse associational patterns. The more complex the patterns, in terms of the number and degree of perceptual associations, the more intelligent the organism. The intellectually superior, therefore, is one who has experienced a variety of events, become sensitive to the perceptual experiences associated with these events, related perceptual experiences through the development of cell assemblies, and elaborated on the cell assemblies by making possible their higher-level association into phase sequences. The development of such associational systems assumes a potential of Intelligence A.

INTELLIGENCE DEFINED In Hebb's terms intelligence may be defined as the *"number of strategies for processing information that have been differentiated and have achieved the mobility which permits them to be available in a variety of situations."* "Number of strategies" refers to the extent to which associational networks (cell assemblies and phase sequences) have been developed. Mobility is an important feature of the definition in that emphasis is placed on the need for flexibility within the system. Not only is it essential that networks be developed; it is equally crucial that the system allow additional perceptions to become associated so that elaboration of cell assemblies can occur. This will lead to a system which, because of its high level of associational patterning, is able to arrive at a variety of solutions to problems since flexibility of the organism allows more complex associations to be formed.

HEBBIAN EXPLANATION FOR MENTAL RETARDATION   Benoit (1957, 1959) has explained mental retardation using Hebb's theory. Certain children are retarded because of deficits in Intelligence A. For a variety of possible reasons, the innate potential of the organism is reduced with the result that the system is less amenable to the development of associational networks. This would be the case for those children with genetic aberrations or gross cortical damage resulting from intrauterine difficulties and for those children who have experienced some type of central-nervous-system damage at birth. In each case, the child's potential for using experiences and perceptions in the establishment of cell assemblies and phase sequences has been damaged or not developed.

The largest group of mentally retarded children exhibits mild intellectual deficits (i.e., IQ between 50 and 80), not because of an inadequate Intelligence A, but because it has not had the opportunity to experience many perceptions around a variety of events within the environment. These children typically come from low socioeconomic situations and are usually classified as culturally deprived. There is no reason to believe that these children do not have basic potential (Intelligence A) for taking advantage of their environment; however, in most instances the opportunity is not provided at an early enough age. These children, because of their paucity of experiences, develop weak and inadequate associational patterns which are extremely limited in scope. Little wonder that they are unable to solve problems effectively, do well in school, or operate as intellectually normal individuals. Indeed, if the lack of opportunity for experiencing a variety of events is severe enough, they will not develop an adequate repertoire of associations and will function as mentally retarded persons.

From research on human beings at various ages, it is well established that plasticity of the organism decreases with increasing age. That is, if an impact is to be made on an organism, it is much more efficient and effective to work with a young individual than with one who is older. Some scientists believe that plasticity decreases substantially after age six. Relating this point to Hebb's theory, there is obvious wisdom in providing the young child with a variety of stimulating experiences in order to foster the early development of associational networks leading to higher levels of intellectual functioning. The difficulty in training and educating a relatively more rigid organism is substantial.

Implications of Hebb's theory for education of the retarded

1 In order to provide the neonate with as robust an Intelligence A as possible, parents, particularly the mother, should receive instruction during the prenatal period. There are certain considerations and cautions about which an expectant mother should be aware prior to the child's birth which could influence the infant's health and robustness. If expectant mothers are unaware or unconcerned about personal health during pregnancy, a variety of difficulties could result in the infant's potential being reduced. This area is of educational concern in a broad sense.

2 One of the most obvious implications of Hebb's theory for the retarded is the need to enlarge the stimulus field of these children. They need to be engaged in a large variety of experiences which provide many distinctive perceptual experiences to facilitate association.

3 To control the development of inaccurate and incomplete associational networks and to take advantage of the greater plasticity characteristic of the young child, emphasis should be placed on early educational programs. There is a definite advantage in working with children when they are young, during the period when new organizational structures are in the process of formation.

4 The teacher will need to provide the child with consistent, clear stimulus patterns during the early phases of training. If the child is presented with different stimuli at different times, each of which is related to the same event, confusion will result, and the opportunity for developing a stable associational pattern will be substantially reduced. The stimulus value of the stable percepts should be increased, irrelevant stimuli decreased in stimulus value, and associations between percepts explicitly called to the attention of the child. To leave such associations to chance is hazardous.

5 Effective and efficient learning will occur only after the child's attention has been focused. If the child is inattentive to the stimuli or receives only a segment of the perceptions of an event, inadequate or erroneous associations will take place. The teacher should first gain and hold the attention of the child before proceeding with an activity.

6 The assumption of a lesser number of healthy neural cells is reasonable in most cases. Assuming this to be the case, the teacher will need to constantly repeat stimuli for associational chains to develop. The repetition of stimuli is desirable not only to develop associational patterns but also to maintain those cell assemblies and phase sequences which have been formed. Obliteration will occur if experience is not reinforced. This is particularly true with the retarded because of their frequently pronounced short-term memory deficit.

7 Early cortical stimulation is desirable for effective subsequent learning. Advantage should be taken of the infant's natural tendency for motor activity by providing the child with opportunities for moving about and experiencing various events within the environment. There is reason to believe that early motor activity will lead to the more rapid development of perceptual skills—a basic ingredient in Hebb's theory. To restrict a child's movement or to reduce stimuli during the early years will negatively influence subsequent cognitive development. This point has both theoretical support and empirical validation.

ASSESSING INTELLECTUAL ABILITY

The measurement of intellectual ability is an area of substantial controversy. Many believe that it is impossible to evaluate adequately an individual's intellectual capacity. Others feel that intelligence tests are so heavily biased against children from lower social classes that the findings are invalid. Some have expressed dissatisfaction with contemporary intelligence tests because they assess only a small segment of what presently is known to constitute intelligence. Some attempts have been made to develop culture-free tests.

Although there is a degree of validity in each of these arguments, one must not lose sight of the primary functions of intelligence tests nor attribute to intelligence tests a function for which they were not originally designed. As Newland (1955) suggests, intelligence tests measure *manifest* and not *basic* capacity. From scores on such tests, the skilled clinician can infer a person's basic capacity. The fact that intelligence tests emphasize verbal ability and not mechanical competencies, in which lower-class children often excel, does not mean that they are biased against culturally deprived children. This is true even though lower-class children are more frequently associated with a less stimulating environment. The reasons for this are the following:

1 Most intelligence tests purport to measure verbal competencies and to predict school performance but not performance in mechanical areas.

2 Intelligence tests are not designed to assess innate potential—only operating capacity. The inadequate environment which causes a child to perform poorly on an intelligence test is at fault and not the test. Intelligence tests measure only the level of functioning rather than try to account for poor performance. To say that the intelligence test is unfair is analogous to saying that the tuberculin patch test is invalid since lower-class children show more positive reactions than middle-class children.

There is truth in the observation that even the more sophisticated tests used to evaluate intellectual ability provide inadequate estimates of the total mental abilities of a child and are based on an incomplete sample of the presently known factors of intellect. No longer should an individual intelligence test, as presently conceived, be used as the *sole* criterion for placing a child in a special class, developing a special education program, or for referring a child to an institution. Factors of intelligence other than those measured by standardized intelligence tests, such as social competency, emotional adjustment, and physical maturity are also important variables when a child is considered for some type of special educational procedures. Moreover, it is apparent that educators and psychologists need to employ measures of intellectual ability in addition to the battery of instruments presently used for providing educational guidelines.

Current standardized intelligence tests do not identify and assess certain intellectual talents such as originality, fluency of ideas, sensing problems, foresight, and evaluation abilities. It is possible, therefore, to have a child who tests low on a standardized intelligence test but who could score relatively higher on other factors of intelligence, such as those associated with creativity. Likewise, the specific learning disabilities of certain children are not always identified using current instruments because of the circumscribed constellation of factors sampled. Therefore, teachers are not informed about appropriate remedial procedures. The need is to supplement standard instruments with tests which evaluate other dimensions of ability.

The function of intelligence tests is essentially threefold:

1 *To predict future school performance*
2 *To assist in classifying children into more homogeneous units for purposes of instruction and research*
3 *To discover certain patterns of ability and disability which are educationally meaningful and which can lead to appropriate curricular and methodological decisions aimed at fostering efficiency and effectiveness in learning*

To attribute any other function to intelligence tests would be inappropriate.

There are certain acknowledged limitations in intelligence tests which should be noted. In the first place, every test inherently has errors of measurement. Test designers work hard on reducing errors such as those caused by invalid items, unclear wording, inadequate directions, or subtests which do not measure the factors they purport to evaluate.

Second, incorrect administration has a substantial limiting effect. To either administer or score a test without proper knowledge and training violates a major assumption underlying these instruments and can substantially alter a subject's score.

Most educators and psychologists realize that children quickly become "test wise." To examine a child using the same test on numerous occasions will often result in wide variation among scores because the subject remembers the dimensions measured and, in some cases, even specific questions. For these and other reasons test-retest reliability of intelligence tests is frequently lower than desired.

Even with all these difficulties, the Revised Stanford-Binet Intelligence Scale remains the best predictor of capacity. When properly administered by a trained psychometrician, this test will fairly, accurately, and reliably measure operating intelligence.

The Wechsler Intelligence Scale for Children is also considered a reliable and valid instrument. Unlike the Binet, which emphasizes only verbal abilities, the WISC has both a verbal and a performance scale. Both these instruments are individually administered intelligence tests and require administration by a person with special training, knowledge, and clinical experience.

SELECTED REFERENCES

Benoit, E. P.: "Relevance of Hebb's Theory of the Organization of Behavior to Educational Research on the Mentally Retarded," *American Journal of Mental Deficiency,* vol. 61, 1957, pp. 497–507.

————: "Toward a New Definition of Mental Retardation," *American Journal of Mental Deficiency,* vol. 63, 1959, pp. 559–564.

Coghill, G. E.: *Anatomy and the Problem of Behavior,* Cambridge University Press, London, 1929.

Dobzhansky, T.: *Evolution, Genetics, and Man,* John Wiley & Sons, Inc., New York, 1955.

Goddard, H. H.: *The Kallikak Family,* The Macmillan Company, New York, 1913.

Gottesman, I.: "Genetic Aspects of Intelligent Behavior," in Norman R. Ellis (ed.), *Handbook of Mental Deficiency,* McGraw-Hill Book Company, New York, 1963, p. 255.

Guilford, J. P.: "The Structure of Intellect," *Psychological Bulletin,* vol. 53, 1956, pp. 267–293.

————: "Three Faces of Intellect," *American Psychologist,* vol. 14, 1959, pp. 469–479.

————, Kettner, N. W., and Christensen, P. R.: "A Factor Analytic Study of Planning: I. Hypotheses and Descriptions of Tests," *Report from the Psychological Laboratory,* no. 11, University of Southern California, Los Angeles, July, 1954.

Hebb, D. O.: *The Organization of Behavior,* John Wiley & Sons, Inc., New York, 1949.

Kirk, S. A.: *Early Education of the Mentally Retarded,* The University of Illinois Press, Urbana, Ill., 1958.

Newland, T. E.: "Psychological Assessment of Exceptional Children and Youth," in W. M. Cruickshank (ed.), *Psychology of Exceptional Children and Youth,* 2d ed., Prentice-Hall, Inc., Englewood Cliffs, N.J., 1963.

Rosenzweig, M. R., Krech, D., and Bennett, E. L.: "Heredity, Environment, Brain Biochemistry, and Learning," *Current Trends in Psychological Theory,* The University of Pittsburgh Press, Pittsburgh, Pa., 1961.

Shirley, Mary M.: "A Motor Sequence Favors the Maturation Theory," *Psychological Bulletin,* vol. 28, 1931, pp. 204–205.

Skeels, H. M. and Dye, H. B.: "A Study of the Effects of Differential Stimulation on Mentally Retarded Children," *Proceedings of American Association of Mental Deficiency,* vol. 44, 1939, pp. 114–136.

Spearman, C.: *The Nature of Intelligence and the Principles of Cognition,* Macmillan & Co., Ltd., London, 1923.

Thurstone, L. L.: *The Nature of Intelligence,* Harcourt, Brace & World, Inc., New York, 1926.

Wellman, B. L.: "Iowa Studies on the Effects of Schooling," 39th Yearbook, *National Society for the Study of Education,* 1940, pp. 377–399.

chapter three

assessing individual differences

The advent of the modern testing movement at the turn of the century resulted in substantial interest in and concern about differences among individuals. The fact that individuals reared in the same type of environment often exhibited totally different psychological and educational characteristics suggested the need for differential educational programs. As sophistication increased in instrumentation and the possibility for assessing precise factors of ability and performance became real, it soon became obvious that not only do individuals differ among themselves (inter-individual variations) but that most people vary substantially within themselves (intra-individual differences) in areas of educational and psychological significance. Kirk (1962) has termed these differences *discrepancies in growth* and applied this concept to the various exceptionalities.

This chapter is intended to review the concept of inter- and intra-individual variation as it applies to teaching the retarded. This notion is basic to clinical teaching and will establish the foundation for subsequent discussions on specific methodological techniques appropriate in the education of the mentally retarded.

RATIONALE FOR CONCERN ABOUT INDIVIDUAL DIFFERENCES

Children not only learn at a different rate when compared with each other, but within themselves tend to exhibit different capabilities in various subject areas. These variations are present for several reasons. First, each individual is associated with a completely unique internal and external milieu. The behavioral patterns we exhibit are based primarily on the way in which we have been reared, the areas of our environment in which emphasis has been placed, our perception of what is important to the groups with which we identify, and our own capabilities. The level of intrinsic and extrinsic motivation concerning the need to achieve and in goal striving are other areas in which wide differences exist between and within individuals. An individual may be highly motivated to learn to read because of a desire to pass a driver's test; whereas the same person may not be highly stimulated to learn long division unless some type of need provides the stimulus for developing a certain level of competence in this area. Another person may very well be motivated in entirely the opposite direction.

Not only does one's potential in part determine areas of strength and weakness as well as personal and social motives, but most of us exhibit greater responsiveness in those areas in which we have maximum development and relatively less interest in those areas which are less well developed. For example, it is typical to observe that retarded children are much stronger in nonverbal than in verbal competencies. Gallagher and Lucito (1961), in summarizing a series of studies in this general area, noted that retarded children on the WISC were *relatively stronger* on performance subtests; whereas intellectually superior children were *relatively stronger* on the verbal than on the nonverbal tests. Intellectually normal children showed no pattern of particular strengths or weaknesses. Surely the fact that children are differentially responsive according to idiosyncratic strengths and weaknesses points not only to the need for greater awareness of individual differences generally, but also suggests the desirability for a more clinical approach in teaching.

To further complicate the picture, particularly with retarded children, wide differences often exist between a person's predicted individual level of ability and his level of performance. If the child's mental age is used as a general indicator of the expected performance level in academic areas, and after being examined on achievement tests, he is found to be working below that predicted level in certain subject areas, the child not only could be generally retarded but also underachieving. Many retarded children are underachievers, most frequently in areas related to communication and reading skills. In addition, wide discrepancies are often observed between levels of performance in subject areas.

Educators must be sensitive to inter- as well as intra-individual differences. To effect maximum performance, children's specific strengths and weaknesses must be ascertained in educationally relevant areas and a specific program planned accordingly. Consistent with this point of view, the effective teacher must learn about and be able to apply more than one method of instruction in order to respond to the wide differences existing among children. The cookbook approach will no longer work.

Moreover, because of the significant differences among and within children which directly affect teaching and learning, the teacher must become skilled in basic educational diagnosis. It would be unrealistic to expect a high level of sophistication in psychoeducational diagnosis from teachers. However, the teacher can be expected to be constantly aware of clues by informally analyzing all aspects of a child's performance. The results of this analysis will suggest the efficacy of adjusting and altering instructional techniques.

THE SIGNIFICANCE OF INTER–INDIVIDUAL VARIABILITY

Inter-individual variability is another concept central to the notion of exceptionality. In describing characteristics of various populations of subjects, professionals in the behavioral sciences use a measure of central tendency, such as the mean (or average), mode, or median. For example, the mean intelligence quotient for children on the Revised Stanford-Binet Intelligence Scale and the Wechsler Intelligence Scale for Children is 100. This average score is not an indication of the manner in which scores spread out or vary from the mean.

Children who deviate substantially from the average in one or more educationally significant areas can be considered exceptional. Mentally retarded children, in addition to often being atypical in other areas, vary enough from the average in their intelligence ability to warrant some type of special educational program. Most typically an IQ score below 84 is considered deviant enough to warrant some type of special education program.

Two major factors must be considered in determining what constitutes a significant exceptionality. First, it is necessary to decide on the importance of the dimension or area in which the individual exhibits weakness. For education an area of deviation from the average may not be as significant as for professionals from other disciplines. For example, an extra digit or two on a child's hand could constitute an exceptionality of substantial interest to the members of the medical profession, but would not be so clear an exception for the educator.

To be more obtuse, a redheaded person or a child with one blue and one brown eye is exceptional since the prevalence of these conditions occurs infrequently in our population. Deviations on these variables are irrelevant for the teacher. On the other hand, if a child has a disability in areas such as visual memory, auditory discrimination, perceptual-motor development, concept formation, or expression of ideas, his general performance will be reduced in areas related to learning. For this reason, when one considers a child to vary significantly from the average, the educational importance of the dimension on which variations are observed must be considered.

Other factors in determining whether a deviation is significant are the degree of disability or weakness the individual exhibits and the nature of the population with which the person has been compared. With respect to the former, the degree to which an individual's condition is disabling enough to demand special education is subjectively determined. In addition to intellectual deviation, other factors must be considered according to the degree to which they contribute to the person's inability to maximize his potential. Many children score around IQ 85 and can perform very adequately in a regular class; whereas other children with the same measured intellectual ability could find it impossible to work effectively in a regular class because of some second disability or because of their lack of skill in certain foundation areas.

The educator and psychometrician should know the reference group with which a child's performance is being compared. Further, not only must the reasons for the diagnosis be clear, but a wise selection of the evaluative instrument(s) is crucial. The important points are that tests be chosen which will supply maximum information on the variables of concern, that the examiner be proficient in administering the tests, that the tests be effective, and that the testing process be efficient. When one wishes to screen a group of children, an individually administered test may be the most effective but not the most efficient technique. Although instruments do not purport to explain a deficit, caution must nonetheless be exercised to interpret a child's performance with an eye to the group on which the test was standardized. For example, to say that a deaf child is mentally retarded because of a poor performance on the Revised Stanford-Binet Intelligence Scale is to be insensitive to the facts that (1) the test is essentially verbal and was standardized on hearing children and that (2) deaf children are typically deficient in verbal communication skills.

Some control, therefore, should be exercised over the various elements which could bias the results of an inter-individual assessment. When experimenter or subject bias is introduced, the validity and generalizability of the findings are reduced. This situation leads to less precision in formulating an educational program for a child or group of children. The teacher should know about these possible sources of bias as educational and psychological reports are interpreted.

THE SIGNIFICANCE OF INTRA–INDIVIDUAL VARIABILITY

Inter-individual assessment uses the performance of other children as the reference for determining an individual's level of competence; intra-individual assessment uses the individual's own ability level and performance as reference points. The child is compared with himself, and a profile of *relative* strengths and weaknesses is determined.

As suggested earlier, most individuals show certain areas of relative strength and other areas of comparative weakness. Even among intellectually normal or superior people uneven competencies are often observed. For example, many people are extremely unskilled in artistic or musical performance and at the same time are highly effective in other areas of performance. Depending on the number of areas assessed, most of us would show an extremely uneven profile.

Awareness of a retarded child's level of ability in academic subject areas is important; however, cognizance of disabilities in very specific areas (e.g., memory, transfer, incidental learning, and vocal expression) will provide a more practical basis for planning an educational program. The entire process of teaching and learning would be simplified if it were possible to provide a method or system which could be prescribed for all retarded children. It is unrealistic and impossible to provide teachers with specific and foolproof techniques because of the heterogeneous characteristics of the retarded. Each child is atypical in his own way and in varying degrees. The need for differential diagnosis and the wisdom in a clinical approach to teaching these children, therefore, is clear.

To illustrate, two retarded children of the same age, operating at the same general level of intellectual ability, may demand entirely different programs. One child may be weak in areas related to visual-motor performance but relatively strong in use of the auditory channel. The other child may show the opposite profile. If the teacher has been trained to use phonics, based on auditory capabilities, the first child will be in a much better position to learn than the second youngster. If, on the other hand, emphasis is placed on visualization, the first child will be penalized. Teachers of these children soon learn that there is no standard way for teaching arithmetic, reading, or any other skill area.

To base an educational program for the retarded solely on inter-individual assessment indicates an insensitivity to differences within children and implicitly supports a cookbook approach to teaching. Instead, moving beyond the inter-individual procedures to a within-individual analysis transcends the use of traditional disability categories and focuses attention, properly, on educationally relevant factors. Special educators most often deal with multiply disabled children who show extremely diverse patterns of ability and disability. The onus is on the teacher to develop an educational prescription according to the unique pattern of each child.

DIAGNOSING STRENGTHS AND WEAKNESSES

There are several levels of diagnosis involved in assessing a child's patterns of ability and weakness. The process involves moving from a gross estimate of the child's general mental ability to a precise determination of very specific areas of weaknesses, including the process a child uses in receiving and interpreting information, relating it to the existing repertoire, and in expressing ideas. Each of the stages in this evaluative process will be discussed in a general sense in this section but more specifically in those subsequent chapters concerned with various subject areas.

Several assumptions are basic to the discussion. We must assume that the examiner is trained and has wisely chosen tests which are valid, reliable, and provide maximum information on the variables being assessed. We must also assume that the program objectives are firmly in mind, that the child is inconsistent in his patterns of learning or is achieving at less than the predicted level, and that the subject has been cooperative throughout the evaluation process.

The first step in the procedure is to establish the child's predicted level of ability. This can be determined with most precision by using some standard individually administered intelligence test. Although a group test is satisfactory, the possibility of increased errors of measurement is a major factor in such tests. Mental age is an important factor in assessing capacity. It provides some general indication of a child's level of expectation in academic areas. The calculation of mental age is easily done using the following formula, in which MA stands for mental age and CA for chronological age:

$$MA = \frac{CA \times IQ}{100}$$

Mental age provides a measure of a child's present intellectual status; whereas the IQ gives an indication of a child's approximate rate of learning. To be sure, mental age is greatly determined by the extent to which a child has had opportunities to experience a variety of events. The performance of a child usually varies somewhere between his MA and CA, with the exception of intellectually superior children whose MA exceeds their CA. The emotional and academic status of retarded children in particular will be close to their MA; their social and physical development will be closer to their CA.

Mental age provides the teacher with an indication of the starting point for a child in terms of classroom experiences and activities. For example, we would expect two children with the same level of intellectual ability, but with different chronological ages, to be able to operate at different academic levels. To illustrate:

Child A: IQ = 75
CA = 11 years 3 months
MA = 8 years 5 months

We would predict that this child is ready to use the first-level reader and has developed some basic skills in simple addition and subtraction.

Child B: IQ = 75
CA = 7 years 9 months
MA = 5 years 10 months

We would predict that this child is ready for reading-readiness activities and has developed some competence in rote and rational counting.

In addition, mental age provides an estimate of a child's attention span, tolerance for frustration, ability in small motor functioning, and in other areas directly related to efficiency in learning. It should be remembered, however, that mental age is calculated from performance on an intelligence test; one must be cautious about possible sources of bias and test weaknesses.

The second step in the diagnostic process is to ascertain the level of achievement of the child in various subject areas. Whereas in the first stage capacity was estimated, in this stage level of performance is evaluated. Children often do not achieve at a level commensurate with their predicted level of ability.

Achievement tests are most frequently used to evaluate performance. The use of standardized instruments provides the most accurate indicator of achievement, although school grades can be used for informal assessment. Tests such as the Metropolitan Achievement Test or the Stanford Achievement Test will allow for a comprehensive evaluation in a number of areas. The Wide Range Achievement Test, which can be administered easily by the teacher, does not take long and provides general information on spelling, reading, and arithmetic achievement.

After a child's performance has been assessed in the subject areas, the scores should be profiled as illustrated in the following diagram.

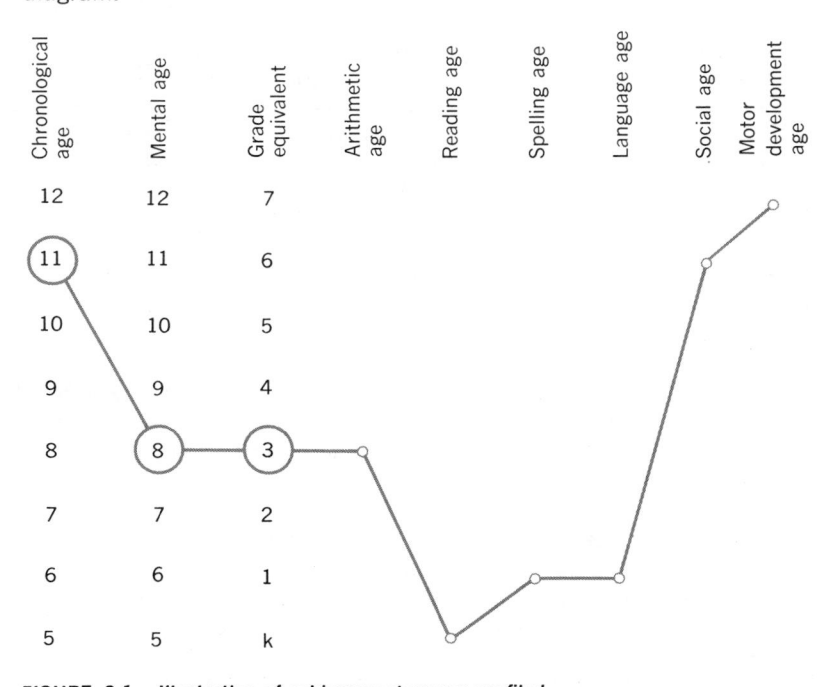

FIGURE 3-1   Illustration of achievement scores profiled.

This profile indicates that the child is educable mentally re-tarded, scoring on an intelligence test with an IQ of approximately 75, and that he has a mental age of 8. This means that the youngster could be expected to perform at about the third-grade level. His arithmetic performance is consistent with expectations. Social age and motor development are nearer his CA than MA, both of which might be predicted. As compared with his predicted capacity, the child has particular difficulty in reading, spelling, and language. The graph does not explain why the child is underachieving in these areas; it does provide, however, a basis for suggesting some *hypotheses* concerning the reasons for this constellation of difficulties. Because reading is particularly low, the child may be experiencing difficulty in spelling and language.

By graphing the child's level of achievement in all the areas and comparing these data with his MA, the teacher is able to identify areas of common strength and weakness. In the absence of achieve-ment scores, school grades can be used in an informal analysis of achievement. If a child exhibits continuity in his performance among the various subject areas, it would not be necessary to proceed with a more penetrating analysis of educational difficulties, which are suggested by steps three and four.

The third step in this procedure involves the determination of areas of difficulty *within* those specific subject areas in which weakness has been demonstrated. One could initially compare a child's scores in areas of reading such as reading readiness, oral reading, speed, silent reading, word knowledge, comprehension, paragraph meaning, and sight vocabulary. A profile could be developed, similar to the one diagrammed earlier, to determine in which areas of reading the child was particularly weak. This, then, will provide the teacher with more specific information concerning how the reading program might be structured for this child. A similar kind of procedure could be used in arithmetic by fractioning down areas involved in the arithmetic process.

A more refined and comprehensive analysis would require the assistance of a trained school psychologist or subject-area specialist. By using certain kinds of instruments, these professionals can detect patterns of difficulties which in turn affect the child's performance at each of the higher levels discussed earlier. For example, if a child has trouble in blending sounds, this difficulty will be manifested by a poor performance in one or several areas of reading as well as in spelling and language. If this difficulty receives some type of special educational intervention, achievement in each of these areas will be increased.

The fourth major step in analyzing a child's pattern of strengths and weaknesses is to survey the technique the individual uses in working through a problem. For example, it is important to know whether a child attacks a word by sounding out, spelling, writing, or through a look-and-say method. Similarly, in arithmetic does the child always count items individually when grouping objects? How much dependence does the child exhibit in his use of concrete reference points as opposed to the abstract? All of these are questions related to an individual's process for responding to a problem.

The importance of this type of analysis cannot be overstated, particularly if a child is employing a process in which a certain weakness is manifested. For example, if a child is able to learn best through use of the visual channel and for some reason is weaker in the auditory-vocal areas, the teacher should know about this and adapt methods of instruction accordingly. The Illinois Test of Psycholinguistic Abilities (Kirk and McCarthy, 1961) is an instrument, individually administered by a trained psychometrician, which allows for the assessment of these important variables. The teacher can informally check on a child's progress through the observation of reading or arithmetic.

In summary, the process of profiling strengths and weaknesses, leading to more effective teaching and learning, moves from a gross inter-individual assessment to a very precise analysis of each child's idiosyncratic process used for learning. The following diagram summarizes the relationship among these stages.

TABLE 3-1 Stages of Educational Diagnosis

Level 1	Inter-individual analysis based on an individually or group-administered intelligence test with the objective of ascertaining the child's predicted level of ability
Level 2	Administration of an achievement battery designed to detect relative strengths and weaknesses among subject matter areas
Level 3	Determination of difficulties within the specific subject area(s) in which the child has shown relative weakness
Level 4	Survey of the techniques the child uses as he works through a problem and a discovery of those channels of communication by which learning occurs most efficiently and effectively

GENERALIZED LEARNING CHARACTERISTICS

The following section presents results from a sample of studies in several areas of learning in which retarded and normal children have been compared. The findings of much of the research in these areas are not in agreement, although on certain learning variables retarded children tend to exhibit relative homogeneity in their characteristics.

There are some problems in conducting research on retarded individuals, the most pronounced of which are problems of sampling, testing, and instrumentation. This is particularly true in doing research with public-school retarded children. Because of this situation, investigators have conducted most of the research dealing with learning variables using trainable or custodial subjects.

Short- and long-term retention

The research literature strongly suggests that retarded youngsters exhibit significant weakness in short-term memory. Their ability to store auditory or visual material over a few seconds or minutes is decidedly poor. Hermelin and O'Connor (1964) found that intellectually normal children remembered an auditory sequence two to six seconds after presentation better than retarded children. No differences were observed between the groups when a longer time interval ensued after the stimulus was presented. Similar findings have been reported by others using visual stimuli and requiring some type of motor response (Headrick and Ellis, 1964; Baumeister, Smith, and Rose, 1965).

With respect to the short-term memory of mentally retarded children, several common threads seem to be evidenced throughout the empirical literature. First, in addition to retarded children being poorer in immediate recall than normal youngsters, they appear to be overly influenced by irrelevant stimuli and have more difficulty focusing on a task (House and Zeaman, 1961). Both normal and subnormal children tend to be hindered in short-term memory by items which intervene between the stimulus presentation and the test for recall. When verbal labels are used in association with the stimuli, significant improvement in the short-term memory of retarded persons has been observed (Barnett, Ellis, and Pryer, 1959; Jensen and Rohwer, 1963). Children, irrespective of intellectual level, do less well in short-term memory when

1 *The complexity of the stimulus is increased*
2 *The delay between presentation and recall becomes excessive*
3 *Some type of psychological threat is perceived by the child*
4 *Anticipation of reward is too great*
5 *Some type of interfering material is presented*

Long-term memory deficits in retarded individuals have not been observed when comparisons were made with intellectually normal subjects (Jensen and Rohwer, 1963; Johnson and Blake, 1960). Generally, retarded youngsters are able to remember material as well as normal subjects if (1) they have overlearned the fact or concept beyond a minimal criterion level and (2) they have had an opportunity to reinforce this learning through constant use. If a retarded child does not have a chance to employ the material which has been learned, there is greater likelihood of obliteration occurring.

Hebb's theory supports the empirical findings concerning the retention characteristics of retarded children. If, for some reason, a child has impaired cortical tissue, it is reasonable to expect that the development of associational networks (cell assemblies and phase sequences) will occur to a very limited degree. Retarded children without obvious organicity may be faulty in short-term memory and in the concomitant development of associational patterns because of the ambiguous nature of the stimuli, the vague or reduced stimulus value of the perceptual events, the short duration period of the stimuli, the lack of clarity in relationship among various types of stimuli concerning an event, the lack of attention on the part of the child, the introduction of irrelevant perceptions at a time when relevant stimuli are presented, or because of faulty peripheral systems such as the auditory or visual. Any or all of these difficulties would result in either a reduction in or a confusion among the various perceptual experiences of an event and lead to the less precise development of cell assemblies and phase sequences. This, then, would result in the child experiencing difficulties in short-term memory.

If the child has developed a stable repertoire of associational patterns, the theory suggests that obliteration or decay will occur only with disuse. There is no reason to suggest that this position would not be true of retarded individuals. The empirical documentation for validating this postulation shows that once the retarded learn a fact or concept they are likely to remember it as well as the intellectually normal, provided they are given opportunities to use the material. By using information available from existing cell assemblies and phase sequences, the individual establishes a firmer entrenchment of the network in the cognitive structure, and an opportunity is provided for elaboration with other old and new assemblies. In using existing networks, the individual will infrequently experience precisely the same stimuli which were initially instrumental in the formation of networks. Because of this, elaboration is extended to other perceptions related to the same event which, in turn, leads to opportunities for greater flexibility and generalization on the part of the individual. The use of existing information in the repertoire, therefore, is important for long-term retention, application, and generalization.

Discrimination learning

Discrimination among auditory or visual stimuli is a skill which is basic for effective and efficient learning. Children must develop skill in discriminating among shapes, configurations, symbols, and sounds in order to learn how to read. Even in social situations discrimination is required of adults. For example, it is often necessary to discern the intentions of people in social interaction.

Studies in discrimination learning have typically offered to subjects several stimuli which are closely related in their characteristics. The subjects are asked to choose one of the objects, and their response is either acknowledged as being correct or wrong according to an a priori decision by the experimenter. For example, in a series of these experiments the correct choice, as determined by the researcher although not explicitly told to the subjects, might be the one object shown each time with two or more rounded corners. From the experiments the investigator can choose any number of variables for study. For example, the speed of learning, various types of punishment or reward schedules, types of rewards (candy versus toys), face-to-face versus machine presentation, influence of labeling objects prior to selection by the subjects, and other variables have been used as dependent variables in discrimination-learning experiments. A number of studies in this area have been done using mentally retarded persons as subjects, and their performance has been compared with intellectually normal children of either the same MA or CA.

The studies which have contrasted retarded and normal children in discrimination learning are inconsistent in the direction of their findings.[1] Several studies indicate that retarded children learn more slowly than normal subjects (Stevenson and Iscoe, 1955; House and Zeaman, 1959; Rudel, 1959); whereas other researchers have found no difference between these two groups in their rate of discrimination learning (Ellis and Sloan, 1959; Stevenson, 1960). The differences in the results of these studies are probably due to methodological variation in the procedures of experimentation more than to differences among subjects. In fact, most of the research in discrimination learning has employed subjects from institutions, comparing these individuals with noninstitutionalized normals. It is difficult to precisely specify their discrimination-learning characteristics apart from considering the possible influence of institutionalization.

Although difficulties in research design have tended to confuse the findings of studies in discrimination learning, the research does suggest that retarded children will learn patterns of discrimination more rapidly if they are encouraged to name or label the stimuli (Zeaman, House, and Orlando, 1958; Dickerson, Girardeau, and Spradlin, 1964), provided with stimuli which are novel (Zeaman, House, and Orlando, 1958), and given a reward for a correct response (Cantor and Hottel, 1955). Caution should be exercised in generalizing these findings to all populations of retarded youngsters since, in many cases, trainable-level children were used as subjects in these studies. The applicability of these findings to the educable child remains somewhat speculative.

Learning set

The term *learning set* refers to the ability of a person to learn how to solve additional problems because of previous experience with similar situations. For example, it takes fewer trials to solve discrimination problems after a person has earlier been required to respond to the same type of problem. The decrease in the number of trials required to learn the techniques for solving subsequent problems indicates that the individual learns how to solve such problems. This phenomenon has been called "learning how to learn."

Studies of learning set show that retarded children generally are capable of learning how to learn. The ability to establish a learning set seems to be directly related to MA, the phenomenon occurring

[1] For a review of a representation of the studies conducted in the area of discrimination learning see Stevenson (1963).

more rapidly for subjects with a higher MA (Ellis, 1958; Stevenson and Swartz, 1958). In studies in which retarded and normal children of the same MA were compared, the retarded children tended to be somewhat slower in establishing a learning set, perhaps because of a tendency toward increased perseveration.

One additional generalization seems warranted from the literature. When retarded youngsters are given an opportunity to solve and master easy problems prior to their being exposed to more difficult problems, the establishment of a learning set is effected more rapidly. The most obvious educational implication of these studies is that the retarded need to be exposed to a sequential presentation of facts and concepts.

Incidental learning

Relatively few studies have endeavored to ascertain to what degree retarded children are able to acquire knowledge from stimuli which are peripheral to those perceptions involved in a directed learning task. The ability to be sensitive to incidental clues from the environment is a competency which will lead directly to the establishment of a more elaborate response repertoire.

Goldstein and Kass (1961) compared educable retarded with gifted subjects of the same MA and found that the retarded children were capable of incidental learning in terms of the number of responses given. The retarded, however, gave significantly more incorrect responses than did the gifted. Hetherington and Banta (1962) indicate that familial retarded and normal children score higher on incidental learning tasks than retarded children with organic involvement.

Although the retarded appear to have the potential for making use of stimuli which are incidental to a direct task, the empirical evidence describing any specific deficit in this area is fragmentary. The retarded are less perceptive and selective of stimuli within their environment and much less able to make use of such peripheral stimuli. If maximum benefit of the potential value inherent in incidental stimuli is to accrue to the retarded, their attention must be directed to perceptual events. The association of these perceptions with stimuli from intentional learning should be encouraged. By intentionally following this procedure, maximum advantage is made of the environment, and the associational patterns developed in the cognitive structure become much more elaborate.

Reaction time

There is almost complete consensus in the literature that the retarded are significantly weak in reaction time. A significant negative correlation between MA and reaction time has been consistently found with various samples of retarded children (Ellis and Sloan, 1957; Bensberg and Cantor, 1957). Studies dealing with reaction time show that retarded children with organicity do less well than familial retarded children. Further, children with perceptual difficulties and attention difficulties appear to be slower in their reaction to stimuli than children without these behavioral traits. Some evidence suggests that greater stimulus intensity will result in more favorable reaction time among the retarded (Baumeister, Vrquhart, Beedle, and Smith, 1964).

Transfer

A certain amount of conceptual overlap exists between the notions of transfer and learning sets. In the following discussion, transfer should be viewed in a more general way. Transfer, therefore, is to be considered as skill in using and applying response patterns and experiences formerly learned to another problem which has components similar to the previous situation. In order to be skilled in transfer, an individual must have concepts and facts stored in the cognitive structure, be able to choose and select those concepts relevant to the problem, and appropriately apply them to another situation.

The research designed to investigate the retarded's ability to transfer indicates that they show a definite tendency to transfer negative rather than positive learnings. The retarded remember with much greater facility what they are *not* supposed to do instead of what they are supposed to do (Bryant, 1965). The reverse tends to be true for intellectually normal children. This finding is of great instructional significance.

Orton, McKay, and Rainy (1964) suggest that educable mentally retarded children perform better in transferring when the instructional presentation is concrete, the materials used can be manipulated, and the tasks involve a minimal need for abstraction. In contrast, bright students transfer best when the method of instruction involves the use of rules, principles, and generalizations.

In teaching retarded children to transfer, the teacher should

1 *Logically sequence instruction and make liberal use of materials and concrete examples before a principle or rule is considered*
2 *Place the retarded youngster in a situation which will be successful for the child, thereby encouraging positive transfer*
3 *Provide a variety of rewards for correct responses*
4 *Identify retarded and potential retardates early*
5 *Stress relationships between situations and problems by explicitly showing the children commonalities which exist*

Productive thinking

The terms *creative* and *divergent* are frequently used as synonyms for *productive thinking*. The research in productive thinking has been based primarily on the work of Guilford (1960) by employing instruments which assess fluency, flexibility, and originality in thinking.

Since low, nonsignificant relationships are known to exist between scores on intelligence tests and factors of productive thinking, researchers have endeavored to evaluate the extent to which retarded children are able to perform in the areas of creativity. Some effort has been directed toward determining the influence of training programs for the retarded which have been especially designed to foster skill in productive thinking.

Tisdall (1962) compared the productive-thinking abilities of educable mentally retarded children in special classes with those of educable-level children in the regular grades. On the verbal tests of productive thinking, the special-class children performed better than the children in the regular classes. Differences did not exist between the groups on the nonverbal measures. Low relationships existed between intelligence-test scores and all productive-thinking scores.

Rouse (1965) gave a group of educable-level children a special training program designed to enhance productive thinking. Their performance was compared with that of a group of educable children who had not received the special training program. As might be anticipated, the trained children were significantly superior in all areas of productive thinking.

These studies indicate that retarded children are poorer in spontaneous productive thinking than are intellectually normal children. They also show that educable retarded children possess the potential for being trained in productive thinking. A planned program in productive thinking would probably enhance the *total* verbal performance of educable children, which is their greatest area of difficulty. Other, somewhat tangential, benefits could accrue in areas of cognition such as in transfer, retention, and establishment of learning sets.

A productive-thinking program for the retarded should not have as an objective the training of these people to be unusually creative. A more appropriate emphasis should be on developing a more extensive repertoire of general information and associations which will allow for flexibility in retrieval at the most appropriate time.

SELECTED REFERENCES

Barnett, C., Ellis, N., and Pryer, M.: "Stimulus Pretraining and the Delayed Reaction in Defectives," *American Journal of Mental Deficiency*, vol. 64, 1959, pp. 104–111.

Baumeister, A., Smith, T., and Rose, J.: "The Effects of Stimulus Complexity and Retention Interval upon Short-Term Memory," *American Journal of Mental Deficiency,* vol. 70, 1965, pp. 129–134.

———, Vrquhart, D., Beedle, R., and Smith, T.: "Reaction Time of Normals and Retardates under Different Stimulus Intensity Changes," *American Journal of Mental Deficiency,* vol. 69, 1964, pp. 126–130.

Bensberg, G. J. and Cantor, G. N.: "Reaction Time in Mental Defectives with Organic and Familial Etiology," *American Journal of Mental Deficiency,* vol. 62, 1957, pp. 534–537.

Bryant, P. E.: "The Transfer of Positive and Negative Learning by Normal and Severely Subnormal Children," *British Journal of Psychology,* vol. 56, 1965, pp. 81–86.

Cantor, G. N. and Hottel, J. V.: "Discrimination Learning in Mental Defectives as a Function of Magnitude of Food Reward and Intelligence Level," *American Journal of Mental Deficiency,* vol. 60, 1955, pp. 380–384.

Dickerson, D. J., Girardeau, F. L., and Spradlin, J. E.: "Verbal Pre-training and Discrimination Learning by Retardates," *American Journal of Mental Deficiency,* vol. 68, 1964, pp. 476–484.

Ellis, N. R.: "Object-Quality Discrimination Learning Sets by Mental Defectives," *Journal of Comparative and Physiological Psychology,* vol. 51, 1958, pp 79–81.

——— and ———: "Oddity Learning as a Function of Mental Age," *Journal of Comparative and Physiological Psychology,* vol. 52, 1959, pp. 228–230.

——— and Sloan, W.: "Relationship Between Intelligence and Simple Reaction Time in Mental Defectives," *Perceptual and Motor Skills,* vol. 7, 1957, pp. 65–67.

Gallagher, J. J. and Lucito, L.: "Intellectual Patterns of Gifted Children Compared with Average and Retarded," *Exceptional Children,* vol. 27, 1961, pp. 479–482.

Goldstein, H. and Kass, C.: "Incidental Learning of Educable Mentally Retarded and Gifted Children," *American Journal of Mental Deficiency,* vol. 66, 1961, p. 245–249.

Guilford, J. P.: "The Structure of Intellect Model: Its Uses and Implications," *Report from the Psychological Laboratory,* University of Southern California, Los Angeles, April, 1960.

Headrick, M. and Ellis, N.: "Short-Term Visual Memory in Normals and Retardates," *Journal of Experimental Child Psychology,* vol. 1, 1964, pp. 339–347.

Hermelin, B. and O'Connor, N.: "Short-Term Memory in Normal and Subnormal Children," *American Journal of Mental Deficiency,* vol. 69, 1964, pp. 121–125.

Hetherington, E. M. and Banta, T. J.: "Incidental and Intentional Learning in Normal and Mentally Retarded Children," *Journal of Comparative and Physiological Psychology,* vol. 55, 1962, pp. 402–404.

House, B. and Zeaman, D.: "A Comparison of Discrimination Learning in Normal and Mentally Defective Children," *Child Development,* vol. 29, 1959, pp. 411–416.

———— and ————: "Effects of Practice on the Delayed Response of Retardates," *Journal of Comparative and Physiological Psychology,* vol. 54, 1961, pp. 225–260.

Jensen, A. and Rohwer, W.: "The Effect of Verbal Mediation on the Learning and Retention of Paired Associates by Retarded Adults," *American Journal of Mental Deficiency,* vol. 68, 1963, pp. 80–84.

Johnson, G. and Blake, K.: *Learning Performance of Retarded and Normal Children,* Syracuse University, Monograph no. 5, 1960.

Orton, K. D., McKay, E., and Rainy, D.: "The Effect of Method of Instruction on Retention and Transfer for Different Levels of Ability," *The School Review,* vol. 72, 1964, pp. 451–461.

Rouse, S. T.: "Effects of a Training Program on the Productive Thinking of Educable Mental Retardates," *American Journal of Mental Deficiency,* vol. 69, 1965, pp. 666–673.

Rudel, R. G.: "The Absolute Response in Tests of Generalization in Normal and Retarded Children," *American Journal of Psychology,* vol. 72, 1959, pp. 401–408.

Stevenson, H. W.: "Discrimination Learning," in Norman R. Ellis (ed.), *Handbook of Mental Deficiency,* McGraw-Hill Book Company, New York, 1963, pp. 424–438.

————: "Learning of Complex Problems by Normal and Retarded Subjects," *American Journal of Mental Deficiency,* vol. 64, 1960, pp. 1021–1026.

———— and Iscoe, I.: "Transposition in the Feebleminded," *Journal of Experimental Psychology,* vol. 49, 1955, pp. 11–15.

———— and Swartz, J. D.: "Learning Set in Children as a Function of Intellectual Level," *Journal of Comparative and Physiological Psychology,* vol. 51, 1958, pp. 755–757.

Tisdall, W. J.: "Productive Thinking in Retarded Children," *Exceptional Children,* vol. 29, 1962, pp. 36–41.

Zeaman, D., House, B. J., and Orlando, R.: "Use of Special Training Conditions in Visual Discrimination Learning with Imbeciles," *American Journal of Mental Deficiency,* vol. 63, 1958, pp. 453–459.

primary methodological concerns

It is imperative that teachers of the mentally retarded be highly efficient and effective in their planning of an educational program. The primary reason for emphasizing this need is that in reality, even under optimum circumstances, the teacher has less actual time available for the formal aspects of the instructional program than does the teacher of intellectually normal children. Because of their subaverage intellectual ability, mentally retarded children do not reach the stage in their development at which specific skills in the tool subjects can be taught effectively until they are approximately eight years of age chronologically. Since these aspects of the educational program are more closely related to MA than CA, retarded children often spend the first few years in school on prereadiness and readiness activities. By the time intellectually normal children are reading at the second- or perhaps third-grade level, retarded children are engaging in readiness activities. Thus, relative to their intellectual peers, retarded children can be considered more inefficient organisms for whom instruction in the tool subjects begins late, but from whom as adults a nearly normal performance is required by society. Indeed, it is paradoxical that the teacher has less time to produce a self-sufficient individual from whom demands by society are in many ways similar to those expected of intellectually normal people. This contradictory situation imposes critical demands on the teacher by forcing the construction of very efficient and effective educational experiences.

SCOPE AND SEQUENCE

Obviously, then, every aspect of the school program for the retarded should be clearly described so that administrators and teachers understand desirable short- and long-term objectives. Efficiency in teaching and learning will occur only after the program scope and sequence have been clearly delineated.

"Scope" refers to the totality of experiences and activities to which an individual is exposed during a specified period of time. It can be viewed from the perspective of the entire school program, a specified year, a month, the amount of time it takes to complete a unit of study, a day, or a single lesson. Time is a crucial factor, and, therefore, the selection of experiences and activities for each of these time intervals should be done with knowledge of prior and subsequent instruction within the total program. Unnecessary repetition among grade levels should be studiously avoided. This can be done when each teacher understands the broad boundaries within which each program component is to operate.

Although the general program scope for all retarded children of approximately the same level can be sketched out, consideration of the type and level of activities will vary among and within students in each subject area. This implies that the teacher must be skilled in informal assessment procedures so that both the common and the unique characteristics of the children can be described and reacted to in the instructional program. A further criterion of scope is the predicted level of performance each child will be able to attain as an adult. If a child has the predicted capabilities for becoming a baker, his program should include various experiences related to weights and measures; whereas if his past performance indicates that at best he will be able to perform as a custodian, it may not be necessary that measurements of the type required of bakers be a major part of his class activities. Although it is desirable that the candidate for custodian be exposed to as much learning as possible, it should be realized that it will take him as long to learn the lesser requirements of a custodian's occupation as it will for the more able retarded child to learn the more complicated skills required of a baker. Thus, for the child of low performance capability, time must not be lost on the irrelevant and inappropriate.

Awareness of the need for sequencing experiences and activities within and between classrooms at each level is a second important consideration if the educational objectives for these children are to be met. To be able to outline the scope of the total and specific parts of their educational program is obviously important, but all will be for naught if the retarded are not presented with an appropriate sequence of experiences wherein one activity provides the basic skills required for the next. Teachers cannot teach independent of co-workers. There must be curriculum and methods planning between teachers in order for the special-education program to have the desired impact.

Deficits cumulate. If a child's experiences are not intelligently sequenced and periodic diagnostic checks are not built into this sequence, specific learning disabilities will often occur in addition to general retardation. Not only must a teacher consider sequence in terms of the process she uses for teaching a specific skill in certain areas, but the teacher must schedule her activities each day, week, and year so that one follows the other. Ordering must occur within each classroom; it is of equal importance that consecutiveness be characteristic between classes throughout the entire program. In addition to the need for the teacher to consider the potential value of each experience in terms of the total program, each activity within the experience must be analyzed to identify those skills necessary for a satisfactory performance. This type of analysis will lead to the identification of appropriate sequences and scope.

EDUCATIONAL OBJECTIVES FOR THE RETARDED

The general objectives of education for the intellectually normal as listed by the Educational Policies Commission (1946) are appropriate for mentally retarded children. These objectives of civic responsibility, human relationship, self-realization, and economic efficiency, when considered in a global sense, are philosophically appropriate for all school children. Such objectives represent an expression of the basic tenets related to education in a democracy. The specifics of program development are less precise.

Kirk (1951) has enumerated eight aims for educating the mentally handicapped, each of which emphasizes occupational adequacy, social competence, and personal adequacy. The point of view taken in this book is not inconsistent with the objectives suggested by others. The emphasis here, however, is that teachers have the responsibility for helping the retarded to develop certain basic skills which can be used with equal facility in all these areas. One might emphasize that the child develop a "style of life" which will result in adequate responses to social, personal, and occupational situations. All of this has the primary aim of developing as self-sufficient an organism as possible.

In this context, the following are viewed as the primary educational objectives for mentally retarded children:

1 *The educational program should be designed to assist the mentally retarded child to develop a repertoire of general information which can be retrieved quickly and at appropriate times.*

2 *The educational program should assist the mentally retarded child to develop skills necessary to become socially, personally, and occupationally self-sufficient through the effective use of a consistent method of problem solving. The following subobjectives are directly related to this primary aim:*

   a *The educational program should assist the retarded child to develop competency in predicting the consequences of his behavior in areas concerned with the effective social, personal, and occupational interaction with his environment.*

   b *Emphasis should be placed on conceptual rather than rote understandings by the child.*

Underlying each of these objectives is the central theme of information processing. Concern should be with the way information is used in responding to a problem situation. Before information can be used, however, the organism must first develop a repertoire of facts, concepts, and associations. Even this is not sufficient; unless the individual has the capacity to retrieve appropriate facts quickly, inadequate, and often impulsive, response patterns will develop. A prerequisite objective, thus, should be to assist the retarded to establish and elaborate their networks of associational patterns. Substantial opportunities must be provided for them to use this "cortically programmed" information in a variety of ways. It is not enough that the retarded child use information in only one context when he could appropriately apply it to a wide range of situations.

If the child has developed an adequate repertoire of general information and is able to accurately and quickly associate segments of this knowledge with a problem, he is immediately faced with the need to assess the consequences of acting or reacting in a certain fashion. With the second objective, emphasis is on assisting the child to generate a number of possible alternatives to problems and to predict the consequences of using each of these possibilities. The evaluation of cause and effect and the consequences of using each of the alternatives will result in less impulsive behavior.

The use of a consistent method of problem solving is an important skill for the retarded to learn. The ability to associate a particular problem with one specific response is not a sufficiently broad educational aim; the retarded must develop conceptual understandings instead of rote responses to problems. They must be shown relationships, and emphasis must be placed on the general applicability of various solutions to an entire spectrum of problems. They should learn to know when and under what conditions a response is most appropriate and not which *one* response is always to be used in a particular circumstance. Their poor ability in retention permits neither accuracy nor enough situations to be covered or learned during their school experiences. The child can be successful if he learns to make his own deductions from standards he understands well. Standards, in this case, means guidelines, such as always choosing the careful over the unsafe, the kind over the rude, and so on.

FUNDAMENTAL PRINCIPLES OF INSTRUCTION

In order for these objectives to be effected with efficiency, the teacher should be aware of certain broad considerations in instructing retarded children. These guidelines are relevant to all subject areas.

Concern with learning phenomena

Although controversy exists concerning basic principles of learning, the following areas would probably be endorsed by most psychologists and educators. Research has tended to support the need for giving attention to each of these principles so that learning can proceed in an orderly and complete fashion.

READINESS FOR LEARNING   Among the factors inherent in the concept of readiness is the general belief that an organism must be mature enough to respond in a consistent and accurate fashion. The validation of this finding in nonverbal areas has been well established. A child needs to acquire certain basic skills before adequate performance can be expected in areas such as walking, drawing, gross and fine motor movements, and other types of visual-motor activities. The influence of maturation on verbal skills, and more generally on cognition, is less well validated, since there is larger inter-individual variation existing in these areas than in nonverbal skills. Some degree of extrapolation from observations in nonverbal areas to those involving more cognitive competencies has occurred, particularly as they are related to maturation. Although without sound empirical documentation, this extrapolation seems to be valid clinically.

   In order to receive incoming stimuli, engage in associational activities, and respond properly, the organism must be in a state of wakefulness. Many believe that general lack of attention, the etiology of which may be multitudinous, is the primary reason that retarded children often do poorly in school activities. No doubt the problem is more complex than simple inattentiveness, other difficulties contributing their share to readiness problems.

In addition to maturation, readiness to learn a skill is based on the degree of competence the child has developed in precursive skills. If the necessary basic skills upon which subsequent learning is dependent have not developed, any new skills will at best develop in an inefficient and disorganized manner, often totally out of context. Since deficits are cumulative, the area of readiness is particularly important. For example, if a child has trouble discriminating between the shapes of two objects, such as a square and a circle, he is not ready to choose the largest square among several sizes of circles and squares, because the skill of discriminating among shapes precedes the two-dimensional discrimination of shape and size.

The methods or processes the child uses for learning are related to readiness. If he has received primary instruction in using an auditory approach to solve problems but is subsequently given a task demanding skill in visual interpretation, the child may have difficulty in performing adequately. Methods of instruction to which the child has previously been exposed are related to readiness.

Finally, the child's emotional adjustment and attitude toward school generally and learning specifically are related to readiness. Those children who are antagonistic toward school activities or toward the teacher will gain little by being forced to participate. Time would be better spent attempting to alter attitudes.

The notion of readiness is also related to concept development. Although it is true that retarded children can be taught to memorize without having developed the basic readiness skills described earlier in this section, this strategy is inconsistent with the objectives of the special-education program. Emphasis should be on the systematic and sequential development of skills leading to conceptual understanding and not rote memorization.

MOTIVATION TO LEARN   The term *motivation* is used frequently, but often erroneously, in educational circles. The most common misuse of the word is in connection with the wornout phrase, "We must motivate the child." Children cannot be motivated. They can be stimulated, which can lead to their becoming eager or motivated to engage in an activity or to learn a concept.

There are several factors contained in the concept of motivation. If learning is to proceed in a stable fashion at an optimum level, children must perceive a need to learn. For example, many primary- and intermediate-level retarded children are often disinterested in activities related to learning basic skills involved in reading. Among the reasons for this attitude is the failure to perceive why they should learn to read effectively. In the early school years, one can "get by" without being highly skilled in reading; this is particularly true if the child is with other retarded children in a homogeneous class in which peer pressures to learn to read are usually minimal. At the secondary level, however, retarded children begin to show a rather intense interest in learning how to read, for it is at this age that obtaining a driver's license becomes important. On several occasions the author has seen dramatic increases in reading performance based primarily on this very clearly expressed need of the child. All reading problems cannot be interpreted using a motivational hypothesis; obviously, many children cannot read because they have more complicated disabilities. The degree of interest in and the amount of need for acquiring a skill, however, are important for learning to be facilitated.

Of early concern is the need to sensitize the children to the benefits of learning about a concept or a subject. Not preparing the class, but blindly launching into a lesson will result in very little learning if the class is generally disinterested. To foster a desire to learn, the following points should be considered:

1 *The children must perceive a need to learn. This can be accomplished by judicious use of peer and social pressures or by the teacher relating a goal that the child has to the area of learning in which an adequte level of interest is not apparent.*

2 *In order for children to develop an interest in learning about something, they must have had a history of success in related areas. Nothing inhibits interest more than failure. To extend this notion, retarded children should be placed in situations in which they can perceive their performance as being very successful. Not only a history of success, but subsequent successful experiences will stimulate in children a desirable level of motivation.*

3 *Long- and short-term goals, established by both the teacher and by the child, should be realistic and sensitive to the child's individual strengths and weaknesses. If a child is placed in a situation in which he is pressed to achieve beyond reasonable expectations, failure will result and he will quickly lose interest in participating. When this occurs frequently, the child will generalize the negative feelings to all school activities.*

IMMEDIATE KNOWLEDGE OF RESULTS AND REINFORCEMENT OF SUCCESS The greatest incentive for any child who has consistently failed to learn is to provide experiences in which the child can be successful, especially at the beginning of a series of tasks. Success is a reward and will lead to a better general performance by the child. Activities should be structured so that the retarded child can be successful, with consistent and immediate rewards provided for an accurate performance.

Delayed reinforcement has been repeatedly demonstrated to impede learning. Immediate confirmation of a child's correct response is essential. This immediate knowledge of results should be accomplished initially by a spoken confirmation of correctness or by some other more obvious reinforcement technique. Gradually, after the child becomes more dependent on using his own feedback and evaluative system, he will be able to monitor his own response and assess its correctness if reinforcement is provided.

The integrity of the child's feedback and monitoring system is important. If a child misinterprets stimuli and responds incorrectly, or if his feedback system is inadequate or inaccurate, much of his time will be devoted to practicing errors. Prompt intervention by the teacher is required before the child has a chance to practice and reinforce errors. Initially the teacher must act as the monitor for him and reinforce responses, feedback, and stimuli until an effective and trustworthy system for analyzing, using stimuli, and giving responses develops. Delay simply cannot be allowed to occur. Success must be emphasized, rewards or reinforcement must be of significance to the child, and a personal expectation for success should be encouraged. The latter point, if successfully effected, will reduce the possibility of the occurrence of emotional distress.

EXERCISE Retarded children are generally less responsive to stimuli than are the intellectually normal. Moreover, the relative inefficiency of the organism results in learning occurring much more slowly and laboriously than would be true for other children. Fundamental in teaching the retarded is the advantage in offering them opportunities to repeat and practice experiences in a variety of ways.

The chance to exercise, practice, or repeat is necessary for two reasons. First, since stimuli will rarely occur again in the same form, children should be exposed to a range of stimuli around an event in order to become aware of the dimensions of a problem and allow for an opportunity to associate relevant stimuli. Second, wide experience on a number of occasions, and in repeated contexts, will direct the child's attention and help in the development of associational bonds. Exercise and varied repetition will assist the retarded to practice correct responses. The true test of whether a concept has been established is if the child can scan his cognitive structure and respond in an appropriate fashion. This aim will be met more effectively if opportunities are provided to repeat responses in a variety of settings.

DISTRIBUTED PRACTICE Even under optimum circumstances, in which the material is interesting and the student is motivated, learning will become inefficient if the length of time for study or practice is massed and not determined according to each child's learning rate. Distribution of practice should vary according to the characteristics of each student as well as in terms of the type of materials being used. With certain types of activities, for example, retarded children might profit most with 4 ten-minute periods of practice; whereas with other kinds of exercises, fewer and longer periods would be more efficient. When the interpretation of symbols is required to obtain meaning, more and shorter sessions will be more profitable than longer periods of study. The reverse is probably true when computational and social-occupational lessons are being considered.

In distributing practice, moving to a different but somewhat related topic is often as effective as a rest period. Similarly, switching the materials used by the children (such as from using a piece of paper to employing the blackboard) will serve the same purpose as moving to another topic or providing a time for relaxation.

Although the evidence supports the value of distributing practice in tasks ranging from pure rote material to complex learning tasks, it should be noted that a possible error can be made in the opposite direction. Practice periods for the retarded should not be too short. The most desirable length of time for practice in the various areas of learning with the retarded has not been empirically determined. The teacher should be aware of the student's restlessness and reduced efficiency so that activity on a task can be stopped and a switch made in order to take advantage of the effects of distributed practice.

ACTIVE PARTICIPATION Most educational psychologists agree that active involvement by the learner will facilitate learning. Such participation has several advantages: (1) It helps to focus the child's attention on the task at hand, (2) it alerts the child to his importance in the teaching-learning process, (3) it fosters greater efficiency in learning, (4) it provides a more dramatic source of feedback, and (5) it serves as a more accurate means of diagnosing the extent of learning which has taken place as well as any unusual weaknesses.

If children are not provided with opportunities to actively participate, boredom will result and the tendency for desired responses to be extinguished will increase. If learning is to be profitable, a certain degree of tension is needed and an optimal level of stimulation must be provided. Too much stimulation should not be provided, since this is just as detrimental to learning as too little stimulation.

OVERLEARNING This concept is defined as the practice of a task beyond the point of initial mastery. Retarded children do not have a complete understanding of a concept after having accurately responded on the first few occasions. Since retarded children often have difficulty in attention, short-term memory, and association, there is a need for overlearning to be an integral part of the special program.

Improvement in learning, retention, transfer, and relearning will be facilitated if overlearning has taken place (Gilbert, 1957; Postman, 1962; Mander and Heinemann, 1956). According to Hebb's theory, overlearning would provide the organism with opportunities to strengthen and elaborate on the associational networks which have developed around an event. The same types of stimulus conditions that were present when initial learning occurred should prevail on subsequent presentations. Gradually, additional perceptions and stimulus variations can be introduced so that the generalization and elaboration of cell assemblies are possible.

When overlearning is allowed to occur, the teacher reduces the possibility of eliciting random responses from the child, enhances retention and transfer, and provides a means for increasing the child's general response repertoire. By presenting previously learned material in a variety of ways on numerous occasions, a more flexible and less rigid organism will develop.

STRESSING ACCURACY   In order to control the chance of children practicing errors, accuracy instead of speed should be stressed. This is especially necessary in the early stages of learning when new and basic concepts, which later will form the basis for subsequent learning, are formulated. Although competition between and within individuals is often beneficial to effect learning, accuracy can be stressed by the teacher, instilling in the children appropriate dimensions upon which such a competitive situation is to be founded. If children compete in terms of the time it takes to complete a task, accuracy will be sacrificed.

The teacher must see that the children develop a stable cognitive structure which is characterized by lack of ambiguity. An early emphasis on speed will result in errors, which in turn will lead to a less clear and less firmly established network of interrelated conceptual patterns. To reduce the possibility of confusion occurring on subsequent tasks, corrections must be stressed and less emphasis placed on speed of response.

REDUCING PROACTIVE AND RETROACTIVE INHIBITION   "Proactive inhibition" refers to interference with learning because of some *prior* experience. For example, a child might find it difficult to learn the frog kick in swimming because of having *previously* learned to use the flutter kick. Knowing how to flutter kick interferes with and decreases skill in learning the frog kick.

"Retroactive inhibition" refers to the interference with learning because of some *subsequent* experience. A child might find it difficult to remember how to do the butterfly stroke, which he had previously learned, because he *subsequently* learned how to swim the breast stroke.

To reduce each of these types of interference, intelligent sequencing of material is necessary. During initial learning, material with different characteristics should be presented in close temporal contiguity. When learning material is too similar in character and presented initially at approximately the same time, there is an increased possibility that one learning task will interfere with the other. After the child develops an awareness of differences and similarities, material which is more similar in character can be presented. The process is evolutionary; therefore, be sure that learning experiences differ enough initially so that each is clearly identified. Gradually, the similarity of the stimuli can be increased as the child's performance level increases. This principle is appropriate at various levels of the program, from a specific series of activities to the entire structure of the special-education program.

Interference can be damaging to subsequent or prior learning. The subtle influence of such confusion will often result in difficulties accumulating and frequently defy even the most astute diagnostician. Teachers must be diligent in logically sequencing their techniques of presentation and curriculum to control these potentially interfering effects.

MINIMAL CHANGE   Retarded children will learn most effectively if materials are programmed so that abrupt shifting between concepts and activities is minimized. Hegge, Kirk, and Kirk (1955) have developed remedial reading drills which follow this principle. For example, instead of a series of drill words quickly shifting to a new series, only the last letter in the new series changes: "s a t," "m a t," "r a t" followed by "s a p," "m a p," "r a p."

All activities cannot be developed to precisely follow the minimal-change principle as illustrated above. Some consideration, however, must be given in a step-by-step progression of activities which do not require the child to make conceptual leaps.

USING THE CHILD'S STRENGTHS   All of us are relatively stronger in certain areas than in others. Retarded children typically show their greatest capabilities in nonverbal activities and exhibit relatively weaker performances in skills requiring verbal competencies. In teaching retarded children with uneven profiles of abilities and disabilities, it is wise to use those areas of relative strength to enhance development in the weaker areas. For example, a child with this type of uneven profile should be encouraged to verbalize about nonverbal tasks. Telling the class what is being done as the child proceeds through an activity, answering questions posed by the teacher and other classmates, and talking about the dramatization of an event illustrate the principle to be followed.

The children should be encouraged to engage in activities

which will strengthen areas of relative weakness. At first, some children may be hesitant to participate because of a history of failure in the weak areas. The focus of the activities, thus, should be on situations wherein the threat of evaluation is minimal. In fact, initially they should be placed in situations in which there are no wrong responses. Gradually, evaluation can be judiciously introduced without penalty.

TEACHING CONSIDERATIONS IN AREAS OF FREQUENT WEAKNESS

Generalized learning characteristics of the retarded were discussed in Chapter 3. These weaknesses are significant in all areas of learning and skill development. Methods the teacher chooses to develop skills should consider these weaknesses. Teaching tactics are presented in nine areas in which the retarded often show particular disability.

Short-term memory

Mentally retarded children are frequently weak in short-term memory. In order for the child to correctly perceive and record stimuli and to form comprehensive associational networks which are remembered, the teacher should plan her presentations with the following in mind:

1 She should see that the child's attention is focused on the task by reducing the environmental stimuli to a minimum and increasing the stimulus value of the task. The working stimuli must be clear, unique, pertinent, and interesting to the student. The class should be located in a quiet section of the building and the students faced away from any external distractions. All irrelevant visual and auditory stimuli in close proximity to the activity should be masked. Auditory and/or visual stimuli directly associated with the activity should be increased in value and emphasized.

2 Every component of the auditory or visual stimuli should be presented in a clear fashion with each aspect initially of equivalent stimulus value. If the children are asked to recall a sentence or a short song, every word of the auditory chain should be loud enough to be heard and articulated clearly. If visual stimuli are to be recalled, whether in a certain sequence or not, the stimuli should be bold enough to allow for a clear view. Gradually, variations from this general rule can be allowed to occur as the children gain competence in recalling stimuli that vary in shape, size, content, or stimulus value. The same perceptions should appear each time with stimulus variation occurring later. In this way, a consistent and stable constellation of cell assemblies can become established; to do otherwise could result in confusion and the obliteration of existing networks.

3 All tasks should move from simple to more complex situations. The children should be initially exposed to and required to remember small groups of stimulus chains. The objects or sounds should be different so that each maintains its unique identity. Objects grossly different from each other are remembered more easily than objects closely alike. For example, in short-term visual memory the teacher might place a spoon, a toy automobile, and a rubber ball in front of a child in no specific sequence. The child is asked to close his eyes and upon reopening them recall which object had been removed. If a pencil, a pen, and a crayon had been placed before him initially, the task would have been more difficult because of the similarity among the objects in terms of shape, size, perhaps color, and function. To further complicate the task, the objects can be presented and the children asked to reproduce the sequence as it previously appeared. A similar gradation in levels of difficulty can be used with auditory stimuli. The maintenance of attention and the degree to which the child experiences success should constitute the principal criteria for deciding if the task is too difficult.

4 If interfering material intervenes between the components to be remembered or between the learning situation and the recall tests, memory will be inefficient and decay.

5 To improve short-term memory, stimuli should be labeled. In the earlier illustration, one-word labels for each object (spoon, car, and ball) will help the child recall what he has seen. Encouraging the child to use verbal labels in a visual task, and vice versa, will help recall and assist in the formation of strong intrasensory associations, such as auditory-visual, auditory-tactile, and visual-tactile.

6 Reward or reinforcement should be minimal since too great an emphasis on doing well or high anticipation of reward are detrimental to the development of short-term money. When a child succeeds, simply saying "fine" or "good" is adequate reinforcement. When a child fails, moving to another task or activity without comment or saying, "Let's try this one now," is wise strategy. Undue attention should not be called to errors since retarded children tend to remember best what not or how not to do something rather than remembering the correct response or proper approach to a problem.

7 Ample time should be provided for the practice of short-term-memory activities. Use of a tachistoscope, flash cards, games, records with sounds or songs, and various types of material recorded on tape will provide a medium for individual and small-group practice. It is important in these kinds of activities that accurate feedback be provided to each child immediately after a response is given. To disregard this principle will result in inefficient learning.

8 Material used in practice should be integrated with other subject

fields as often as possible and thereby make use of the successful experiences of the child. If a retarded youngster is particularly interested in arithmetic, it would be advantageous to use numbers auditorially or visually in short-term-memory tasks. If, on the other hand, the child particularly dislikes arithmetic, it would probably be more desirable to use material from some other area having greater positive valence for the child.

9 A great deal of dramatization of skills involving short-term memory should become methodologically central to the program. Remembering and executing commands of an auditory or visual nature and using sociodrama are illustrations of this technique.

Long-term memory

Mentally retarded children have less difficulty with long-term than with short-term memory. This finding supports those Hebbian postulations which suggest that once networks of association are established, their maintenance becomes vital and can be accomplished through the constant use of the information contained within the networks. Although the long-term-memory performance of the retarded is relatively good, it is necessary to constantly review, use, and elaborate upon previously learned facts and concepts so that forgetting will not occur easily. To this end, the following general teaching suggestions apply to various subjects areas:

1 Primary emphasis should be put on overlearning, during which time the concept being learned must be put to use in a practical and meaningful way. Repetition of the material being learned will occur more easily when a variety of sensory modalities are employed. Telling about and dramatizing an event which has been seen or done will make maximum use of intersensory association and facilitate the development of transfer abilities. Acceptable criteria for overlearning demands more than one appropriate response by the child.

2 Since context, e.g., remembering how to or what to do in a social situation, remembering a story sense or an arithmetic process, etc., is of much greater importance in long-term than in short-term memory, the teacher should reduce each task to its simplest components and present material in a logical sequence. For example, one would not want to teach addition before teaching grouping, since the latter is basic to an adequate understanding of the former.

3 For maximum long-term retention, the use of meaningful materials is more desirable than those which are nonmeaningful; the employment of pleasantly toned materials is preferred to the neutral or unpleasant; and recitation during learning activities should be incorporated into the general teaching strategy.

4 Being consistent in the presentation of materials, activities, and tasks is necessary. Retarded children who have learned a concept after having been exposed to a certain set of stimuli and who are later exposed to a different set of perceptions, may have great difficulty arriving at the correct answer because no explicit association was made between the series of stimuli. For example, if a child is taught to read the word g o l d e n using a "look-and-say" approach but, at a later date, is transferred to the room of a teacher who emphasizes reading through a phonics method, it might be expected that a severe reading problem could result. Established networks of association must be maintained, although elaboration on these assemblies by anchoring new perceptions to the presently existing cognitive structure is desirable.

5 The material committed to memory should be used in practical situations. If information is remembered and applied appropriately, the major reason for learning is realized. In this way additional benefits accrue, i.e., the increased opportunities for the child to repeat and reinforce learned material in lifelike circumstances. The further elaboration of cell assemblies and phase sequences, therefore, is effected.

Discrimination learning

Learning to discriminate among objects or sounds assumes that the peripheral systems are intact. If they are functioning adequately, the child's attention must be focused on the relevant stimuli in order to observe differences and similarities. Discrimination is important if the significance of information is to be correctly perceived, appropriately recorded and associated, and properly used in subsequent situations. For these operations to occur, the following should be considered:

1 Background interference and interruptions should be reduced to a minimum and those stimuli of the task increased in stimulus value. It will often be necessary to deliberately mask irrelevant stimuli.

2 Labels should be attached to each stimulus with emphasis given to making use of all sense modalities. For example, in discriminating among three objects, the child could be asked to choose the appropriate object and also to tell its name and hand it to the teacher. The unique characteristics of the object and how it is similar to and different from the other objects might also be discussed with the child.

3 Stimuli should initially be distinct and novel with gross discriminations used first. The dimensions on which the children are to discriminate should be clear. If the teacher wants discrimination by size, the colors and shapes of the alternatives should be the same as those of the correct choice. As the child gains skill in differenti-

ating along various dimensions and begins to understand and correctly use the related language (e.g., larger, smaller, round corners, green, etc.), more complicated and finer discriminations can be required. In the beginning stages of instruction, objects which are either large or small are preferred to intermediate-size stimuli.

4 The need for a sequential presentation of material according to the difficulty of the discrimination task should be understood. Difficulty can be increased either by requiring finer discriminations with the alternative choices being more closely alike or by asking for discriminations on more than one criterion. For example, the task might be to select the object that is green, largest, and longer than it is wide. Some of the options could be green but smaller than the correct choice, and other choices could be large but yellow.

5 Discrimination should logically lead into an understanding of classes and categories of things. To assist in the development of this skill, verbal and visual stimuli should constantly be related.

6 The learning phenomena which were discussed earlier, such as immediate reinforcement, success, active involvement, and spaced learning, are important for the development of skill in discrimination.

Incidental learning

Incidental learning does not typically occur without conscious or concentrated effort. All of us are aware of certain peripheral stimuli within our environment; those who are intellectually normal tend to absorb this information into their response repertoire with greater relative ease than do retarded children. Unfortunately for the retarded child, much of this peripheral information is basic and often establishes a foundation upon which subsequent learning is based. Consequently, some intentional teaching effort must be devoted to this important area. Although it is true that the retarded do not seem to be as weak in incidental learning as in other areas of cognition, the following teaching considerations will allow them to exercise their maximum capabilities in this area.

1 Retarded children must be given opportunities to experience a great number of events. The diversity of stimuli and events within their environment must be explicitly called to their attention and clearly related to other events and stimuli. In short, those aspects of the environment learned incidentally by the normal must become areas of intentional learning with the retarded. The special-education teacher, therefore, should frequently, but judiciously and with specific objectives in mind, take the children on meaningful field trips. Preparation before each trip and follow-up should be an important part of the experience.

2 Questioning and group discussions will help to make the students more aware of their surroundings. Questions asked must initially

be open-ended with every answer being correct. For example, there is a difference between asking, "What else did you see this morning on your way to school?" and, "What color is the flower in front of the school?" Gradually, more specific questions can be asked as the children become more alert to their surroundings.

3 Games and other types of competitive situations can be used as the students develop incidental learning skill. Studies seem to suggest that incidental learning will be enhanced when reward or incentives are used.

Initial learning

When retarded children face a new learning situation, they have less chance than normal children of initially learning concepts inherent in the tasks. This is because of their limited intellectual ability, a history of failure, and their traditionally low generalized expectancy for success. They fail to see the rewards in learning which normal children characteristically perceive.

Research indicates that mentally retarded children, when matched with normal children on CA, do poorly at the outset but show rapid improvement with continued practice. Although MA seems to determine the upper limit of task competency that can be mastered in areas related to cognition, assuming that the task is within the individual's range, sufficient practice could overcome certain initial performance disadvantages. It is within reason, therefore, to suggest that although retarded children learn slowly at the beginning, they have some potential for overcoming this slow initial performance speed to some degree if they are provided with opportunities for success and practice. Studies have shown that after the failure on problems, the retarded have difficulty solving easier problems with which they were earlier successful. If a child has success with easy problems, he stands a better chance of successfully and more quickly performing harder ones than if he begins with the difficult problems.

Practice, too, has its part in even the most simple initial learning task for the retarded. These periods of practice must be varied and interesting, allowing the child to give full attention to the task. To form comprehensive associational networks in learning, the retarded will profit from repetitions, exposure in a great variety of contexts, and from using all the senses in concert. More specific suggestions for helping the children in initial learning are:

1 New learning should be presented early in the day when the children are more alert. Early presentation of such material in each work period is also desirable.

2 The children must be impressed with the personal significance of their learning the material. This preparation phase is important and may take more time than is consumed in teaching the new material.

3 New learning should be related to past learning and experiences. It is wise to provide them with a reference or anchoring point to which the new material can be directly related.

4 The children should have chances to react to and explain in their own words the major concepts inherent in the new material. Illustrations of the practical application of the new learning should be solicited from the students.

5 New learning should be repeated in a variety of ways and applied to a variety of situations in order to stress the applicability, generalizability, and usefulness of the information.

Attention

Many feel that if the retarded were able to inhibit the effects of extraneous stimuli, learning could proceed in a much more orderly and effective manner. These children typically have very short attention spans, which directly affects their ability to grasp material quickly. It should be pointed out here that attention span for the retarded, as for the nonretarded, is a variable which is often a function of the type of task the retarded are required to perform. The average child, however, will typically attend to a task long enough to understand the major concepts involved in a lesson; the mentally retarded child frequently loses interest and drifts away from the grasp of the teacher and material. Helping the retarded to develop skills in attending to relevant stimuli is important for instructional effectiveness. Factors which will increase or decrease the attention of the retarded include:

1 Reducing extraneous stimuli by sectioning the room with partitions when small groups are at work, seating the children away from doors and windows, controlling interruptions, and by establishing patterns of work and conduct which the children gradually perceive as appropriate behavior. For example, using the same classroom and seating positions will help to create a more stable atmosphere and eliminate irrelevant stimuli which would occur when physical changes are made.

2 Emphasizing relevant stimuli and varying the mode of presentation by employing illustrations, examples, demonstrations, or audiovisual aids. The materials should be handled by the children and a definite attempt made to stimulate as many channels of communication as possible during the lesson. For example, when doing rational counting, have the child place a peg in a hole or drop a ping-pong ball into a jar. When saying a word, have the youngster trace the letters.

3 Spending very short periods of time on new, more difficult activities. The teacher should be alert to (a) situations in which children are reaching their tolerance for frustration because of lack of success

and (b) the point at which they are becoming restless or inattentive because the material is too difficult, boring, or unstimulating. Activities should be varied to offset these difficulties.

4 Encouraging questions during the activity and group interaction. This technique will keep interest high and provide for a more complete understanding of the material. Introducing mildly competitive situations is desirable when all the children are performing at approximately the same level. Attention-maintaining devices such as saying, "Follow my finger with your eyes and don't let it get out of sight," will help mask irrelevant stimuli.

Association

The ability to associate concepts or facts is part of intelligence. This permits us to react to stimuli in a rapid and proper manner. For example, when we are driving and see a red light, we stop. We react to this stimulus because in the past we have developed a complex network of perceptual associations which result in the action of stopping a car. It is clear that in order for associational bonds to become established, the individual must have clearly received the various perceptions common to an event. The teaching considerations mentioned earlier apply to the development of association skills. In addition to these, the following should be considered:

1 The first association activity should require students to group together things which are alike. At first the criterion for "likeness" should be very general. For example, have them name all the animals they have seen. Cutting out pictures from magazines of things they can ride in, eat for dinner, or wear to school will help relationships to develop. The children should always be encouraged to verbalize about the various aspects of their activity. The teacher could ask a child why the various pictures were put together just to have him verbalize and see the relationships which exist among events.

2 Children should learn that some events naturally precede other events. The idea of sequence can be developed by showing a story illustrated on cards. Mixing the cards and asking a child to reconstruct and simultaneously tell about the story will help in the development of sequencing skills.

3 At a higher level, there is need for the retarded to relate cause to effect. This task demands more conceptual skill than simply seeing likeness. For instance, the child might be told not to cross the street unless the light facing him is green or the crossing guard is there to help. He might also be taught that he should look both ways for cars on those streets that do not have traffic lights or crossing guards. A clear explanation of the reason for this desired behavior must be presented. The child should realize that if he does not understand this relationship, an accident might result. Always in-

form the children why a certain act will cause another. Frequent use of the question, "Why?" will guide them to see the important components in cause-and-effect situations.

4 *The school program should not be structured so that the retarded are led to believe that knowledge in reading does not have applicability in other areas, such as in arithmetic or occupational information. Cell assemblies and phase sequences will become strongly established if commonalities among activities are explicitly pointed out.*

Expression of ideas

Ideas can be expressed either vocally or by gestures. Mentally retarded children tend to be poor in both these areas. This situation is probably due in large part to their not being exposed to stimulating contacts in the early years and because there have been insufficient models in the home which are necessary for developing skills in expression. To overcome this difficulty, the teacher should consider the following:

1 *The classroom atmosphere should be conducive to stimulating vocal and gestural expression. The children should feel that their productions will not be evaluated and criticized.*

2 *The teacher must take time to listen to the children and must provide a good example of speech and language by speaking clearly and talking about subjects which are enjoyable and pleasant to the children. Many of the retarded do not have an opportunity to listen to an adult speak unless the adult is reprimanding or punishing them. In other instances, children are not given an opportunity to express themselves because their parents, knowing that they are retarded, do not require enough of them.*

3 *Vocal and gestural expression can be stimulated by making use of a variety of materials such as hand puppets, flannel boards, and costumes. Dramatization will aid expression and help the children to increase their general information repertoire. For example, the children could stage a make-believe visit to the doctor, supermarket, dentist, or to another city to visit a friend. Pantomime can be used and a game played with the other students by trying to guess what or who the child is depicting.*

4 *The way questions are framed will often either enhance or stifle responses of children. Questions should be open-ended and allow for a variety of responses in order to increase expressive performance. The children will not be encouraged to express themselves when asked a question for which a "yes" or "no" response is sufficient. Questions designed to enhance expression can be formulated in a fashion so that there is no wrong answer and any response is acceptable. This approach should be used until the child reaches a*

point at which enough security is gained to tolerate corrections and suggestions related to the content and technique of the answer being expressed.

SELECTED REFERENCES

Dunn, Lloyd M.: *Exceptional Children in the Schools,* Holt, Rinehart and Winston, Inc., New York, 1963.

Educational Policies Commission: *Policies for Education in American Democracy,* National Education Association, Washington, D.C., 1946, p. 47.

Ellis, Norman R. (ed.): *Handbook of Mental Deficiency,* McGraw-Hill Book Company, New York, 1963.

Gilbert, Thomas R.: "Overlearning and the Retention of Meaningful Prose," *Journal of General Psychology,* vol. 56, 1957, pp. 281–289.

Hegge, T., Kirk, S. A., and Kirk, W.: *Remedial Reading Drills,* George Wahr Publishing Company, Ann Arbor, Michigan, 1955.

Kirk, S. A. and Johnson, G. O.: *Educating the Retarded Child,* Houghton Mifflin Company, Boston, 1951.

Mandler, G. and Heinemann, S. H.: "Effect of Overlearning of a Verbal Response on Transfer of Training," *Journal of Experimental Psychology,* vol. 52, 1956, pp. 39–46.

Peter, Laurence J.: *Prescriptive Teaching,* McGraw-Hill Book Company, New York, 1965.

Postman, L.: "Retention as a Function of Degree of Overlearning," *Science,* vol. 135, 1962, pp. 666–667.

Robinson, Halbert B. and Robinson, Nancy M.: *The Mentally Retarded Child,* McGraw-Hill Book Company, New York, 1965.

Stevens, Harvey A. and Heber, Rick (eds.): *Mental Retardation: A Review of Research,* The University of Chicago Press, Chicago, 1964.

Wiseman, Douglas: "A Classroom Procedure for Identifying and Remediating Language Problems," *Mental Retardation,* vol. 3, no. 2, April, 1965, pp. 22–23.

perceptual-motor development:
the foundation for subsequent learning

If an organism is to learn anything or to engage in various types of cognitive behavior, such as problem solving, the mechanism responsible for information gathering must operate effectively. Physical information from the environment is received by the sense organs and converted into message units which are understood by the nervous system. After this conversion, the impulses are channeled to the brain where they are dealt with by either being directly sent to a response system or modified in some fashion prior to encoding. In the final stage of this process, the organism responds in some manner.[1] If an individual has difficulty in one of the peripheral systems, such as a hearing or visual problem, reception of information from the environment will be impaired and result in a diminution of the efficiency of subsequent stages in the process. The integrity of the various seg-

[1] For a discussion of the perceptual process and a review of the empirical literature in this area, the reader is referred to Forgus (1966).

ments of the perceptual process must be maintained if learning is to occur and if the individual is to benefit from experience.

Consistent with the Hebbian point of view and in agreement with the research in mental retardation which suggests that lack of attention is a primary disability among retarded children, the thesis of this book is that perceptual-motor skills are basic to all subsequent learning. If a child is to learn by gathering information from his environment and to remember, associate, and use this information in an appropriate fashion, it is essential that perceptual sensitivity, selectivity, and stability be established. This means that the child must be able to attend, select from his environment those perceptions which are relevant to the situation and problem at hand, organize the input by associating relevant perceptions with appropriate material existing in the repertoire, respond in a suitable fashion, and use responses as feedback for further perceptual selection and the modification of subsequent response patterns. Surely, then, learning is dependent on and subsumed under perceptual-motor skills. As an individual's experience increases, his perceptual set broadens; he becomes more selective in extracting the most relevant stimuli from the environment; and learning becomes more efficient and effective.

SEQUENCE OF PERCEPTUAL–MOTOR DEVELOPMENT

The process by which perceptual-motor skills develop is complex. It is difficult to precisely identify the components of the process since they are not discrete entities and substantially overlap. In a general sense, there are four major components of the process, viz., input, association or integration, output, and feedback.

The receptive element of the perceptual process consists of the extraction of information from the environment by the sense organs and the translation of these perceptions into a message system appropriate for the cortex. A certain level of arousal is necessary for perceptions to be received. The brainstem reticular formation has the function of awakening the higher centers so that information can be processed. If the organism is lethargic for some reason or damaged to the point that arousal is not possible, information will not be received or subsequently processed. Similarly, if the organism is too highly aroused and the extreme activating effect of the brainstem reticular formation is not inhibited by those sections of the cortex responsible for this function, behavior will be hyperactive, inattentiveness will be manifested, and inappropriate perceptions will be received. Lack of attention or too high a level of arousal will impede the accurate reception of information from the environment.

The receptive component of the perceptual process normally develops in early infancy and operates at a meaningful level before a commensurate degree of skill is manifested in areas of association and expression. The meaning and significance of commands and admonitions are usually understood first; the integration of concepts occurs more slowly and must often be intentionally taught. As the organism gains skill and satisfaction in the reception of stimuli, incidental learning begins to play a greater role in learning. With retarded children, who often have difficulty extracting relevant stimuli from their environment or who are exposed to a restricted range of stimuli, learning cannot be left to chance and must be more intentional than incidental.

Perceptions must be received before association and integration can occur; there must be something to program into the repertoire. The integrity of the receptive components of the perceptual process is fundamental to the development of associational networks. Moreover, to inhibit the development of random patterns of association, stable and relevant stimuli must be presented in the early stages of learning. If a child receives different perceptions each time the same event is experienced, integration among the perceptions will not be facilitated and associational bonds will be unstable.

Early learning should intentionally be structured so that new information is directly associated with existing, stable associational networks. It is usually necessary to call to the attention of the retarded relationships between new and old learning so that bonds between perceptions can be more easily and accurately formed. There is some potential advantage in the organism being exposed to stimuli from all the sense modalities. This will result in associations which develop more quickly and allow for the increased probability of appropriate responses given to various stimuli. This intersensory association suggests the need to combine auditory, visual, and tactile procedures into activities involving new learning.

The development of association skills follows closely the establishment of and growth in receptive capabilities. Infants quickly learn that the bottle means food and that this, in turn, results in comfort. Visual, auditory, and intra-individual stimuli associate rapidly; and in homes in which a routine has been established, the infant will develop stable associational networks quickly. These networks provide anchoring points to which subsequent verbal and nonverbal learning can be related and subsumed. For example, if a child associates milk in a glass, the quenching of thirst, and general comfort, at an early age the parents can introduce the vocal expression "milk." This allows the child to relate the appropriate label to the proper, well-established associational pattern. The introduction of additional perceptions to an established network can be done by using this same strategy.

The expression, or output, phase of the perceptual process occurs after the organism perceives that some type of response is appropriate or necessary in a situation. The organism must scan the repertoire for those responses which are correct for each situation and assess each of the possible alternatives for the most appropriate answer at that time. A response is made after the repertoire has been surveyed. Individuals will vary substantially in their ability to perform this operation.

A response can be made vocally, gesturally, or in combination. Meaningfulness expressed vocally does not typically occur until a child reaches the mental age of approximately eighteen to twenty-four months. Gestures and other nonverbal expressions constitute the primary means of production prior to that time. A great amount of earlier development must occur before a child reaches the stage of vocal expression of ideas.

Initial responses by the child are motoric. Patterns of output are developed, systematized, and elaborated upon according to the perceptions the child receives from the environment. These motor patterns gradually become strengthened and generalized to more elaborate responses. For example, sitting leads to a variety of types of locomotion, such as crawling, walking, running, skipping, and jumping.

It is critical that the perceptual process contain an effective system for monitoring the appropriateness of the output in order to be in harmony with the problem and other information received from the environment. Apparently, some aspects of the output are internally fed back to the receptive components of the system. This monitoring results in any necessary modifications within the system and leads to greater discrimination, selectivity, and differentiation in the reception of subsequent stimuli. Other adjustments are often effected in the associational process as well as in subsequent output.

An important goal of special education is to assist the retarded to develop an internal monitoring system. These children have difficulty in using their output to adjust the various components of the perceptual process. Initially their attention should be called to the degree of consonance between their responses and the problem. The teacher will often need to act as the child's monitor during the early stages of learning, until sensitivity to and skill in using feedback are developed. Gallagher (1960) suggests the use of tutors for those retarded children who exhibit monitoring problems so that proper remediation can be given to this specific area of disability.

RATIONALE FOR EMPHASIZING
PERCEPTUAL–MOTOR DEVELOPMENT

Children with specific or general difficulty in one or more of the components of the perceptual process exhibit a reduction in efficiency and effectiveness for learning. The causes of these difficulties can be traced to (1) the erroneous or random reception of stimuli including the misunderstanding of a problem or situation, (2) the introduction of irrelevant perceptions into associational networks, (3) the obliteration of existing networks because information has been programmed which is antagonistic to established associational chains, (4) too little or too much arousal in the higher centers, (5) an ineffective mechanism for surveying the cognitive structure to locate appropriate alternative responses related to a situation, (6) improper response patterns, and/or (7) an inadequate mechanism for monitoring output and providing internal feedback.

Learning will not occur effectively if children have difficulty in receiving information, making associations properly, perceiving differences between figure and ground, making spatial-to-temporal translations, accurately perceiving objects in space, developing coordination between eye and hand, and in sequencing. All these skills are prerequisite to adequate perceptual-motor development and basically dependent on the effectiveness of control an individual has over the movement of his own body. Information is not received nor are responses transmitted in a vacuum. An individual perceives accurately only after having developed some reference against which comparisons and checks can be made. Consistent and efficient motor patterns permit an individual to explore his environment and systematize his relation to it. An individual, therefore, compares aspects of the environment to himself and only after much experience is he able to receive and translate environmental stimuli without constant reference to his own body.

To illustrate, assume that an individual is asked to compare the size of two objects and to indicate which one is the larger. A young child who has not developed skill in perceptual orientation will find it necessary to compare each of the objects with his own body in order to judge the larger of the two objects. If, however, the youngster has completed knowledge of his own body in relation to the outside world and is able to project this information and compare it with objects, he will no longer find it necessary to constantly check his perceptual experiences by referring back to himself. In short, for children with unstable perceptual organization, discriminations and comparisons between objects must be checked with themselves and their own position in space. As control of the body is gained and the individual begins to understand his relationship with external objects, more rapid comparisons between objects can be made without establishing the constant time-consuming reorientations. If a person has not learned about his own body and its spatial position, an inadequate perception of outside objects will result.

Kephart (1960, 1963, 1965) has suggested that children develop understanding of themselves and thus, a reference against which perceptions can be compared at an early age through the development of skill in the use of motor-activity patterns. He has suggested that four basic motor patterns of (1) balance and maintenance of posture, (2) locomotion, (3) contact, and (4) contact with a moving object with propulsion constitute important areas in which competence must be developed for effective interaction and evaluation of the environment. Accordingly, if an individual has difficulty in any of these basic motor patterns, a stable reference point for comparing perceptions external to the organism will not be developed. This situation will lead to errors in any or all the components of perception (reception, association, and expression) and subsequently result in learning difficulties.

The table on page 77 summarizes the postulated hierarchy of perceptual-motor development.

An example may help to explain this sequence. Suppose we have two pieces of pipe, one of which is large enough for a young child to crawl through and the other of which is too small. The objective is that the child eventually reach the point at which a correct judgment will be made concerning which of the two is larger in diameter. Prerequisite to the task is that the child be able to perceive sensations and transmit this information to the already awakened cortex. The child must also be able to move about and engage in enough motor movements to allow for the manipulation and exploration of the objects in space.

Assuming that the systems necessary for these functions are intact, the child will respond initially by indicating that one of the pipes is larger than the other totally on the basis of a comparison of each with himself. Pipe A may be large enough to crawl through; whereas, pipe B may be too small to go through. The child responds purely on the basis of comparison with his own body. Gradually, after having experienced this type of event on several occasions, the child will be able to begin using one of the pipes as the reference point against which other objects are compared. No longer will it be necessary to make a perceptual-motor match between himself and objects in space. Logically, then, this skill will result in learning which occurs in a more rapid, functional, and efficacious manner.

HEBBIAN RELATIONSHIPS

In relating this phenomenon to Hebb's theory, it is reasonable to expect that early cell assemblies develop primarily on the basis of motor exploration. All the requirements needed to adequately perform the basic motor patterns are programmed into the repertoire as the child attempts to manipulate the various parts of his body. These networks of association are gradually elaborated as the individual

**TABLE 5-1 Hypothesized Hierarchy for Perceptual-Motor
Development**

Level 1 Integrity of the peripheral sensory mechanisms including vision, hearing, speech, and tactile senses.

Level 2 *Development of basic motor patterns.*
   a balance
   b locomotion
   c contact
   d receipt and propulsion

Additional and more precise motor patterns.
   a gross motor movements
   b fine motor movements

Level 3 *Development of a concept of one's own body in space.*

At this stage the individual makes use of the body as a reference point for experimentation with the environment. Responses are formulated solely in terms of the position of the body in relation to the perceptions being received. For example, laterality is the internal appreciation of left and right with which all objects in space are compared. In short, at this stage of development of the child, the object is not perceived in itself as having a left or right since all comparisons are made in terms of one's own body and its position in space.

Level 4 *Matching perceptions with established motor patterns.*

As perceptual stability progresses and the organism gains experience, perceptions are compared with information the repertoire has programmed from previous motor learning. As these perceptual matches occur between the sensory experience and the motor experience, the object being perceived begins to have meaning in terms of general and unique characteristics. Eventually, the organism no longer has to depend on a perceptual-motor match when characteristics of objects are accurately perceived, and reference to one's own body is unnecessary.

Level 5 *Accurate perception leads to efficient and effective learning.*

As soon as the organism has reached the level of development at which perceptual stability is established and a dependable system for processing perceptual data created, effort can be devoted to increasing associational networks, further elaborating on the capabilities to establish external sources for reference, establishing a consistent means for evaluating alternative responses to problems emanating from the perceptual experiences, and responding in a precise and appropriate manner.

continues to relate objects in space to his own body. As experience broadens, in this respect, networks become more firmly established and dependable.

The organism eventually gains enough cognitive stability so that it is no longer necessary that direct comparisons be made between the motor and perceptual components of the cell assemblies; enough maturity will have already occurred to allow the individual to depend primarily on using the more efficient perceptual parts of the network for reference. With experience, therefore, the individual will no longer need to resort to using the highly inefficient motor components of associational networks as reference points.

Many children have trouble developing the basic associational networks upon which subsequent cognitive development is founded. These motor-based patterns are poorly formed because the children are either damaged in some fashion and are unable to perform basic motor movements, or they lack the opportunity to engage in appropriate types of activities because of living in a restricted environment. In each instance, the children will not develop an adequate foundation with which perceptions received from the environment can be compared. This results in a perceptual reference point not developing, perceptual stability being reduced, and inaccurate and incomplete cell assemblies being formed. Since the basic associational networks upon which elaboration occurs are so important and because first learning is motoric, establishing the basis for the development of first cell assemblies, the need for more attention to be given to these basic motor patterns seems greater than ever.

The parallels between the theories of Hebb and Piaget have been discussed by Hunt (1961). The degree of commonality between these two points of view is striking. The Hebbian explanation emphasizes the central role of perceptual development; Piaget indicates that motor behavior structures the central processes. Both theorists agree that intelligence and behavior are determined by the central processes, which can be altered dramatically through interaction with the environment. The theories of both suggest the vital determinant of early experience in establishing the rate of subsequent development.

The behavior characteristic of Piaget's stages of development denotes the emphasis he places on early motor experience. During the first stage, in which there are six sensory-motor operations, and in the second stage of development, which encompasses three levels of concrete thinking operations, emphasis is placed on the need for the child to organize and manipulate the surrounding environment. Each of these operations is tied to some type of concrete action. These activities provide the basic cognitive foundation which will subsequently lead to the child's being able to deal with abstract concepts, formulate hypotheses, and engage in reasoning. The close parallel which exists between the theories of Piaget and Hebb adds credence to the idea that educators should first show concern for perceptual-motor development of the retarded child before launching into more difficult material which exceeds his conceptual capabilities.

PERCEPTUAL–MOTOR DEVELOPMENT OF THE RETARDED

Investigators studying perceptual-motor development with the re-tarded have been in frequent disagreement concerning the param-eters of study. Spivack (1963), for example, in reviewing the litera-ture on perceptual processes, elected not to include studies in which subjects were required to engage in some type of visual-motor per-formance. He felt that one cannot accurately study perception without being aware of nonperceptual components involved in response. This scientist contends that it is necessary to differentiate between perceptual reception and discrimination on one hand and perceptual-response patterns on the other. Similarly, the nature of motor skills in the retarded has been studied (Malpass, 1963). Investigations in this area have exercised minimal control over perceptual input by focusing on dimensions of motor proficiency. Still others have re-ported on research in which both input and output have been con-trolled and measured (Lipman, 1963).

Spivack (1963) and Benton (1964) surveyed the contemporary research describing the perceptual-input characteristics of the re-tarded. To summarize conclusions from the studies they review in depth, it was found that retarded children tend to have difficulties in (1) auditory and visual discrimination, (2) right-left discrimination, (3) locating the site of stimulation applied to various parts of the body, (4) color discrimination, and (5) in the general identification of complex stimuli. Because of methodological difficulties, includ-ing the use of brain-injured and non-brain-injured subjects in the same sample, the findings from investigations designed to assess perceptual-input characteristics of the retarded are ambiguous and often confusing. Spivack (1963) has presented an excellent summary of these possible methodological difficulties.

The results of research dealing with motor skills of the mentally retarded have been reported in depth by Malpass (1963) and Denny (1964). There is consistent agreement in the literature that the re-tarded are generally deficient in motor ability, including skills related to speed of performance or reaction time, precision, and strength or force required to successfully perform a task. In specific motor skills, such as in rail walking, finger dexterity, and various types of hand manipulations, the retarded do less well than intellectually normal subjects.

Denny (1964) has summarized the research in motor educability of the retarded. The evidence suggests that when retarded children are provided with a program aimed at developing simple motor skills and given opportunities to practice, they will often be capable of performing at a level commensurate with their CA. It is important, however, that the perceptual-motor program be sequentially structured so that tasks build on and emanate from previously developed skills. Moreover, it should be pointed out that as the motor task increases in difficulty, the influence of intelligence becomes more apparent.

Studies of perceptual-motor performance and development in which input and output are relatively controlled and measured have typically required subjects to perform on tasks such as card sorting, rotary pursuit, block turning, mirror drawing, maze learning, or formboard work. Lipman (1963) has reviewed and interpreted the major research in these areas. In general, the data seem to suggest the following:

1 *The retarded often exhibit initial performance difficulties which frequently can be overcome with practice if the task is not too complex.*
2 *A relationship seems to exist between the complexity of the task and intelligence.*
3 *In certain perceptual-motor tasks, the subject's CA appears to determine the upper limit of capability; whereas, on other tasks MA determines the upper limit.*
4 *Establishing goals and providing verbal praise results in an elevation of a child's performance level.*
5 *The data have not clearly indicated the relationship between MA and competence on the various perceptual-motor tasks typically used in these experiments.*

ASSESSMENT OF PERCEPTUAL–MOTOR COMPETENCE

Both formal and informal techniques are available to evaluate perceptual-motor capabilities of children. Instruments which are of a formal nature are standardized, have data from a normative group against which a subject's response can be compared, and require administration by a trained psychometrician. Some of the instruments attempt to assess the entire spectrum of perceptual-motor factors; others focus on a specific skill such as perceptual input or response.

Whereas most of the formal instruments require administration by a qualified examiner, there are several scales (principally those involving motor performance) which do not require a trained administrator. Irrespective of the test, the examiner should always be sure that he has the proper background and training required to administer the instruments. In most instances the manual of instructions will outline these requirements.

Table 5-2 describes a sample of instruments which evaluate various areas of perceptual-motor performance.

TABLE 5-2 Examples of Instruments Designed to Evaluate Various Factors Related to Perceptual-Motor Development

Name of test	Age range	Factors assessed
Moore Eye-Hand Coordination and Color-Matching Test	2 yrs.–adulthood	Eye-hand coordination, color matching
Marianne Frostig Developmental Test of Visual Perception	3–8 yrs.	Eye-hand coordination, figure-ground discrimination, form constancy, position in space, spatial relations
Merrill-Palmer Scale of Mental Tests	24–63 mos.	Fine motor movements as well as intellectual development
Arthur Point Scale of Performance Tests	4.5 yrs.–adult	Various perceptual-motor competences as well as general intelligence
Perceptual Forms Test	6–9 yrs.	General visual perception
Embedded Figures Test	10 yrs. and above	Dimensions of a field-ground nature
Bender-Gestalt Test	4 yrs. and above	Perceptual-motor skills in addition to personality factors
Progressive Matrices	5 yrs. and above	General visual perception and intelligence
Porteus Maze Test	3 yrs. and above	Visual-motor ability and intelligence
Spiral Aftereffect Test	5 yrs. and above	Spiral aftereffect
Pre-Tests of Vision, Hearing, and Motor Coordination	12 yrs.–adult	Visual-motor and auditory-gestural association and coordination

TABLE 5-2 *(Continued)*

Name of test	Age range	Factors assessed
Brace Scale of Motor Ability	8 yrs. and above	Motor agility, balance, control, flexibility, minimizes importance of size and strength
Edmiston Motor Capacity Test	6 yrs.–adult	Hand-eye coordination, estimation of distance, and general perceptual judgment
Lincoln-Oseretsky Motor Development Scale (revision of Oseretsky Tests of Motor Proficiency)	6–14 yrs.	Gross motor skills, speed, coordination, dexterity, rhythm, balance, jumping, manual ability, with strength and power minimized
Rail-Walking Test	5 yrs. and above	Locomotor coordination and general control of body while moving
Cureton Physical Fitness Test	Adolescence and above	Balance, flexibility, agility, strength, endurance, power

In addition to the above instruments, perceptual-motor development has often been evaluated by using tasks which involve rotary pursuit, mirror drawing, coding, maze tracing, card sorting, assembling objects, formboards, pegboard apparatus, ball and slot, and other similar activities. These procedures are used when the researcher wants to compare one group with another and is not primarily interested in evaluating an individual's performance in terms of a comparative normative group.

Informal procedures have also been developed to assess perceptual-motor development. These techniques, which most frequently are not standardized, can be used by the classroom teacher or physical-education specialists. There typically is no specified time limit for their administration, and, in fact, the tasks can be given in part, in total, or in any combination. This flexibility is bought at a price; intra-individual comparisons can be easily made, but inter-individual comparisons and evaluations are more imprecise when informal procedures are employed. They do, however, provide excellent means for checking on a child's progress in those important basic perceptual-motor areas which are directly related to success in academic areas.

One of the most comprehensive techniques for informally assessing perceptual-motor development is the Purdue Perceptual-Motor Survey which was developed by Kephart (1960, 1966). The scale is designed for children ranging in age from six to nine and surveys a rather complete spectrum of auditory and visual perceptual-motor abilities. Tasks in the scale are easy to administer and any aspects of the child's performance to which the examiner should pay particular attention are well delineated in the literature describing the procedures. Emphasis is placed on the response aspect of the perceptual-motor process. Table 5-3 summarizes the tasks included in the Purdue Perceptual-Motor Survey and the dimensions each evaluates.

TABLE 5-3 Dimensions Evaluated by the Purdue Perceptual-Motor Survey

Name of activity	Primary functions observed
1 Walking board	a Balance b Postural flexibility c Laterality
2 Jumping, skipping, and hopping	a Symmetrical behavior and body control b Laterality c Body image d Rhythm
3 Identifying body parts (auditory stimulus-motor response)	a Body image b Understanding significance of what is heard c Proper translation of an auditory stimulus to a gestural response
4 Imitation of movements	a Laterality b Body control c Directionality
5 Obstacle course	a Body image in terms of its position in space b Body control
6 Angels in the snow (visual stimulus-motor response with frequent auditory-vocal associations)	a Body image b Laterality c Directionality d Body control

TABLE 5-3 (Continued)

Name of activity	Primary functions observed
7 Stepping stones (visual-motor)	**a** Laterality **b** Body control **c** Eye-foot coordination **d** Directionality
8 Chalkboard work	**a** Laterality **b** Directionality **c** Motor movement **d** Visual memory
9 Ocular pursuits (lateral, vertical, diagonal, rotary, monocular)	**a** Ocular control **b** Laterality
10 Visual achievement forms (copying various forms presented by the teacher)	**a** Form perception **b** Figure-ground relationships
11 Kraus-Weber Tests	**a** Gross motor coordination **b** General postural adjustment **c** Muscular fitness

The above is a summary of the material presented in Roach and Kephart, *The Purdue Perceptual-Motor Survey*, Charles E. Merrill Books, Inc., Columbus, Ohio, 1966.

It is frequently desirable to check quickly on the progress of a child in one or more of the perceptual-motor areas. For these quick checks one does not need to comprehensively evaluate in a fashion that is implied when using the Purdue Perceptual-Motor Survey. Observation of a child in routine classroom activities or in physical education will often suffice. This will allow consideration of specific areas of weakness and general patterns of development. When time is available for a more complete assessment, periodic use of Kephart's scale is recommended.

DEVELOPING PERCEPTUAL–MOTOR SKILLS

This section is devoted to a discussion of broad teaching considerations appropriate to assist the retarded in developing those basic perceptual-motor skills required for later success in school. Any decision regarding which areas need more attention than others is arbitrary. Techniques outlined in each section are often appropriate in developing skills in other areas. For example, when attention is given to training areas of input, factors involving association and response are strengthened simultaneously.

Training of receptive ability

It is reminiscent of Montessori to devote a section to a consideration of the need to train retarded children to be alert and attentive to relevant stimuli in their environment. For certain, if this area is not considered, there will always be a high probability of erroneous perceptions becoming a part of the retarded child's response repertoire. This situation could lead to difficulties throughout the entire perceptual process and perhaps precipitate subsequent learning problems.

In a modern translation of Montessori (1965), suggestions have been made for helping children develop receptive capabilities. The instruments and materials which are used to teach the youngsters are of a graded nature and manipulated solely by the child. The perceptual input of children is refined through repeated exercises. Table 5-4 presents an illustration of activities recommended by Montessori for training various types of perceptual sensitivity. Unfortunately, it is not possible to give unqualified endorsement to these suggestions because consistent empirical documentation of their efficacy has not been presented. This situation is not atypical in special education and should not deter the teacher from experimenting with these procedures in the classroom.

Many of the types of activities suggested by Itard, Séguin, and Montessori are appropriate today in training receptive skills of the retarded. By becoming familiar with materials and techniques suggested in their educational programs, the teacher can easily elaborate on the basic principles inherent in the activities they suggest.

The following suggested activities and pedagogical considerations will help the retarded to develop keener receptive capabilities. Each of these suggestions can be modified according to the ability level and age of the children.

1 *The teacher should have some assurance that the children have no difficulty with the peripheral systems. If a child continually misperceives, an examination by a medical specialist should be scheduled.*
2 *If the sensory mechanisms are to accurately perceive, manipulating the environment within the classroom is necessary in order to reduce tangential stimuli and force the child to attend to relevant stimuli.*
3 *Auditory receptive skills can be developed by engaging the children in activities such as the following:*
   a *Have the children listen to various types of sounds they have heard during a class walk. They should be asked to identify the source of each sound and to give it an appropriate label.*

TABLE 5-4 Illustrations of Perceptual Training Suggested by Montessori

Sensory channel affected	Illustration of an appropriate activity
Tactile sense	The children touch materials with various types of surfaces, starting with those requiring discriminations between two highly different surfaces (sandpaper and silk) and gradually reducing the degree of difference between the surface characteristics.
Thermic sense	The children feel the outside of two metal bowls each of which contains water of a different temperature. Slowly the difference between the bowls is reduced, requiring a finer discrimination by the children.
Baric sense (sense of weight)	The children are required to estimate the difference in weight among small blocks each of which is of the same size, texture, and degree of smoothness; however, the blocks are made of different types of wood and thus are of different weights.
Sterognostic sense (recognition of objects through the simultaneous help of the tactile and muscular senses)	The children are presented with a large pile of cubes and bricks each group of which has different composition characteristics. The task is to make two piles by placing the bricks on one side and the cubes on the other, while blindfolded.
Taste	The tongues of the children are touched with various solutions which have different characteristics such as salty, sweet, sour, bitter, acid, or neutral.
Olfactory sense (smell)	The children learn to recognize various odors, first by associating the smell with the appropriate label. Later they are asked to discriminate among various odors while blindfolded.

TABLE 5-4 *(Continued)*

Sensory channel affected	Illustration of an appropriate activity
Visual sense (a variety of dimensions related to visual perception is assessed such as size, thickness, color, shape, length, contour, etc.)	Various objects of graded size, dimensions, and color are used with the children manipulating the objects according to a variety of possible criteria, such as the longest, the larger, red colored objects, or placing them in the appropriate geometric inserts in a formboard.
Hearing sense (the primary concern in this category is in the discrimination of sounds, auditory acuity, pitch, volume, and various modulations of the voice)	In discriminating among sounds, the children are asked to strike a bell in one of a double series of thirteen bells and then to locate the same sounding bell in the second series. At a very early stage, the children are taught about silence by being asked to sit in absolute and complete silence for periods of time. Later, very small noises are introduced such as the tick of a clock or the buzz of a fly or bee. Comparisons are frequently made between noise and sound. Eventually, musical education is incorporated into this aspect of the program.

b Ask the children to distinguish between various characteristics of sounds, such as between loud and soft, high and low, pleasant and obnoxious, and happy and sad. The use of a tape recorder will often help to standardize the sounds and give the children an opportunity to check their responses. The tape recorder also provides an opportunity for the retarded to make their own happy, sad, loud, soft, low, or high sounds. This will help receptive abilities and also help to develop basic expressive skills.

c Have them follow auditory commands by using a gestural or motor response.

d Have the children listen to nursery stories, rhymes, and songs, and pick out details and other information or generalizations. The children at first can be asked to listen for certain sounds or words on the records and eventually be required to repeat the sounds or words heard. This activity will help to develop association and response skills.

e Ask questions of the children in order to make them more aware of the world around them.

f Give them opportunities to play with musical instruments and rhythm-band equipment. Work on the perception of rhythm through musical games.

g Have quiet periods during which time they are to listen for various sounds.

4 Visual receptive skills can be developed by giving the children experiences such as the following:

a Have them identify common objects by name, giving their proper use and telling to whom each object belongs. Emphasis should be placed on tasks involving visual reception wherein the stimuli are obvious or intentionally presented and not based on stimuli which must be perceived incidentally.

b Have the children examine various objects and toys and report on their color, shape, size, texture, and the materials used in their construction. By comparing these objects in some way, visual association skills will also be enhanced.

c Let them stand in front of a mirror each day and comment on what they see.

d Have the children interpret pictures in terms of the objects seen, colors, sizes, motion, or by noticing details.

e Give them opportunities to copy, cut and paste, and draw.

5 Tactile receptive skills can be developed by:

a Showing the children different scraps of cloth and allowing them to handle these scraps and learn the names of each. Place several scraps in a bag. Have each child feel the material and select the roughest, smoothest, largest, smallest, or most wrinkled. See if they can give the name of the scrap chosen. It would be best to introduce this activity by using objects which are grossly dissimilar.

b Having the children identify shapes and sizes of objects while blindfolded.

6 The olfactory sense can be trained in a way similar to that used by Montessori. Odors can be sniffed as the children are walking on a tour or field trip. Even in the classroom, bottles with various distinctive odors will provide an excellent medium for playing unusual games.

Training in perceptual-motor association

Seeing relationships among stimuli is an important skill to be developed. The degree to which associations are established will dictate, in a large measure, the extent to which intellectual development will occur. On numerous occasions each day, we are called on to make judgments concerning differences and similarities among objects. Moreover, individuals are frequently required to consider relationships between a series of perceptions received and the appropriateness of the response given. These skills must develop early; and, if stimulated at a young age, children will develop an extensive repertoire of associations. Additionally, it is desirable that association between sense modalities be stimulated. Auditory, visual, and tactile perceptions should become closely related to each other. The following are illustrations of activities which will promote this association:

1 *Children will learn to hear likenesses and differences among auditory stimuli by observing sounds and words that are alike and playing games by making up silly words. The tape recorder or record player will help in these activities.*
2 *Rhythmical moving to music will help children to establish relationships between input and response.*
3 *Have them follow directions, play "Simon Says", sing songs, or make up stories in response to a situation or picture.*
4 *Cut construction paper of different colors into squares, triangles, circles, and oblongs; paste small strips of felt to the back of each and have the children group them according to color, size, or shape. The children can play a game by grouping objects in various ways after having received vocal directions.*
5 *Initiate and practice the development of sequence using such techniques as sentence completion. For example, "After we arrive at school on the schoolbus we. . . ."; "Before lunch we must. . . ."; or "Before we go home from school we. . . ." This can be done by using both auditory and visual stimuli.*
6 *Gradually, various relationships between time, space, quantities, quality, and other similar dimensions should be introduced into the program.*
7 *In all these activities, it is important that perceptual stability be emphasized so that children receive and associate perceptions which are clear and unambiguous.*

Training in responding

The major theme of this chapter has been that motor skills are prerequisite to development in all areas. Accordingly, attention must be given to assisting children to develop skill in gross and fine motor movements including balance, posture, eye-hand coordination, locomotion, and similar skills. Kephart (1960) has suggested specific activities for developing these skills. Radler and Kephart (1960) discuss the effect on general perceptual-motor development of stimulating motoric types of playtime activities. They suggest experiences such as:

1 In developing gross motor skills, games should be planned so that the children are allowed to walk, run, slide, gallop, skip, hop, run over uneven areas, dance freely and spontaneously, practice other methods of movement (cat, elephant, duck, crab, measuring worm), balance and walk along board or brick fences, crawl through openings, play stepping stones, and use a variety of playground equipment. Action songs or other types of rhythm music should accompany many of these activities. Total use of the body should be encouraged in all activities with particular attention given to the children making use of both sides of their bodies. Initially, the teacher should encourage the children's participation through imitation, since spontaneity on the part of many retarded youngsters may be lacking.

2 Fine muscle movement and coordination between the eyes and hands can be developed by having the children draw on a blackboard or large piece of paper, by doing pegboard work, cutting and pasting, working on puzzles and lotto games, manipulating toys, handling and sorting small objects, throwing balls, climbing ropes, hanging from playground equipment by their hands, copying patterns, coloring, tracing, working with buttons and zippers, and engaging in rhythm activities. In their use of paper or the blackboard, it is wise to encourage a left-to-right progression whenever appropriate. When demonstrating, for example, the teacher should move in a left-to-right direction from the perspective of the class.

3 In many of these activities, vocal expression previous to, simultaneously with, or immediately following the motor response is natural and desirable. Every attempt should be made to relate vocal expression to the appropriate motor response.

4 After the child has established a stable spatial world, some effort should be directed to emphasizing spatial-to-temporal translation. Adequately performing complex activities such as batting a ball, kicking a can, drawing a triangle, and reading requires that the child translate an object in space into an appropriate temporal sequence. For example, in batting a ball, the child must do certain things before swinging the bat. He has to throw the ball in the air, estimate how rapidly it will fall in relation to his own body, and judge the speed at which he should swing the bat. Unless the temporal translation of these spatial entities is accurate, an error of some type will occur. As soon as gross and fine motor skills develop, attention should be directed toward working on spatial-temporal translations.

SELECTED REFERENCES

Benton, A. L.: "Psychological Evaluation and Differential Diagnosis," in H. A. Stevens and R. Heber (eds.), *Mental Retardation: A Review of*

Research, The University of Chicago Press, Chicago, 1964, pp. 16–56.

Denny, M. R.: "Learning and Performance," in H. A. Stevens and R. Heber (eds.), *Mental Retardation: A Review of Research,* The University of Chicago Press, Chicago, 1964, pp. 128–132.

Forgus, Ronald H.: *Perception,* McGraw-Hill Book Company, New York, 1966.

Gallagher, James J.: *The Tutoring of Brain Injured Mentally Retarded Children,* Charles C Thomas, Publisher, Springfield, Ill., 1960.

Hunt, J. McV.: *Intelligence and Experience,* The Ronald Press Company, New York, 1961.

Kephart, N. C.: "Perceptual-Motor Concepts of Learning Disabilities," *Exceptional Children,* vol. 31, 1965, pp. 201–206.

————: "Perceptual-Motor Correlates of Education," in S. A. Kirk and W. Becker (eds.), *Conference on Children with Minimal Brain Impairments,* University of Illinois, Urbana, Ill., 1963, pp. 13–25.

————: *The Slow Learner in the Classroom,* Charles E. Merrill Books, Inc., Columbus, Ohio, 1960.

Lipman, R. S.: "Learning: Verbal, Perceptual-Motor and Classical Conditioning," in Norman R. Ellis (ed.), *Handbook of Mental Deficiency,* McGraw-Hill Book Company, New York, 1963, pp. 391–423.

Malpass, L. F.: "Motor Skills in Mental Deficiency," in Norman R. Ellis (ed.), *Handbook of Mental Deficiency,* McGraw-Hill Book Company, New York, 1963, pp. 602–631.

Montessori, Maria: *The Montessori Method,* translated from the Italian by Anne E. George, Robert Bently, Inc., Cambridge, Mass., 1965.

Radler, D. H. and Kephart, N. C.: *Success through Play,* Harper & Row, Publishers, Incorporated, New York, 1960.

Roach, E. G. and Kephart, N. C.: *The Purdue Perceptual-Motor Survey,* Charles E. Merrill Books, Inc., Columbus, Ohio, 1966.

Spivack, G.: "Perceptual Processes," in Norman R. Ellis (ed.), *Handbook of Mental Deficiency,* McGraw-Hill Book Company, New York, 1963, pp. 480–511.

developing areas of communication

If retarded children are to function adequately in society, they must be able to make themselves understood by their contemporaries. To do so requires that they understand the significance of incoming stimuli, relate these perceptions to existing knowledge, and express themselves in an appropriate and clear fashion. Speech, language, and written expression are three major components of communication. The teacher of retarded children must give emphasis to the development of skills in each of these areas. Blending into society is typically no major problem for the retarded child until he is forced to communicate with others; if unable to do so adequately, the child will immediately be identified and labeled as a defective person. If, on the other hand, the child is able to benefit from systematic training in communicating with others, the number of potential problems in other areas will be minimized.

This chapter discusses some of the major facets of communication as they apply to the retarded and suggests procedures which teachers can use to help these children to develop capabilities in speech, language, and written expression.

THE SIGNIFICANCE OF SPEECH FOR EFFECTIVE VERBAL COMMUNICATION

Speech is the manner in which sounds are made. A poor speaker is one whose audience pays more attention to how he talks than to what he is saying. Retarded children typically have more difficulty developing adequate speech patterns than do intellectually normal children. The reason for this situation is directly related to the extent to which certain basic requirements for effective speech development characterize the individual child.

Auditory discrimination abilities

Comparing and contrasting correct and incorrect sounds in isolation and in connected speech is a basic requisite for the development of speech. Children who have difficulty differentiating among sounds will subsequently be unable to reproduce various components of speech. There are several possible reasons for a child having a disability in auditory discrimination. Poor hearing involving some general or specific difficulty in the peripheral or central mechanisms, which reduces auditory acuity, will impede discrimination capabilities. The literature reveals that retarded children tend to have substantial hearing disturbances (Birch and Matthews, 1951; Kodman, 1958). It should be pointed out that research in this area has been done primarily with trainable-level children who reside in institutions. Among these studies some inconsistency has been observed in the criteria used for determining a hearing handicap.

Inattentiveness on the part of the retarded will account for difficulty in auditory discrimination. This problem may be the direct result of too many peripheral stimuli, confusion or lack of clarity in the stimulus presented to the child, and previous lack of success in related tasks.

Discrimination difficulties may also be present because the child has some type of expression problem. The individual's difficulty could be on the expression side and not in the reception area; however, the fundamental problem could be camouflaged by another type of associated disturbance.

Auditory discrimination is essential for ear training. To develop adequate speech and reap the benefits of any subsequent speech therapy, children must be able to isolate sounds in various positions.

Effective speech therapy dictates that the speech-defective child be able to hear differences between his productions and the expressions of others. Speech development and the remediation of speech difficulties are based, in large measure, on the auditory discrimination capabilities of the child.

Several studies have reported results which suggest that training programs designed to assist the retarded in effectively utilizing their hearing will enhance the auditory capabilities of those children (Goda and Rigrodsky, 1962; Schlanger, 1962; Glovsky and Rigrodsky, 1963). It is indeed promising that capabilities of this nature can be learned; the implication is that activities to train auditory discrimination should be a major part of the classroom program.

Adequate feedback and monitoring systems

From one perspective, feedback can be viewed as a conditioned reflex which is automatic and self-regulating. This physiological process regulates the manipulation of the articulators so that the individual does not consciously think about the rapid movement and repositioning of the articulators as words are expressed. As the articulators move, signals are sent to the appropriate nerve centers for subsequent and sequential innervation and deactivation of the various muscle groups. Although these processes are of academic interest, educators do not need to be concerned about nor understand their complex interaction.

Other aspects of feedback and monitoring are of a learned nature and should be of interest to individuals working with speech defective children. If they have not learned to make use of their vocal output, modifications which are subsequently required for speech productions will be less well effected. Even with an intact speech mechanism, retarded children frequently do not listen to themselves; that is, they do not make use of their own vocalizations to improve future utterances. Unless some type of intervention by a speech therapist or teacher is introduced, the child practices his own errors. When this occurs to a substantial degree, poor patterns of speech become established in the child's cognitive structure through repetition. This situation, in turn, leads to a hard-core remedial problem which, if severe enough, is frequently beyond the training and experience of the special-education teacher.

Adequate and effective models

Speech is a learned activity which takes place through example and activity. The child needs to have a reference point against which utterances can be compared. This requirement is directly related to auditory-discrimination skills, the use of feedback, and the child's capabilities in monitoring his productions for purposes of altering future speech.

Children, such as many of the deprived, who are born into homes in which the parents and siblings often have faulty speech will typically exhibit the same patterns of poor speech. Young children quickly take on their parents' style and characteristics of expression because of inadequate models or poor speech standards in the home. In fact, if the child's speech problems are severe enough, the parents may be the only ones able to understand his vocalizations. In a sense, such families develop their own systems of communication.

Even within families that offer satisfactory stimulation to children, errors are often made in providing satisfactory speech patterns by placing undue pressure on children or penalizing them for poor productions. Instead of demonstrating to the child how to make a sound or say a word in an appropriate fashion, parents will frequently nag the child by demonstrating how not to say something. This procedure results in alerting the child to his deficiencies and does not provide the kind of support and model essential for subsequent success. Parents and teachers must not be impatient with their children's speech development or push them beyond their level of capability.

Adequate speech mechanisms

Adequate speech development is dependent on the effective operation of those mechanisms responsible for speech. There is no specific organic entity devoted exclusively to speech; the individual makes use of a variety of parts of the body which, in addition to speech, serve other functions. For example, the tongue and teeth are vital to the development of effective speech; yet they serve other important functions, such as mastication. Any number of malformations of these organic components could result in poor speech development. Difficulty in respiration, vocal cord nodules, a short soft palate, lip abnormalities, central-nervous-system disturbances, or muscular difficulties are a few of the vast number of physical problems that may impede the development of speech.

The basis for speech disturbances can be environmental, organic, or a combination of the two. Typically the teacher is not trained to deal with organically based defects. These severe difficulties require the expertise of a trained speech therapist; however, the classroom teacher must continue to provide an environment wherein functional difficulties do not become added to the existing organic-based problem.

Minimum intellectual capabilities

Learning to speak is an intellectual function which is based on adequate employment of the cortex, or higher neural centers. This is a complex process requiring a certain minimum level of intellectual ability as well as the rapid and unconscious manipulation of the various articulators. Thus, it is not astonishing to find that retarded children are slower in speech development, speak at a slower pace, and finally attain a lower level of success in speech than the intellectually normal.

It would be difficult to identify the minimum level of intellectual ability below which speech will not develop. Likewise, it would be hazardous to suggest that speech will develop adequately in children who are above a certain intelligence level. In a general sense, the retarded have more difficulty with speech as well as with the peripheral mechanisms associated with communication.

STAGES OF SPEECH DEVELOPMENT

To a substantial extent, speech and language develop simultaneously. As a child proceeds through the various stages of sound emission and gains skill in manipulating the articulators, he is at the same time gaining an understanding of the meaning of words and expressions. In considering the speech development of children, two major factors are worthy of emphasis: (1) Speech and language do not develop in isolation from each other although a child can be disabled in one but not necessarily in the other, and (2) the stages of speech development are not mutually exclusive, discrete entities but overlap substantially. Indeed, a child can easily be operating in more than one stage at the same time.

There is some inconsistency in the literature regarding appropriate labels for describing stages of speech development. Table 6-1 summarizes the major stages of speech development and the characteristic behavior associated with each. The student interested in a more complete and detailed description of each stage is referred to the excellent discussion by Van Riper (1965).

SPEECH CHARACTERISTICS OF THE RETARDED

The literature shows evidence of a substantial amount of research activity concerning the study of speech in retarded children. It should be emphasized, however, that it is often difficult to separate speech studies from those investigations of language because of the intimate relationship existing between these areas. Moreover, great

TABLE 6-1 Summary of the Stages of Speech Development

Stages and behavioral characteristics

Reflexive Sounds

The first sounds the child makes are related to either crying or comfort. Wide variation exists among infants during the first few months in terms of the type and extent of these vocalizations. Both crying and cooing allow the child to manipulate his articulators and form sounds, although more sounds relevant to speech emanate from cooing than from crying. Subsequent development of speech will depend to a great extent on how effectively the infant uses his tongue during sucking and swallowing.

Babbling and Vocal Play

This stage usually begins around the end of the second month and is typified by the child emitting a variety of sounds, primarily front vowels with a few consonant productions. Most frequently the child babbles during periods of relaxation and when alone. Interruptions will often stifle the child's continuation of babbling. Toward the half-year mark, the child begins to interact more completely with his environment and develops a type of social vocalization. At this point he will make sounds at objects, repeat syllables, and begin making combinations of consonant-vowel blends such as "da-da" or "ma-ma." Eventually, the child develops a variety of capabilities including variation in volume, inflection, and tone. The repertoire of sounds increases, and the child uses his own feedback for repetition as well as exhibiting a tendency toward imitating sounds from other sources. During the latter half of the first year, the child develops skill in using the back vowels and elaborating on his consonant production.

First Words

Emerging from the myriad of sounds are the child's first words. When stimulated and appropriately responded to, he develops an understanding of the significance of the first few words over which he has control. "Ma-ma" or "da-da" take on meaning, elicit a pleasurable response from the two observers to whom the word becomes attached, and thus, provide a system of rewards to the child. Repetition of these sounds only brings more satisfying experiences. By judicious use of stimulation, the parent can foster a firmer establishment of these vocalizations and their meanings. It should be emphasized, however, that comprehension of the meaning of words is often a slow process and does not necessarily occur in close temporal contiguity with the first words. Comprehension of the meaning of

TABLE 6-1 *(Continued)*

Stages and behavioral characteristics

words can be aided if the parents use gestures, so long as the child does not substitute this type of behavior for vocalizations. By the end of eighteen months, the child has typically developed a repertoire of ten to fifteen meaningful words, usually choosing from those which most effectively manipulate his parents.

Jargon

Midway through the child's second year, he will devote much time to vocal productions which are characterized by the term *word salad.* Distributed throughout these vocalizations are a few intelligible words with interesting patterns of inflection. Indeed, this seems like double talk. This period of speech development is often perplexing to parents because it contrasts sharply with the few intelligible words the child is able to use.

Echolalia

Emerging from the stage of jargon is a second period of vocal play which is of greater breadth and sophistication than the earlier stage. At this point, the child plays with and repeats words, syllables, and combinations of words and phrases. The children parrot themselves and their parents. Fortunately, for the parents, it typically lasts for a short time.

More Elaborate Speech Development

The two-year-old child is able to communicate meaningfully in two- and three-word sentences. His articulation is typically not good, and variation occurs from normal rhythm, voice, and volume. By the time the child reaches ages three and four, speech and vocabulary have progressed at a dramatic rate. The child's skill in syntactical understanding is growing at this point, and he usually is not hesitant to attempt an explanation of most anything. Articulation capabilities continue to develop because of maturity of the child's own feedback and discrimination abilities as well as his propinquity to appropriate models. Progress continues in articulation development, although the child typically does not master all sounds until about the age of eight, assuming a relatively normal environmental situation prevails.

inconsistency prevails among studies dealing with speech because of the wide variation in the criteria used to determine and classify poor speech, the lack of consistent assessment procedures, the use of subjects for study from trainable and institutionalized populations, and the hesitation of investigators to study speech of the retarded in a comprehensive and logical fashion.

These difficulties notwithstanding, there is consistent evidence indicating that the retarded have more defects in speech than the intellectually normal (Goertzen, 1957; Matthews, 1957; Spradlin, 1963; Kirk, 1964), although the literature reports a wide range in the percentage of speech problems among the retarded. In fact, percentages range from 5 to 100 depending upon the degree of retardation manifested by the subjects, type of speech examination used, speech factors studied, age of the subjects, criteria used in determining that speech was defective, and whether the subjects were institutionalized or living at home. In considering the prevalence of speech defects among the retarded, one must be attentive to the divergency among these factors.

Some effort has been devoted to studying the types of speech problems most characteristic of the retarded. There are difficulties, again, in generalizing from the prevalence studies. The evidence seems to be clear in two areas: (1) The mentally retarded acquire speech much more slowly than do the intellectually normal, and (2) the greatest percentage of errors in speech among the retarded appear to be of an articulation type, with voice problems constituting the second area of greatest difficulty. The latter finding differs in no way from the data on the intellectually normal.

The types of articulation errors made by the retarded have been investigated. Karlin and Strazzula (1952) and Bangs (1942) report that the kinds of articulation errors made by the retarded are similar to those characteristic of a normal population, although Bangs (1942) suggests that the retarded make more errors of omission in the final position.

The influence of speech therapy with the retarded has received relatively little attention and, thus, does not allow for the formulation of clear generalizations. Those studies which have been reported suffer from methodological weaknesses which raise questions concerning their validity. Clinically, there is reason to believe that higher-level retarded children can benefit from speech correction. Similarly, the younger retarded child who comes from an environment in which good speech models are consistently available typically shows a more favorable prognosis than does the older institutionalized retardate. There is consensus in the literature that speech therapy with the retarded will prove beneficial in some measure irrespective of the degree of speech defect or the individual's intellectual capability. The question requiring an answer is whether intensive speech therapy with the retarded, particularly the more severely disabled, is worth the effort in light of the usual heavy case load of normal and dull-normal children with speech problems. To be sure, some expert attention must be given to educable children with speech problems since they will eventually become active members of the community and be required to develop adequate communication skills.

In summary, the literature reveals that

1 *Speech problems are related to MA with more communication defects occurring among subjects with moderate or severe intellectual disability than among the mildly retarded.*
2 *Articulation disorders, followed by problems of voice, constitute the greatest percentage of speech defects.*
3 *The influence of speech therapy has not been adequately assessed, although the evidence suggests the greater benefits of special corrective procedures with educable-level children than with the trainable and severely retarded.*

ASSESSMENT OF SPEECH DIFFICULTIES

Formal procedures

An adequate assessment of a child's speech capabilities should involve periods of observation in a variety of settings in which verbal communication is necessary. These observations should be done by a trained speech clinician who is skilled in identifying patterns of specific weaknesses. Standardized testing procedures and other instruments should be used to supplement data gathered through observation. The observation period should never be sacrificed in favor of using only a standardized test.

Van Riper (1965) has presented a complete dossier of examinations and forms for recording relevant speech information. This material suggests procedures for examining children in voice production, articulation defects, stuttering, and in the general collection of information. Techniques are given for "fractioning-down" speech processes into component parts. Although this information is of interest and instructive to teachers of the retarded, caution should be exercised in the use of these materials, especially if one has not had proper training.

Tests such as the following provide data which support observations by the trained speech correctionist.

1 *Templin-Darley Screening and Diagnostic Tests of Articulation*
2 *Speech Articulation Test for Young Children (Revised)*
3 *Weidner-Fensch Speech Screening Test*
4 *Speech Diagnostic Chart*
5 *The Arizona Articulation Proficiency Scale*
6 *Clark Picture Inventory*
7 *Boston University Speech Sound Discrimination Picture Test*

Informal procedures

The teacher should be aware of her frequent lack of formal preparation in the assessment of speech difficulties. In addition, many teachers do not have adequate speech services available for the children in their classes. Among the reasons for this unfortunate situation are (1) the lack of enough trained speech correctionists, (2) the unusually heavy case load of therapists, and (3) the difficulty in working with the retarded, who often show disappointing results even after extensive therapy. These problems precipitate the need for teachers becoming aware of the informal procedures they can use to assess and analyze speech defects in the rearded. Moreover, teachers should be informed concerning those guiding principles which will assist in the development of speech among the retarded.

As has been emphasized earlier, teachers must realize the limitations of their training and experience as the task of analyzing a child's speech difficulties is considered. Since the retarded tend to exhibit more difficulty with articulation than with other speech problems, focus should be on this area.

Perhaps the most practical and informative procedure the teacher can use to analyze the children's speech difficulties is to systematically record the types of errors the children make in speech. Errors of articulation can be tabulated in various ways. It is important to know the specific types of consonant and vowel misarticulations that each child makes and if these errors occur in the initial, medial, and/or final positions in words. Moreover, a record should be kept of the type of error characteristic of each phonemic sound and position, such as substitutions, omissions, and distortions in any of the three positions. From these records, the exact nature of a child's articulation weaknesses soon becomes obvious. Table 6-2 presents stimulus words which can be used by the teacher to test consonant and vowel difficulties either as a single word, in a picture, or in a sentence. These will help to systematize the collection of data and should be included in each child's folder.

It is important not only to check on and tabulate a child's articulation errors in isolation but also to evaluate his performance in connected speech. Articulation errors may not necessarily occur with isolated sounds but may be present only when words are used in some type of a relationship. These errors may be the result of slow and sluggish articulators which do not move and reposition quickly enough for the production of a new sound. The teacher should have the child repeat sentences or phrases and listen for atypical sounds during periods of casual conversation. Pictures also can be used as a stimulus for eliciting vocal productions. From all these procedures the objective of the teacher should be to classify the types of articu-

TABLE 6-2 Articulation Test Words

Consonants				Consonant Blends	
	Initial	*Medial*	*Final*		
[r]	rake, rabbit	carrot	door	[dr] [pt]	dripped
[l]	lamp	telephone	ball	[kr] [dl]	cradle
[s]	saw	glasses	house	[sm] [ʃt]	smashed
[z]	zipper	scissors	nose	[tw] [lv]	twelve
[k]	cat	cookies	book	[θr]	three
[g]	gun	wagon	flag	[br] [ðð]	brother
[w]	window	sandwich		[ldʒɚ]	soldier
[θ]	thumb	birthday cake	mouth	[gr] [vz]	groves
[ð]	that	feather	smooth	[rtʃ]	church
[j]	yellow	onion		[sn] [fl]	snuffle
[f]	fork	elephant	knife		
[v]	vase	shovel	stove		
[ŋ]		monkey	swing		
[ʃ]	shoe	dishes	fish		
[ʒ]		measure	garage		
[ʍ]	wheel				
[tʃ]	chair	matches	watch		
[dʒ]	jelly	soldier	orange		
[t]	table	letter	boat		
[d]	dog	ladder	bed		
[p]	pencil	apple	cup		
[b]	bus	baby	tub		
[m]	mouse	hammer	drum		
[n]	nose	banana	train		
[h]	hat				

Vowels		Diphthongs	
[i]	tree	[ɑʊ]	cow
[ɪ]	pig	[ɑɪ]	pie
[ɛ]	bell	[ɔɪ]	boy
[e] [eɪ]	cake		
[æ]	hat		
[ʌ]	gun		
[ɑ]	car		
[o] [oʊ]	comb		
[ɔ]	ball		
[ʊ]	book		
[u]	shoe		

FROM: *Handbook of Speech Pathology*. Edited by Lee Edward Travis. Copyright © 1957 by Appleton-Century-Crofts, Inc. Reprinted by permission of Appleton-Century-Crofts, Division of Meredith Publishing Company.

lation errors the child makes and note any specific circumstances from which these errors may be precipitated.

If it is suspected that a child misarticulates because of environmental, rather than organic, factors, a visit to the home would help to discern the kinds of models available for speech. If the child is associated with a person or family providing a faulty model, it may be necessary to consider offering speech services to other members of the family. The teacher is in the most advantageous position to ascertain these potential problems.

As is true in other areas of speech assessment, a comprehensive examination of voice disorders requires the services of a trained speech clinician. Teachers, however, should be alert to difficulties children have in discriminating among various pitches, producing and duplicating a given pitch, inflecting appropriately in speech, carrying a tune, and in the spontaneous change of inflections and pitch. Intensity difficulties can be assessed by asking the child to engage in activities requiring changes in volume. The range might extend from whispering to calling hogs and vary according to pitch. Moreover, some attention must be given to changes in the voice patterns of children especially in terms of hoarse voices, huskiness, gutteral qualities, nasal or denasal productions, breathy patterns of speech, and other differential abnormal speech patterns of voice related to consonants and vowels.

Data that the teacher gathers on the speech patterns of children will be of benefit only to the degree that a systematic approach is used in their collection. The important point to be remembered is not that the *isolated* and *infrequently* poor production be focused upon but that patterns of *consistent* speech weaknesses be identified. To this end, observation should be made in a variety of speech situations with a standard form used for recording information. By doing this, patterns of strength and weakness will become self-evident. Again, it must be recognized that deep and penetrating speech evaluation are typically outside the training and experience of the special-education teacher. Nevertheless, the exigencies of the special class situation often make it necessary that the teacher do some preliminary screening of speech problems among the retarded.

PROCEDURES FOR CORRECTING SPEECH DIFFICULTIES

The speech correctionist

Specific principles and methods for dealing with speech problems suggested for use by the trained speech correctionist have been discussed in a comprehensive and clear fashion elsewhere (Van Riper, 1965) and are not of central concern to this book. The employment of suggested procedures for remediating hard-core speech problems requires substantial clinical training and experience. This is typically the responsibility of the speech therapist or correctionist.

Ideally, the speech correctionist should provide the direction for the remediation of the retarded child's speech defects and guide the teacher in deciding on the activities and tasks most suitable for resolving each child's problem. Additionally, the speech correctionist should make the teacher aware of the general posture to assume in reacting to a speech problem. For example, because of lack of specific training, questions such as the following often perplex the teacher of the retarded:

1 *How much attention should I call to the child's speech problem by stopping the child during recitation for a second attempt at articulating a difficult sound?*

2 *How much peer pressure should be exerted to help a child speak well?*

3 *How can I make the other children understand speech defects and accept the individual with this type of disability?*

4 *What proportion of group and individual work should be given in speech?*

5 *How can I work with the families to provide more adequate speech models?*

The speech correctionist should clearly serve as a consultant to the teacher of the mentally retarded. Answers to specific and general questions should be given, materials and suggested procedures provided, the child's speech development frequently reassessed, and small-group or independent work provided for the more severely speech disabled. Unfortunately, this ideal situation is more the exception than the rule, with the result that teachers of the retarded are being provided with only minimal services for their children, the most frequent of which is some type of speech screening assessment. Because of this situation, much of the responsibility for dealing with speech problems of the retarded has fallen on the teacher's shoulders. What can the teacher do to improve the speech of the retarded?

Techniques used by the teacher for improving speech

To promote good speech and alleviate a variety of potential difficulties, the teacher will need to demonstrate and establish an understanding of speech problems among the children. The rapport the teacher develops with the students will serve as a model for how the children should react toward one another. If the teacher unknowingly or unnecessarily rebukes, embarrasses, or reprimands a child for speaking poorly or for not trying to articulate properly, one could expect to see other children exhibit the same type of reaction to speech problems. The teacher, then, must establish the class tone so that the children feel free to experiment with speech and to spontaneously try to develop greater skill in being understood. If the teacher chooses not to work on the development of this type of atmosphere, the results from even specific units designed to develop speech will be minimal at best. In a sense, then, the teacher becomes a model for acceptable behavior toward others with difficulties.

The teacher becomes a model in another sense by consciously, skillfully, and continuously illustrating proper techniques for speech. In a way, the teacher should present a standard against which comparisons can be made. By being a good model, standards of acceptability in speech are implicitly established. A certain behavioral set for speaking must be emphasized; children should realize through example that speaking can be enjoyable and fun. Presenting material in an informal fashion in association with a relaxed environment, which allows for periods during which speech productions are emphasized, illustrates the kind of situation which will encourage communication. In trying to provide a good speech model, teachers often fall into the trap of overarticulating. This hyperprecision is atypical and will call undue attention to defective speech. This should be avoided by the teacher.

Certain implications logically follow from these generalizations. It would seem wise for teachers not to handle speech errors at the time they occur. To stop a lesson will destroy the natural rhythm and sequence of the material being presented, and it will also serve to alert children to their weaknesses, or those difficulties of others, at a time when particular attention to remedial procedures cannot be given. This strategy will also result in embarrassment to the child.

Since many retarded children need individual or small-group instruction, certain times each day should be given exclusively to speech activities. This should come after the teacher has a general overview of the nature of the speech problems within the class. A variety of activities can be included as part of this period. A tape recorder, record player, and telephone will help provide the means for listening, stimulating speech, and working on specific speech problems.

Although seeming too obvious to mention, time should be set aside for children to talk and discuss. Teachers often feel that it is desirable to establish and maintain control of the class through the use of constant verbalization. When this occurs, the children have little opportunity to talk and find themselves in a situation in which listening to the teacher constitutes the central activity in communication. Although the verbal stimulation of children is desirable, having the children respond is equally important.

Table 6-3 lists specific activities in which teachers of the

TABLE 6-3 Speech Activities Appropriate for the Classroom

Primary areas for development and suggested activities and other teaching considerations

Exercise of the Articulators

A Blowing, sucking, licking, and chewing exercises will help the retarded to develop more coordination of his articulators. The child can be asked to imitate various movements with the tongue such as curling, clicking, moving from side to side, and rotating.

B Drooling can be controlled, swallowing saliva encouraged, and the tongue strengthened by having children chew gum or taffy, suck through straws, or lick peanut butter from the roofs of their mouths with their lips closed.

C As the children do mouth and tongue exercises, a mirror should be available to them so that they can appreciate the results of their activity. Moreover, using a mirror will provide the students with immediate knowledge of the results of their efforts, establish a more stable pattern for subsequent behavior by reinforcement through the visual modality, and provide immediate reward.

Ear Training and Imitation

A Have the children identify sounds while blindfolded. Direct their attention to sounds around them, and ask the children to identify the unique characteristics of each. Turn the task around and have the children make sounds of various animals or other things in their environment.

B Encourage the understanding of differences between sounds in terms of loud-soft, high-low, happy-sad, or noisy-clear.

C Begin exercises with gross sounds such as are produced by bell, wood blocks, piano, or drums. Gradually, bring the sounds closer together in terms of their characteristics, and require finer discriminations by the child. Eventually, speech sounds in isolation and in words should be introduced.

D Pictures and objects can be used as stimuli for a variety of speech activities. Pictures or objects beginning with various sounds, such as the b sound, can be selected. Games can be played with the the pictures and objects. For instance, have the children find hidden objects which begin with the b sound or paste pictures which begin with the b sound on a large piece of paper.

E The tape recorder or special records presenting auditory discrimination tasks can be used by the teacher.

TABLE 6-3 (Continued)

Primary areas for development and suggested activities and other teaching considerations

F Imitating sounds and words will help to establish standards for good speech. This can be done through music and rhythm activities. Follow-the-leader games will also be beneficial if vocalization is included, as well as the nonverbal activities.

G Reciting funny poems, nursery rhymes, and singing songs will help to develop imitation skills.

Correcting a Defective Sound

A Assuming that the child has the physiological capability to make sounds correctly, the teacher should first work on the discrimination between sounds so the child is able to identify both the correct sound and the incorrect one. The child's ability to discriminate between correct and incorrect productions can be checked by having the teacher say words in which either the correct or incorrect sound is used. The child is then asked to indicate when the correct production is given.

B The correct sound should be produced in isolation at first and gradually employed and practiced in words. Practice should be given in the use of correct sounds in various positions in words, phrases, and sentences.

C The use of a tape recorder will help an individual assess his own productions to determine if new sounds are being correctly used in conversation.

D Speech activities should be done within the context of the classroom activities.

Teaching New Sounds and Stabilizing Their Use

A Assuming that the physiological mechanisms for speech are intact, the children can be asked to listen to a sound and try to imitate what they hear. This activity can be reinforced through games. For example, they will find it interesting to blow a tissue in attempting to make plosive sounds.

B After the sound has been articulated successfully in isolation, repeated, and reinforced through use of the visual channel, the sound should be used in a variety of nonsense words in various positions.

TABLE 6-3 (Continued)

Primary areas for development and suggested activities and other teaching considerations

C Gradually the sounds should be used in several words which are familiar to the child. His repertoire should not be expanded until the sound has been correctly used and overlearned. Additional words incorporating the new sound should be introduced at this point.

D Eventually a group of key words which incorporate the new sound are given to the child who learns to use these and other words in sentences. Reinforcement should always be provided by varying the task after the sound has become stabilized.

E With retarded children this entire process will take time and often result in a number of regressions. The teacher should maintain stability in stimuli, be reasonable and consistent in expectations of the student, and be cautious not to progress too rapidly. Determination of success is based on how accurately the child can consistently use the new sound in a variety of situations involving spontaneous communication. Whenever possible, all sensory channels should be used to reinforce new learning.

retarded can engage their students to improve both speech and language.

LANGUAGE: THE PRIMARY MEANS FOR COMMUNICATING IDEAS

Language is the ability to express ideas and concepts. Most often it is viewed as ability in the vocal expression of ideas wherein the evaluation of one's performance is not based on how well sounds are made but how effectively ideas are expressed. Ideas can also be expressed using nonverbal modes of communication. This is an important component of language for the retarded since it is the one area in which they exhibit their greatest relative strength.

Since the middle 1950s, research on language with the retarded has escalated at an astonishing rate. This has been precipitated by (1) the prevailing view of many educators that language capabilities are directly related to performance levels of the retarded in other areas, (2) the development of linguistic models to which new instruments and experimentation can be directly related and validated, and (3) encouraging reports from investigations which have directed attention to studying remedial procedures in language with the retarded.

The language studies, and the implications emanating from this line of research, have resulted in a greater emphasis on a learning-disabilities approach in the education of the mentally retarded. This, in turn, has stimulated among professionals expressions of dissatisfaction with traditional disability categories. This movement is consistent with the theme considered in this book; viz., that emphasizing a clinical approach in teaching the retarded will result in the occurrence of learning at a level and rate which is more consistent with the capabilities of the retarded.

The range of needs which were discussed as needs vital for speech development are equally essential for the development of language. Discrimination skills, the availability of appropriate stimuli, the presence of adequate models, and the establishment and maintenance of an adequate feedback and monitoring system contribute to language development. Speech and language do not develop in isolation but are the result of dynamic interaction between an individual and his environment. Prerequisite to the development of language is the degree to which the retarded are able to attend to stimuli and listen effectively. Suggestions for maintaining attention in these children have been detailed in previous sections.

Language is an omnibus term which encompasses several major dimensions not mutually exclusive or discrete, but highly interrelated. Deemphasizing the notion that language can be assessed only in terms of the length and/or complexity of a verbal production, Myklebust (1956) has suggested reception, association, and expression as the three major components of language. These factors are similar to components of the perceptual-motor process. Although much of the research dealing with the language characteristics of the retarded has not been intentionally directed toward studying the three processes of language, contemporary experiments have employed theoretical positions or models which allow experimenters to focus on one or more of these language processes. Results from these studies will be discussed in the following section. The research of Mueller (1964*a*, 1964*b*) and Bateman and Wetherell (1965) is particularly applicable because of their use of the Illinois Test of Psycholinguistic Abilities with various populations of retarded subjects.

LANGUAGE CHARACTERISTICS OF THE RETARDED

Dimensions of language development and ability have been comprehensively reviewed and interpreted in other publications (Goertzen, 1957; Harrison, 1958; Smith, 1962; Peins, 1962; Spradlin, 1963; McCarthy, 1964). Although the major presentation by each of these reviews deals with language, there is some difference of opinion among writers in their delineation and definition of language and communication factors. For example, some authors include speech development in their review; whereas others do not consider this area germane to language. The reader should be aware of these differences in the literature.

Receptive language

This component of language involves two processes: (1) the receipt of auditory and visual stimuli by the peripheral organs and (2) the ability of an organism to gain understanding from these sensory experiences.

Individuals with problems in one or more of the peripheral systems will misperceive sensory data and, consequently, have difficulty in the subsequent stage of the process involving the meaningful interpretation of sensory images. Studies have suggested the difficulty that the retarded frequently exhibit in making optimum use of the auditory channel, because of the high incidence of hearing difficulties, auditory discrimination problems, memory disturbances, and environmentally induced inhibiting factors. Relative strengths or weaknesses in the visual channel in these areas have not been reported in the literature.

The research that has compared language capabilities of retarded children at various intellectual levels and mental ages has strongly suggested that the retarded seem to have less *relative* difficulty understanding and interpreting auditory and visual stimuli at a meaningful level than at nonmeaningful levels. It should be recognized that this relative strength is in comparison to their performance level in other areas of language, for the total language age of the retarded is typically lower than their mental age. The literature is consistent in suggesting that nonorganically involved retarded children are stronger in visual reception and interpretation of stimuli than in the auditory. Children exhibiting the "Strauss Syndrome" show the opposite profile. That is, they are relatively stronger in auditory than in visual reception.

Associating meaningful material

"Association" refers to the internal manipulation of symbols of language. The ability to deal with incoming symbolic information and appropriately associate this cognitive material with the existing repertoire is an important component of general language performance and apparently related to MA. McCarthy (1964) characterizes this skill as "thinking in words."

The results of research dealing with the language association skills of the retarded parallel the findings of investigations concerned with receptive capabilities. Although not outstanding in general language performance, the culturally disadvantaged retarded child tends to be relatively poorer in auditory-vocal than in visual-motor association. Again, the opposite profile is seen for Strauss-Syndrome children. Relative to their MA, retarded children score less well than one would predict in both areas of association.

Expressive language

The effective translation of ideas into vocal or motor expression involves a complex constellation of capabilities among which are (1) surveying the myriad of neurological networks for a response pattern which is appropriate, (2) the proper sequencing of the components of expression, (3) the choice of an effective mode for communication (vocal and/or gestural), and (4) the effective monitoring of earlier responses using this feedback system to alter subsequent patterns of expression. Expressive components of language are complex and often erroneously viewed as rather circumscribed.

Investigations of the vocal and gestural expressive abilities of retarded children using the Illinois Test of Psycholinguistic Abilities indicate that educable children tend to do better in the vocal expression of ideas than in gestural expression. As intelligence decreases toward the trainable level, this pattern of expressive abilities reverses, with the gestural modality showing greater relative strength. It should be recognized that other variables apparently influence encoding skills of the retarded. For example, living in an institution or residential facility seems to be associated with a reduction in vocal expression; whereas this same pattern is not true for retarded children in public schools who often exhibit greater *relative* skills in vocal than in motor expression.

To place these results in their proper perspective, it should be noted that the performance of the retarded children was compared with mental age norms, that differences among the areas of language are relative differences, and the indication that the retarded are relatively stronger in vocal expression should in no sense be interpreted as meaning that their vocal expressive skills are necessarily consistent with normal children of the same MA or CA.

Automatic-sequential aspects of language

There are certain aspects of language which do not have meaning in the sense of embracing a concept, although these skills are necessary to effectively communicate ideas. These automatic and imitative rote-learned aspects of language involve the development of skill in the use of grammar, visual memory, and auditory memory. Intellectually normal children learn these skills incidentally. The evidence suggests that the automatic-sequential factors constitute the areas of greatest difficulty for the retarded. It is ironic, indeed, that the retarded have *relatively* less difficulty with the meaningful aspects of language but show much greater difficulty with nonmeaningful, imitative, and rote-learned factors. The literature has been inconsistent in demonstrating greater relative disability in either auditory or visual memory. Both areas appear to be lower than MA and CA in educable and trainable children.

ASSESSING LANGUAGE DIFFICULTIES

Formal procedures

The development of formal, standardized techniques for assessing factors of language has escalated rapidly since the middle 1950s. More attention has been given to relating measurement and instrumentation to accepted theoretical models and constructs. The theoretical position of Skinner (1957) as well as Osgood's (1957) mediational hypothesis have contributed immeasurably to the construction of formal language measures.

Several of these instruments, the dimensions of language evaluated by each, and the age range of the standardization subjects are summarized in Table 6-4. The administration of these instruments and their interpretation requires a trained and experienced clinician.

TABLE 6-4 *Examples of Formal Language Tests*

Name of test	Age range of normative sample	Dimensions assessed
Illinois Test of Psycholinguistic Abilities	2–6 to 9–0	a Auditory-receptive language b Visual-receptive language c Auditory-vocal association d Visual-motor association e Vocal expression f Gestural or motor expression g Automatic use of language structure h Visual memory i Auditory memory

TABLE 6-4 *(Continued)*

Name of test	Age range of normative sample	Dimensions assessed
Parson's Language Sample	6–0 to 15–0	**a** Object and picture naming **b** Digit and sentence repetition **c** Question answering (verbal response) **d** Imitation of motor acts **e** Completion of motor task by vocal and gestural instuction **f** Question answering (gestural response) **g** Question asking by subject
Differential Language Facility Test	2–0 to 6–0	**a** Labeling objects **b** Labeling pictures **c** Word association **d** Object association **e** Mutilated pictures **f** Tracing visual form **g** Gesture sequence matching **h** Speech sound mimicry **i** Gestural conversation **j** Nonsense grammatical mimicry **k** Picture series description **l** Vocal close
Peabody Picture Vocabulary Test	1–9 to 18–0	Auditory word comprehension and association with an appropiate visual stimulus

Informal procedures

If a language program is to be effective, the teacher should have some idea of the different types of language difficulties peculiar to each child. A formal language assessment can be given only periodically in most settings. To frequently check on the progress of each child, a systematic sample of the language performance of children will need to be taken. From these diagnostic efforts, modifications can be made on a day-to-day and week-to-week basis. If children are having difficulties in the various areas of language, it is appropriate that each child's performance be compared with the other children in the class. For example, the fact that most of the children in a class can remember the words of a song indicates that this is a reasonable performance criterion against which the achievement of others in the class can be compared. If a child or a small group of children are unable to measure up to this performance level, it would be indicative of a possible disability in either understanding what they are hearing, discriminating among the various words of the song, or remembering an auditory sequence. When specific difficulties are identified, teachers can systematically provide remedial experiences, which are often similar to those tasks used to diagnose the difficulty. Effort has been made to provide teachers with a compendium of informal diagnostic and remedial tasks related to factors of language; the most notable among these has been the work reported by Wiseman (1965).

Table 6-5 illustrates the types of activities teachers can use to check on those areas of language in which the retarded may show significant weaknesses. These assessment activities can be used for groups as well as for the individual child.

PROCEDURES FOR DEVELOPING LANGUAGE SKILLS

The broad guidelines used to encourage the retarded to develop skills in language are no different from those used to support their performance in other areas. It is of concern that the children be exposed to an environment which is conducive to free expression in order to stimulate oral communication. Moreover, an accepting attitude of each child's functional level should be clearly demonstrated by the teacher. These suggestions are consistent with the need to minimize all hints of external evaluation. If the retarded are to be stimulated to give spontaneous productions, they must be secure enough in their realization that criticism will not take place. The classroom teacher should provide an appropriate model for establishing this atmosphere of acceptance by other children. If the teacher is prone toward constant and open evaluation, the children can be expected to mimic this same style of behavior.

The environment must be manipulated in a fashion which will allow the retarded to be placed in situations in which verbal communication is necessary and natural. Any child whose communication is satisfactorily accomplished by pointing or gesturing does not

TABLE 6-5 Informal Assessment Procedures of Language

Language area and appropriate diagnostic activity

Understanding What Is Heard

A Ask the child to follow your verbal commands such as, "Place your hand on the top of your head." "Hold your right hand in the air and wave to the people sitting on both sides of you." "Go to the table at the rear of the room, take a piece of paper out of the tray, return to your desk, and crumple the paper into a ball."

B Have the child respond to the directions sung on records such as "Ball and the Jack."

C Ask the child various questions such as, "Do books walk?" "Does chalk write?" "Do elephants eat?" Have him respond by standing up or raising a hand if the answer is "yes" and do nothing if the answer is "no."

D Play records containing various sounds and have the child identify who or what makes each sound. Ask the child to listen for certain components in stories or nursery rhymes, or have him tell the story again in order to determine if he understands what is being said.

E Present the child with a series of unambiguous pictures which appear on a single piece of paper, say the appropriate word or words describing one of the pictures, and have the child point to the correct picture.

Understanding What Is Seen

A Show the child a picture of an animal, e.g., a cow, and give him the appropriate label for the animal; then, present the child with a series of pictures and ask him to point to all the cows. It is possible to vary this exercise by using different objects and pictures. For instance, the selection by the child can be according to those objects that are moving, things that are red, pictures that show children, or things that are round.

B Have the child inspect a picture containing an object with a certain shape or characteristic which is a hidden part of the total scene. Show a picture of the object and see how many he can locate in the total picture. The backs of cereal boxes frequently contain these types of pictures.

C Present the child with a group of chips which are of various geometric shapes or which have pictures printed on each. Have the child locate and make piles of all of the squares, triangles, or pictures of donkeys. The same exercise can be done with letters of the alphabet.

TABLE 6-5 (Continued)

Language area and appropriate diagnostic activity

D Show a silent film, filmstrip, or series of cards which tells a story. Ask questions concerning the general story sense as well as specific details, such as what people were wearing on their heads, how many cars were in the picture, if children appeared in the sequence, and so on.

E Have the children interpret pictures by looking for details in a story, sensing implied facts, and seeing cause and effect.

F Present a series of pictures; then, have them sequence the pictures according to a story and tell about the story sequence.

G Show a silent film or filmstrip and ask the students to tell about the story. Dramatization by role playing will help to determine any difficulties they might have in decoding visual stimuli.

Associating Auditory Stimuli

A Play a group of recorded sounds and ask the children to identify all those sounds made by birds or animals. A variation of this is to name an object for the children, following this with a series of sounds. Ask the students to indicate which sound is made by a train. The task is made complicated by reducing the dissimilarity among the sounds or by providing more than one sound made by a train.

B Ask the children to vocally list all the things they can think of that can carry other things, that have ears or hair, or that can be built from bricks.

C Present a series of objects, and ask the students to tell in which ways the objects are similar. A graded series of these tasks can be developed which range from obvious similarities to more obtuse likenesses. Initially, it may be necessary to present a visual picture of each object as the appropriate word is said.

D Present an incomplete story or show part of a short film, and have the children tell what they think will happen, how the story will end, and why.

E Present vocal absurdities such as, "What would happen if we were born with three fingers and no thumb?" or "What would happen if we suddenly could walk only on our hands?" This will help check on how well the child is able to see cause and effect situations.

F Have the child complete sentences such as, "I opened the window and _____."

TABLE 6-5 (Continued)

Language area and appropriate diagnostic activity

G Ask them to interpret or tell you the general sense of a story which they have been told. Determine if the child can discern cause and effect by asking him "What would happen if . . . ?" types of questions.

H Give the students an opportunity to supply an ending to a story.

Associating Stimuli Presented Visually

A Present the children with cards containing pictures of absurd situations, such as a child trying to brush his teeth with a hair brush or comb. Ask them to tell you why the picture is silly, or have them point to the funny part of each picture.

B Have the children look through old magazines or catalogs and cut out all the things they can find which are green, have wheels, or have buttons. Present them with a group of pictures or objects and have the students group the objects according to some criterion, such as those things that are used for work, contain at least two colors, could hold water, or grow in the ground. Gradually ask for grouping on multiple criteria, such as those objects that are round, green, and can be eaten.

C Using one of the commercial story puzzles, ask the children to arrange the pieces of the puzzle so that the story is told. At first, they should be shown the entire sequence and later be allowed to reassemble the components of the story.

D Show a picture and ask the children to verbally or gesturally indicate what would happen if "such and such" had occurred. For example, a picture of cars stopped at an intersection for a red light could be used and the children asked to tell or show the possible consequences of a car going through the red light.

E Prepare a sheet with pictures of objects which have characteristic sounds. From tape, present the children with a sound and have them relate the sound to one of the pictures.

F Present a picture of an object followed by a second series of pictures showing a group of objects. One of the group should be the same as the initial picture, or a variation thereof, shown from a different perspective. Ask the child to choose the one which is the same as the first picture.

TABLE 6-5 (Continued)

Language area and appropriate diagnostic activity

Remembering What Is Heard

A Ask the child to repeat digits of varying lengths forward and/or backwards.

B Present words or sentences of different lengths and complexity, and ask that they be repeated in the way that they were originally presented.

C Observe how well the children remember rhymes and songs.

D Read a story to the group and have each child recall specific and general aspects of the story.

E Sing or play records using music that allows for adding on, such as "Old MacDonald Had a Farm." See how well children remember the paired relationships within the song. For example, the cow goes "moo" and not "quack-quack."

F See if the students can follow a series of directions which increase in length and complexity. For example, say, "Charlie, I would like for you to get up from your chair, take this piece of paper to the trash can, go to the blackboard, draw a circle, place the open book on the table, and return to your desk."

Remembering What Is Seen

A Show a group of objects which initially are quite dissimilar in their characteristics. Have the students close their eyes while one of the objects is removed, and after they have opened their eyes, have them recall what is missing. This task can be increased in complexity by increasing the number of objects presented, exhibiting objects with similar characteristics, removing more than one object, or by requiring that a child replace the objects in the same initial sequence.

B Present a series of cards with paired-associate types of tasks, mix the cards up, and ask a child to reconstruct the pairs. For example, you might have a series of colored chips with the name of each color printed on separate cards. The child learns to associate the blue chip with the card containing the printed word "blue." Several of these types of pairs can be presented with the child requested to match the appropriate word with the correct color after the objects have been mixed up.

C Show a picture and have the students remember all the objects they saw.

TABLE 6-5 *(Continued)*

Language area and appropriate diagnostic activity

D Remembering and reconstructing a pictorial sequence such as in a comic strip will help to assess visual memory and the visual interpretation of stimuli.

Vocal Expression of Ideas

A Observe how well children do during the "show-and-tell" period or in their description of an object, event, or process.

B Have the children respond to questions which emphasize verbal fluency wherein any response a child gives is correct, such as, "How many ways can a toothpick be used?" "What would happen if everyone lived in a house made of glass?"

C Show a picture and have the children tell about the picture, what went on before the picture was taken, and what happened afterwards.

D Have a child tell how to do something such as catch a fish, teach a dog to fetch a stick, or cut the lawn.

E Show a simple object and ask for a description of the object.

F Observe the extent of each child's vocabulary, the length and complexity of sentences used, and how correctly words are used.

Motor Expression of Ideas

A Have the children dramatize an event which has been seen or heard, such as threading a needle, sewing on a patch, cooking dinner, driving a car, or riding a horse.

B Have them listen to a record containing a short story or song and draw a picture on the blackboard or on a large piece of paper describing what was heard.

C Observe how effectively children communicate ideas in finger plays.

D Ask the group to draw objects having certain characteristics, such as things that have three corners, objects that carry other things, or illustrations of things that can be eaten.

E Ask the children to show how many ways musical instruments can be played.

F Observe the use of gestures in describing a happening or object during show-and-tell.

G Creative dramatics and role playing will provide excellent situations for assessing ability in motor expression.

H Present an object or show a picture. Ask the children to show what people usually do with the object.

need to engage in vocal communication. This behavior is often observed in young children whose parents or siblings immediately respond to an unintelligible sound and gesture when some need is felt by the child. This same phenomenon occurs with the retarded when the teacher or someone else speaks for a student. In such instances, there is no need for learning to talk. It is quite important, therefore, that this type of communication not be rewarded, and that the children be placed in situations in which language is needed and required. At the same time, each attempt at oral expression should be rewarded. Specific periods should be set aside for language arts, and the children should become involved in the vocal communication of ideas.

Activities appropriate for an informal assessment of language reception, association, memory, and expression were presented earlier. These suggestions are equally appropriate for remediating the areas of language ability which each evaluates. The activities which were suggested can be used as presented or elaborated upon and extended to more complex tasks accordingly. Other suggestions which the teacher should consider in formulating a language program include the following:

1 *Auditory and visual discrimination and memory should be emphasized through a systematic training program.*

2 *Frequent formal and informal discussion periods should be scheduled to encourage the retarded to express themselves and listen attentively to others. Critical evaluation should not be a part of this activity.*

3 *As language skills develop, the teacher should be more direct in helping the students to organize their thoughts and expressions so that they are logical, parsimonious, and appropriate.*

4 *Activities planned for the children should emanate from real situations which the teacher believes to be significant to the students. For example, allowing teen-age children to use the telephone will provide an excellent and realistic situation from which language activities can develop.*

5 *In all language activities, the association of the various senses early in each child's development should be encouraged. Stimuli can be presented to children using both the auditory and visual modalities. Likewise, it is also desirable that vocal expressions be encouraged at the same time nonverbal productions are given, and vice versa.*

6 *Liberal use should be made of musical activities including recordings of songs and stories, tapes of children's voices, rhythm-band activities, add-on or sing-along songs, and recordings requiring activities by the children. These high-interest materials offer a relaxed environment and at the same time provide appropriate stimulation for encouraging communication by shy retarded children.*

7 Show-and-tell periods often become a daily ritual and, if handled intelligently, will provide an excellent stimulus for encouraging language. Even older retarded children find it interesting to bring something to show their classmates, and they frequently are eager to instruct other students in procedures for correctly working a machine or performing some process, such as rowing a boat.

8 Games and activities in which any response given by a child is correct offer excellent stimulants for encouraging verbal and nonverbal fluency. Questions such as the following can be used: "How many ways can you think of to use a screwdriver?" "What would happen if everyone had springs in his shoes?" In nonverbal areas, the children can be asked to draw as many different things as possible on a sheet of paper containing 30 one-inch squares.

9 Choral reading, reciting, and singing encourage participation from those students who have not developed minimal skills in expression.

10 Creative dramatics and role playing are good techniques for encouraging the development of nonverbal language skills.

DEVELOPING SKILLS IN WRITTEN COMMUNICATION

Handwriting, spelling, and the written expression of ideas will be focused upon in this section. The procedures used by the teacher in providing instruction in these areas are basically similar to those used by the regular classroom teacher. In the regular class, many of the skills involved are learned incidentally; however, special-class instruction in these fundamental subject areas must be conducted intentionally and be intelligently sequenced. Entrance into adult life requires that the retarded acquire a certain level of skill in each area.

Handwriting

As is true with intellectually normal children, instructing the retarded in handwriting requires that they have a certain minimal level of muscular coordination. Children must be able to grasp a pencil or piece of chalk and maintain a certain posture while it is manipulated. Procedures for aiding the retarded to develop basic motor skills were suggested in Chapter 5.

Children should initially be given experiences which allow for the practice of basic writing movements. The configuration of circles and straight and slanted lines can be developed by encouraging freedom of movement in art and drawing. At first, it is unwise to force the students to do small motor tasks with a pencil or pen until they first have practiced the strokes on a blackboard or a large piece of paper with a soft pencil, felt pen, chalk, or crayon. Gradually, as they develop control, the children are taught to combine these circles and other strokes, formerly used for drawing, into the formation of letters and words.

After these basic skills develop, the retarded can be engaged in activities requiring the use of small motor skills. Tracing letters on paper by following appropriately placed arrows will help them develop a systematic procedure for properly constructing letters. Full attention should be given to the development of a clear image of the letter and an appropriate sequence for making the strokes. Paper with horizontal lines is recommended for this stage.

A word of caution should be given at this point. Care should be exercised so that the children focus on the total configuration of the letter rather than the line segments being traced. The mode of presentation and the activities at this stage of development should be varied so as not to encourage emphasis which is tangential to the main objective of the tracing activity. Moreover, long periods of close work should be avoided and special attention should be given so that the children do not need to constantly refocus from near point to far point and vice versa.

Combining letters into words requires a close relationship between activities of reading, spelling, and oral expression. To construct words, the child needs to be able to sequence and space letters appropriately as well as correctly read and spell the word. Many teachers believe that whole words with real meaning should be introduced into the handwriting program at a very early stage. This strategy will increase the possibility of maintaining the child's interest in writing activities.

There is no empirical documentation to suggest that the handwriting program for the retarded should stress manuscript or cursive writing. It seems logically reasonable that less confusion would result in using manuscript writing because of the close relationship this has to material from books and the typewritten reproductions teachers frequently prepare. There is a clear advantage in relating all these activities and skills. Professional opinions vary on which writing style is preferred. Strauss and Lehtinen (1947), for example, suggest the use of cursive writing early in the children's career because it facilitates the children's seeing words in their totality.

Accuracy and not speed should always be stressed. Retarded children should not be placed in competitive situations in writing. The able teacher should focus on intra-individual evaluations by demonstrating variations in each child's performances. Comparing students with each other will foster poor habits and reduce the legibility and accuracy of the retarded child's performance. Principles of learning presented earlier should be viewed by the teacher as basic and necessary to handwriting instruction.

Most educable mentally retarded will eventually be able to make the transition from manuscript to cursive writing. The appropriate time for this event will vary according to each child's manipulative capabilities, their success in other areas such as reading and spelling, and their level of development in manuscript writing. With normal children, cursive writing is typically introduced in the late second or early third grade. Anderson (1964) has suggested the need to proceed from the simple to the complex by introducing lowercase letters in the following sequence: *l, e, i, t, u, n, m, h, k, w, o, b, v, x, y, j, f, s, p, r, c, a, d, g, q, z.* Capital letters can be taught as the need arises, such as when a name is written.

Spelling

It is reasonable to expect that most educable mentally retarded children will achieve in spelling at about the fifth-grade level. As in any subject area involving the use of complex skills, expectations for spelling achievement will vary according to any unique weaknesses an individual child exhibits. For example, children with visualization difficulties may have substantial problems in spelling. In like manner, children with auditory discrimination problems could have spelling weaknesses because they may be unable to hear the sounds peculiar to spelling words. For those who seem to have unusual difficulty in spelling, an informal assessment of each child's performance in the basic skills should be conducted. Some of these fundamental areas are (1) auditory and visual reception, (2) auditory and visual memory, (3) auditory and visual discrimination, (4) association auditory and visual stimuli, (5) motor expression, and (6) vocal expression. Techniques for evaluating children in each of these areas have been presented in an earlier section of this chapter.

Teaching considerations which are paramount for effective instruction in spelling include the following:

1   *There is a need to establish and maintain a close relationship between instruction in reading, writing, and spelling. Procedures appropriate for teaching reading to the retarded will help to strengthen their spelling performances.*

2   *In teaching spelling to the retarded, all sense modalities should be used in concert. Children should trace or write a word, say the word, and observe its configuration when written by someone else. Using all the sense modalities will help to develop firm patterns of association. In this regard, the suggestion of Kirk and Johnson (1951) for using the Fernald system seems to be wise.*

3   *Because English has such a confusing phonemic structure, teaching spelling through the use of rules will be less effective and more confusing to the retarded. As is true in no other area, rote instruction in spelling rather than emphasizing conceptual development and understanding is necessary. For a small number of the higher-*

level educable retarded, however, introducing a few basic spelling rules may help to elevate their general spelling performance.

4 Words which have utility for the children should be selected for the spelling program. Material which is to be learned should be appropriate and of potential use to retarded children.

5 The retarded should not be given a chance to practice their errors. Immediate knowledge of results with appropriate rewards for a correct response will control this possibility. Teachers must be sure that an effective and accurate monitoring device for feedback is available. This could take the form of a programmed device, a teacher's aid, or some type of team or buddy system. In this way, children can be given the necessary feedback required for reinforcing success and obliterating patterns of error in spelling.

6 If the child knows how to write, instruction in spelling will probably make more immediate impact. By knowing how to write letters, the child will provide his own reinforcement and encourage greater intermodality facilitation. However, knowing how to write is not absolutely necessary if the child can discriminate among letters. Children can be given a group of letters each of which is printed on a separate card in a procedure similar to that used in a chart story. Each child can be asked to spell out a word using his own group of letters and to compare his performance with the teacher's model. By moving their fingers over the letters placed in sequence, they will develop skill in seeing the sequence of letters in words and strengthen their writing performance.

7 The teacher should keep a log of words the children use and those each child has particular trouble with in reading, spelling, and writing. If an individual seems to be particularly bothered by a certain group of words which have a common characteristic, the teacher may find it helpful to teach the child the rule or principle appropriate for those situations. Clinical teaching, then, requires the maintenance of a careful record of specific weaknesses in spelling.

8 Spelling is often a boring and tiresome activity. Attempts should be made to provide interesting activities during the spelling period. Retarded children who can spell at a third- or fourth-grade level enjoy participating in spelling bees as long as the rewards and penalties are not too high. When too much pressure is exerted, their performance will decline.

Written expression

With the exception of the comprehensive study by Cartwright (1966), little research attention has been given to investigating written language abilities of educable mentally retarded children. Cartwright's research showed that the retarded are significantly weaker than the intellectually normal in composition length, sentence length, type-token ratio (number of different words divided by the composition length), grammatical correctness, and spelling correctness. Apparently the degree of disability that the retarded exhibit in written expression is directly related to their level of performance in oral expression. Written language, then, is an extension of oral language.

Too much direct emphasis on grammatical structure and other technical aspects of writing should not constitute a large segment of the retarded child's program. Spending too much time and effort on developing these skills will result in shortchanging other more important areas. Moreover, the vast majority of educable children will not be able to develop substantial skill in the appropriate use of written syntax. There are, however, certain procedures teachers can take to upgrade the retarded child's performance in written expression. Among these are the following:

1 *As in the case of oral communication, mentally retarded children will profit in their acquisition of skill in written expression by being exposed to a good model. Since most parents of children living in disadvantaged communities do not provide this type of model, it will be necessary for the teacher to expose the retarded to a wide spectrum of examples of written and oral expression.*

2 *Emphasis should be placed on interrelating oral and written communication. Vocal expression should be translated into written communication, and vice versa.*

3 *Any writing done by the child should be of a practical nature and viewed as significant by the retarded youngster. It will often be necessary to devote time to changing the attitudes of the children before they can be asked to participate in written exercises.*

4 *Attention should be given to making use of the retarded child's relative strengths in nonverbal areas to facilitate development in written production. Dramatizations of some type of process, such as catching a fish, can be described in written discourse. This activity will make clear their need to develop more skill in written expression.*

5 *The teacher can help the child in written communication by encouraging the appropriate sequencing of ideas. Exercises to strengthen the presentation of written material in a logical fashion should be incorporated in all areas of the instructional program, particularly in those portions involving oral communication. The retarded should learn what ideas should logically come before or after a thought, expression, or activity.*

SELECTED REFERENCES

Anderson, P. S.: *Language Skills in Elementary Education,* The Macmillan Company, New York, 1964, p. 108.

Bangs, J. E.: "A Clinical Analysis of the Articulatory Defects of the Feebleminded," *Journal of Speech Disorders,* vol. 7, 1942, pp. 343–356.

Bateman, B. D. and Wetherell, J.: "Psycholinguistic Aspects of Mental Retardation," *Mental Retardation,* vol. 3, 1965, pp. 8–13.

Birch, J. W. and Matthews, J.: "The Hearing of Mental Defectives: Its Measurement and Characteristics," *American Journal of Mental Deficiency,* vol. 55, 1951, pp. 384–393.

Cartwright, G. P.: *Written Language Abilities of Educable Mentally Retarded and Normal Children,* unpublished doctoral dissertation, University of Pittsburgh, Pittsburgh, Pa., 1966.

Glovsky, L. and Rigrodsky, S.: "A Classroom Program for Auditorially Handicapped Mentally Deficient Children," *Training School Bulletin,* vol. 60, 1963, pp. 56–59.

Goda, S. and Rigrodsky, S.: "Auditory Training Procedures of Certain Mentally Retarded Children," *Training School Bulletin,* vol. 59, 1962, pp. 81–86.

Goertzen, S. M.: "Speech and the Mentally Retarded Child," *American Journal of Mental Deficiency,* vol. 62, 1957, pp. 244–253.

Harrison, S.: "A Review of Research in Speech and Language Development of the Mentally Retarded Child," *American Journal of Mental Deficiency,* vol. 63, 1958, pp. 236–240.

Karlin, I. W. and Strazzula, M.: "Speech and Language Problems of Mentally Deficient Children," *Journal of Speech and Hearing Disorders,* vol. 17, 1952, pp. 286–294.

Kirk, S. A. and Johnson, G. O.: *Educating the Retarded Child,* Houghton Mifflin Company, Boston, 1951.

———:"Research in Education," in H. A. Stevens and R. Heber (eds.), *Mental Retardation: A Review of Research,* The University of Chicago Press, Chicago, 1964, pp. 57–99.

Kodman, F.: "The Incidence of Hearing Loss in Mentally Retarded Children," *American Journal of Mental Deficiency,* vol. 62, 1958, pp. 675–678.

McCarthy, J. J.: "Research on the Linguistic Problems of the Mentally Retarded," *Mental Retardation Abstracts,* vol. 1, Washington, U.S. Department of Health, Education, and Welfare, 1964, pp. 3–27.

Matthews, J.: "Speech of the Mentally Retarded," in L. E. Travis (ed.), *Handbook of Speech Pathology,* Appleton-Century-Crofts, Inc., New York, 1957, pp. 531–551.

Mueller, M. W.: "Comparison of Psycholinguistic Patterns of Gifted and Retarded Children," *Selected Convention Papers,* National Education

Association, Council for Exceptional Children, Washington, 1964*a*, pp. 143–149.

————: "Language Profiles of Mentally Retarded Children," *Selected Convention Papers,* National Education Association, Council for Exceptional Children, Washington, 1964*b*, pp. 149–153.

Myklebust, H. R.: "Language Disorders in Children," *Exceptional Children,* vol. 22, 1956, pp. 163–166.

Osgood, C. E.: *Contemporary Approaches to Cognition: A Behavioral Analysis,* Harvard University Press, Cambridge, Mass., 1957.

Peins, M.: "Mental Retardation: A Selected Bibliography on Speech, Hearing and Language Problems," *Asha,* vol. 4, 1962, pp. 38–40.

Schlanger, B. B.: "Effects of Listening Training on Auditory Thresholds of Mentally Retarded Children," *Asha,* vol. 4, 1962, pp. 273–275.

Skinner, B. F.: *Verbal Behavior,* Appleton-Century-Crofts, Inc., New York, 1957.

Smith, J. O.: "Speech and Language of the Retarded," *Training School Bulletin,* vol. 58, 1962.

Spradlin, J. E.: "Language and Communication of Mental Defectives," in Norman R. Ellis (ed), *Handbook of Mental Deficiency,* McGraw-Hill Book Company, New York, 1963, pp. 512–555.

Strauss, A. A. and Lehtinen, L. E.: *Psychopathology and Education of the Brain-Injured Child,* Grune and Stratton, Inc., New York, 1947, pp. 184–190.

Travis, L. E. (ed.): *Handbook of Speech Pathology,* Appleton-Century-Crofts, Inc., New York, 1957, pp. 286–287.

Van Riper, C.: *Speech Correction: Principles and Methods,* 4th ed., Prentice-Hall, Inc., Englewood Cliffs, N.J., 1965, pp. 74–101, 467–502.

Wiseman, D. E.: "A Classroom Procedure for Identifying and Remediating Language Problems," *Mental Retardation,* vol. 3, 1965, pp. 20–24.

instructing in reading

The reading process is exceedingly complicated. An individual must master a series of complex skills to effectively perform and receive the maximum advantage from reading. Adequate reception, discrimination among sounds and symbols, association among various components involved in reading, remembering a visual and auditory sequence, understanding material, applying facts and concepts to earlier learned material, and the effective expression of ideas comprise some of the major factors involved in reading. The complexities involved in adequate mastery of these skills provides a reasonable explanation why retarded children often have such great difficulty learning to read. The added ambition of helping them to develop a conceptual instead of rote competency only increases the magnitude of the problem.

Perhaps in no other area does the teacher need to place greater emphasis on skill development than in reading. There are several noteworthy reasons for emphasizing reading. First, the basic skills contained in reading constitute the most significant common denominator for adequate achievement in other important areas. Without an elementary ability to read, retarded children will be adversely affected in arithmetic, social and personal development, communication, and vocational performance. Satisfactory achievement in each of these areas presupposes a certain minimum level of reading skill. Although the influence of reading disability may not be severe enough to make an impact in the early school years, when the child is old enough to function in a self-sufficient manner, his inability to read will become obvious and register a deleterious influence.

Second, reading must be emphasized to provide the retarded with a means for gathering general information. The enhancement of the child's response repertoire is a primary objective through the stimulation of higher-level associations among the existing cognitive structures with those perceptions continually being received. Reading provides a breadth of general information which can be assimilated into the response repertoire with a minimum of outside direction and influence if the youngsters have developed the basic skills involved in the reading process. This additional information will allow for the generation of alternative solutions to problems.

Third, reading depends on the use of a consistent style or method for systematically analyzing each reading situation. The transfer, generalization, and elaboration of such a style should characterize the manner in which the child solves problems in other areas of life. The thesis expressed here is that reading demands a consistent approach and that such a general tactic used by the child in reading situations will lead to a similar type of strategy being employed in other areas, thereby reducing impulsive and random responses to problems.

In the fourth place, reading will provide opportunities for pleasurable out-of-school activities. Further, ability to independently perform in these activities will logically lead to a more positive self-concept. The side advantage of other children, within a family living in a culturally disadvantaged environment, seeing the value in developing reading skills is worthy of note.

Finally, skill in reading lessens the possibility of the occurrence of physical harm and provides an insulation against severe social and emotional difficulties. The adverse influence of these environmental difficulties alone amply justifies emphasis being placed on the reading program.

BASIC READING OBJECTIVES

The basic objectives of the reading program for the retarded differ little from those appropriate for intellectually normal children. Obviously, the teacher will want to help every child develop as high a level of sophistication in reading as each is able. Variation will exist between the ability and performance of each child. The following specific objectives should be emphasized in the reading program for the retarded:

1 Development of a basic sight vocabulary with elaboration on the existing speaking and listening vocabulary
2 Development of a consistent method for word attack which is appropriate for each child and based on his idiosyncratic strengths and weaknesses
3 Development of skill in and a desire to read independently for information, pleasure, and personal satisfaction
4 Development of an adequate level of reading competence to allow for effective social and vocational participation in society

The first two objectives are consistent with the earlier expressed need to focus on the development of skill in the fundamental processes of reading. By using the children's existing speaking and listening capabilities to develop a sight vocabulary, the teacher can capitalize on the intrinsic motivation of the activities and experiences with which they have had success. The approach that the teacher uses to help in word attack is basically dependent on whether the child shows relative strength in the auditory or visual channel. There is often a wide discrepancy between their skill in using each of these modes. Ideally, therefore, a formal, but at the very least an informal, assessment of every child should precede a decision as to whether a visualization, auditory, or combined approach should be employed for word attack. A further requisite is that consistency be maintained throughout the process.

The latter two objectives emphasize the areas to which a child's developing skill in reading should be applied. A utilitarian theme should be stressed early in their program. This is not to imply, however, that pleasureful reading is to be minimized; indeed, for the retarded, this type of reading is useful and of immediate, tangible value.

EVALUATING READING SKILLS

This section is devoted to a discussion of the major considerations related to assessing various dimensions of reading. Evaluation of capacity, readiness for reading, level of achievement, and reading processes employed by the children are presented. Each of the sections describes formal and informal procedures for evaluation. Since teachers typically have not had the required preparation and experience necessary for administration of the formal standardized instruments, less time will be devoted for their administration and interpretation procedures. Attention will be called to the factors each test measures and to the major characteristics of each. Relatively more emphasis will be given to informal assessment procedures which every teacher can employ within the classroom. Throughout the discussion, the reader should keep in mind that the principal aim of evaluation is that it lead logically to specific suggestions for most effectively and efficiently teaching each child to read. This is the heart of clinical teaching.

Estimating potential for reading

FORMAL PROCEDURES The use of an individually administered, well-standardized intelligence test will most accurately indicate a child's predicted potential for reading. These instruments will provide a reasonable estimate of the approximate grade level at which a child should be achieving in reading at the time the test is administered. From most individual intelligence tests, one can calculate mental age which, in turn, allows for making a judgment concerning a child's predicted reading age.

The Revised Stanford-Binet Intelligence Scale (Form L-M) is generally considered to provide a satisfactory prediction of capacity. This test, which requires administration by a skilled psychometrician, is primarily verbal and was revised and restandardized in 1960. The Wechsler Intelligence Scale for Children (WISC) is also frequently used to assess intellectual potential in children, although scores from this instrument are not readily translated into mental-age equivalents. There is an advantage in using this test because both verbal and nonverbal areas of performance are tapped. It is often advantageous to have estimates of capacity in each of these areas with retarded children. Other tests, such as the Peabody Picture Vocabulary Test, are frequently chosen by psychologists to be administered to retarded children for reasons which are related to the specific child and situation. However, if time permits and the conditions warrant it, the Stanford-Binet Scale is recommended.

Group intelligence tests can be used to assess reading potential. These tests are chosen when a skilled psychometrician is unavailable, a less precise estimate of capacity is satisfactory, or lack of time requires a group administration. These instruments can be administered to students individually.

If properly administered by the teacher, tests such as the California Test of Mental Maturity, Lorge-Thorndike Intelligence Test, or the Otis Quick-Scoring Mental Ability Test will provide a stable indication of a child's reading capacity. Careful review of the manual for administration and interpretation should precede the administration of these instruments.

INFORMAL PROCEDURES   In the absence of test data, the teacher may need to estimate the approximate reading capacity of each child. Informal procedures are obviously a poor second to the more rigorous approach previously suggested. Of the less formal techniques, estimating reading potential on the basis of progress in other subject areas is probably best. Arithmetic performance, principally of a computational nature, can be used. An attempt should be made to select those subject areas which the teacher predicts to be more closely related to mental than chronological age. Moreover, the subject areas chosen to be used as a basis for judging reading potential should not depend heavily on reading skills. For example, arithmetic computation does not require a certain level of reading competency and provides a more reasonable estimate of capacity than arithmetic reasoning wherein children are often required to solve word problems which have as a prerequisite the need to read.

A second technique for estimating reading is a bit more crude and imprecise. Since retarded children learn at a rate of approximately 50 to 75 percent that of the normal child, the teacher can roughly judge mental age by calculating a percentage, within this range, of the child's chronological age.

Assessing levels of readiness

FORMAL PROCEDURES   Appraising the prereading readiness of retarded children is particularly necessary because of the need to be certain to place the children in situations in which they will succeed. The retarded will avoid activities in which they are unsuccessful. It is unwise, therefore, to require that they try to read without being sure that the necessary procedures have been developed. Table 7-1 summarizes factors evaluated by several readiness tests.

Length of attention span, emotional development, and personal adjustment are other important readiness factors requiring evaluation before exposing children to a formal reading program. Personal and emotional readiness can be assessed using a variety of personality inventories, each of which typically requires administration by a trained and skilled clinician. Attention span does not lend itself to formal assessment. This factor can be evaluated with reasonable accuracy, however, by systematically observing the amount of time a child attends to a task or the degree to which he can become involved in an activity. Willingness to complete a task is a good indication of attention and interest.

TABLE 7-1 Examples of Formal Tests Which Assess Various Readiness Factors Necessary for Reading

Name of test	Factors assessed
Illinois Test of Psycholinguistic Abilities	**a** Visual memory **b** Auditory memory **c** Vocal expression **d** Gestural expression **e** Auditory and visual association **f** Understanding the significance of what is heard and seen
Lee-Clark Reading Readiness Test	**a** Letter symbols **b** Concepts **c** Word symbols
Watson Reading-Readiness Test	**a** Social readiness **b** Emotional readiness **c** Physical readiness
Scholastic Reading Readiness Test	**a** Knowledge and understanding of facts and events **b** Visual discrimination **c** Sound-symbol association
The Standard Reading Test	**a** Visual discrimination and orientation **b** Auditory discrimination **c** Oral word-recognition test
The Purdue Perceptual-Motor Survey	**a** A variety of perceptual-motor dimensions (reviewed previously in Chapter 5)

INFORMAL PROCEDURES Teachers often do not have standardized tests available to assess readiness for reading. These considerations are important and cannot be left to chance because future success in reading is based on earlier developed readiness skills. It will often be necessary, therefore, for readiness levels to be assessed using informal procedures. Table 7-2 summarizes several major areas of readiness and suggests procedures for observing each.

Establishing the general instructional level for reading

FORMAL PROCEDURES Survey tests that are a part of a general achievement battery can be used to assess the level at which a child is able to read. These tests sample a variety of reading skills includ-

TABLE 7-2 Informal Techniques for Assessing Reading-Readiness Skills

Readiness factors and assessment procedures

Auditory Discrimination

A Present the children with sounds which are consistent in intensity but which vary in pitch. Ask them to tell which sound is higher and which is lower. Have them try to reproduce the sound. Gradually, bring the sounds closer together in pitch so that discriminations become more difficult. Hold pitch constant, vary intensity, and ask them to choose the louder or softer sound. Eventually, vary both intensity and pitch.

B Read a story or poem with similar sounds. Ask the children to listen to the beginning sound of each word and to tell which is used, for example, "Carl cast copper coins into the creek."

C Ask the children to recite a poem or to sing a song which they have learned earlier. Pay particular attention to whether the children exhibit a consistent pattern of difficulties in discrimination.

D Tape record a series of sets containing two sounds, some of which vary substantially and others of which are alike. Using a numbered piece of paper, have the children listen to each sound and place a mark next to the number of each set which sounds alike. Gradually, develop a taped inventory of sets of words, musical selections, and sounds which differ on more than one dimension. This can be used as an assessment device as well as a procedure for training auditory discrimination.

Visual Discrimination

A Observe the children grouping three-dimensional objects which differ in only one way, e.g., in shape, size, or color. Gradually, introduce variation on more than one dimension, such as by asking the children to choose the largest green box from a variety of other objects which differ in size and color.

B By using jigsaw puzzles, check on visual-discrimination skills. This same technique can be used to assess the degree of spatial orientation children exhibit in placing a puzzle piece in the appropriate spot.

C Ask the children to locate and cross out all the *b*'s in a short passage. Later the children can be asked to cross out words containing the letters *p* and *b*.

TABLE 7-2 (Continued)

Readiness factors and assessment procedures

Attention

The informal assessment of attention is similar in nature to the formal procedure suggested earlier. Observation of the child's general behavior and ability to attend to a task until completed will provide an indication of attention span.

Auditory Memory

(See Table 6-5, page 118)

Visual Memory

(See Table 6-5, page 118)

Perceptual-Motor Development

(See Table 5-4, page 86)

Understanding the Significance of What Is Seen

(See Table 6-5, page 115)

Understanding the Significance of What Is Heard

(See Table 6-5, page 115)

Vocal Expression

(See Table 6-5, page 119)

Gestural Expression

(See Table 6-5, page 119)

Association

(See Table 6-5, page 116)

ing oral and silent reading, vocabulary, word knowledge, paragraph meaning, and comprehension. They can be administered by the teacher either to individuals or groups. Table 7-3 lists instruments which reflect the most recent developments in this area.

TABLE 7-3 Survey Tests Which Assess Reading Achievement

Name of test	Dimensions evaluated	Grade level
California Reading Tests	Vocabulary Comprehension Total	1–14
Developmental Reading Tests	Vocabulary Comprehension Reading for retention Reading for organization Reading for appreciation Reading for evaluation	1–6
Gates Basic Reading Tests	Reading to appreciate general significance Reading to understand directions Reading to note details Vocabulary Comprehension	3–8
Gates Primary Reading Tests	Word recognition Sentence reading Paragraph reading	1–3
Iowa Silent Reading Tests	Rate Comprehension Directed reading Word meaning Paragraph comprehension Sentence meaning	4–14
Metropolitan Achievement Tests	Word knowledge Word discrimination Reading	2–9
SRA Achievement Series: Reading	Comprehension Vocabulary Verbal-pictorial association	1–9
Stanford Achievement Test: Reading	Word meaning Paragraph meaning	4–9
Wide Range Achievement Test	Reading	K–college

INFORMAL PROCEDURES   The evaluation of reading achievement infrequently during the school year can be done using one of the tests mentioned above. The advantage of using a well-standardized, systematically organized series of tasks based on a normative group against which the child can be compared should be recognized. Achievement tests do not typically require a highly trained examiner and can be administered satisfactorily by teachers who are familiar with the testing and scoring procedures.

There are times during the year, however, when the administration of formal tests is not possible or feasible. Nonetheless, the teacher may be interested in estimating the progress the children are making in reading. A similar need exists when a new child is enrolled in a class midway through the year. The teacher must decide at which level to start the student in reading. These situations suggest the need for an informal inventory of a child's performance level in reading.

Johnson and Kress (1965) have outlined a variety of techniques teachers can use to informally survey achievement in important areas of reading. They include techniques for surveying skills in listening, word attack, word recognition, oral reading, silent reading, and levels of readiness. Betts (1963) has also suggested techniques for administering informal inventories.

It is often helpful to inspect test scores from the years preceding the enrollment of students in your class to determine whether a unique pattern of strengths and weaknesses, particularly in reading, is obvious. For example, a child may have continuously shown strengths in word attack but weakness in sentence and paragraph meaning. These data provide information concerning his general level of reading performance, and suggest the need to provide special and extensive remediation in one or more areas. Additionally, previous records will give vital information in judging where further assessment should be directed.

An inventory involves asking the child to silently and orally read selections from a graded set of basal tests. The child's general level of word knowledge is first sampled by requiring the reading of a selection of words which appear at the end of the text initially chosen for the informal assessment. If no outstanding difficulty with the words is exhibited, the child's vocabulary skills are assessed using the text at the next higher level. If the child manifests some hesitation, he should be asked to read several paragraphs aloud to the teacher and answer questions about the content. During this reading, the examiner should observe difficulties related to word attack, hesitations, pronunciations, omissions, and lack of comprehension. The same procedure is used in silent reading, after which the child is asked to read the passage aloud. Approximately 80 percent of the teacher's questions should be answered correctly. The youngster should be able to read comfortably without manifesting confusion and unnatural and inconsistent patterns of recognition and word attack. If the book seems too easy or too hard, the teacher should make the necessary adjustment until the proper level of text is identified which allows for comfortable reading with some degree of challenge.

Teachers can simplify the process by selecting vocabulary samples and paragraphs from each of the basal series, typing the material on cards, drafting questions for the paragraphs, and administering the series to students throughout the year. Having several forms of this material available will allow the teacher to frequently check on the progress of each child without becoming overly concerned about the children memorizing the evaluation selections or becoming test wise.

Diagnosis of specific reading deficits

The evaluation procedures reviewed in the previous discussion were concerned primarily with assessing the level at which a child operates or his state of reading development in terms of a reference group. This primarily involves an inter-individual assessment. Children have difficulty in learning to read for any number of reasons. For example, two children may be underachieving at the same level, one having difficulty because a consistent means of word attack has not been developed, the other having a serious reversal problem. The problems are different, although when compared with other children, both read at the same level. Such inter-individual assessment will not typically lead to the development of a specific prescription for remediating reading difficulties. A more penetrating intra-individual assessment is required to determine which symptoms of poor reading are present, the manner in which the child approaches the reading task, the strengths and weaknesses of the child in terms of auditory and visual use of stimuli, and the degree to which other manifestations of disability are present in reading skills, such as in poor auditory fusion, sound blending, closure, visualization, and laterality. It is for these specific reasons that children often have problems in reading and require study extending beyond comparisons solely between children.

FORMAL PROCEDURES A number of formal procedures have been developed to diagnose specific reading difficulties of children. These diagnostic batteries vary according to individual and group administration. A basic requirement in using these instruments is that the test administrator be familiar with procedures of administration, scoring, and interpreting. The implication is that any teacher choosing to use these tests should have had specific training and experience in diagnosing and correcting reading problems. In most instances, the services of reading specialists should be requested by

TABLE 7-4 Diagnostic Reading Tests and Their Characteristics

Name of test	Characteristics
Gray Oral Reading Tests	This individual oral diagnostic test has four forms and consists of thirteen passages arranged according to level of difficulty from preprimer to adult. The passages are not only useful in assessing general level of reading but also provide an objective measure of growth in oral reading. In addition, they offer the opportunity to evaluate specific problems in oral reading, such as in vowel and consonant sounds, reversals, omissions, substitutions, additions, and specific position difficulties.
Spache Diagnostic Reading Scales	This scale, which requires individual administration, consists of three parts: three graded word lists, twenty-two graded paragraphs from preprimer through grade eight, and six phonics tests. Information is yielded in terms of a child's adequacy in silent reading, sight vocabulary, system for word attack and analysis, oral reading, phonics performance, and listening comprehension.
Gates-McKippop Reading Diagnostic Tests	Both forms of this test require a high level of skill in administration and interpretation by the examiner. A series of graded paragraphs to be read orally, tests for perception and word attack, and an oral vocabulary test all provide specific information concerning errors in oral reading and word attack. A total of twenty-eight scores provide measures of difficulty in areas such as omissions, additions, repetitions, mispronunciations, position, recognition of usual forms, oral reading, syllabication, spelling, and sound blending. This is a revision of the Gates Reading Diagnostic Tests.

TABLE 7-4 (Continued)

Name of test	Characteristics
Doren Diagnostic Reading Tests of Word Recognition Skills	This group, silent-reading diagnostic test can be administered to an entire class and offers a class profile which will assist in planning instruction and in grouping.
Silent Reading Diagnostic Tests	This well-standardized instrument requires administration by an experienced examiner and assesses various dimensions related to content and word-attack skills.
Roswell-Chall Diagnostic Reading Test of Word Analysis Skills	This individually administered word-attack diagnostic test is designed to evaluate a child's ability to blend sounds into whole words. Words are presented slowly to the child, who in turn tells the word to the examiner.
McCullough Word Analysis Tests	This group of individually administered instruments yields ten scores from a battery which consists of 7 thirty-item tests, five of which assess phonetic-analysis skills, with two for diagnosing structural-analysis skills. This instrument is appropriate for children who are achieving above the fourth-grade level.

the teacher to help in the diagnosis and to suggest corrective procedures. Table 7-4 summarizes the major characteristics of a sample of these tests.

INFORMAL PROCEDURES The continuous appraisal of progress and specific weaknesses in the reading performance of children is necessary. The use of tests mentioned in the above table is often not possible; therefore, teachers should know of informal procedures available to them for obtaining this information. In some instances, with the older retarded children principally, friendly discussions or astute questioning by the teacher will reveal possible sources of difficulty. The teacher can often estimate the eagerness of the child to read independently or his personal attitudes concerning developing skills in reading. These may be restricting or interfering to some degree with his progress.

More objective information can be obtained, and systematically recorded, when the teacher frequently appraises the nature of the oral reading errors made. The teacher should listen to the child read and attempt to detect errors of omission and substitution, repetitions, reversals, additions, and intonation problems. Strang (1964) has provided a systematic checklist for recording errors in oral reading.

A child's progress in silent reading can be checked by having the teacher ask questions related to the details and main ideas contained in a passage, inferences from information given by the passage or teacher, contradictory statements of fact or content, mood or characterization of the characters, and various possible reasons for the points of view expressed in the passage. This will reveal the extent to which the youngster has developed mature reading habits. Moreover, asking key questions will help to determine if the child is able to gain understanding from independent reading. Possible areas of difficulty can be checked by asking the student to reread portions of the passage orally.

Analyzing errors on workbook pages and in other types of work requiring independent reading provides an excellent procedure for assessing comprehension and work-study skills. The teacher can constantly assess specific areas of particular difficulty in this fashion. These exercises should have meaning, be related to the specific objectives of the lessons, and be evaluated by the teacher on a consistent basis. Children should not be led to assume that their seatwork is unimportant; the teacher can minimize this potential problem by carefully checking seatwork during and after the period devoted to this activity.

Comprehension and speed of reading can be evaluated by timing the children as they silently read a passage of known difficulty. Asking questions either before or after the reading will emphasize the need to read for comprehension of ideas. The teacher must be selective in the choice of a passage so that it is not too difficult for any one child. To do otherwise will sacrifice success for higher rates of reading speed.

Informal tests of auditory and visual discrimination and memory should be employed when it appears that a child is particularly weak in any of these areas. These tests are no different from those suggested in previous sections. Eye-voice span of the child can be checked by sliding a card over a page being read and asking for all the words seen prior to being covered by the card.

Finally, it is important that a systematic procedure be employed for reporting and summarizing information gathered by both formal and informal reading evaluations. Bond and Tinker (1957), Cleland

(1954), and Strang (1964) have suggested various techniques and checklists for recording such information. Special attention should be given to providing subsequent teachers with complete data on children from these evaluations.

PROCEDURES FOR READING INSTRUCTION

There is no special method for teaching reading to retarded children. The earlier discussion emphasizing the need for clinical assessment of each retarded child in terms of the components of reading alludes to the varied nature of the problems characteristic of this group of children. It should be recognized, therefore, that no single reading procedure will adequately serve all retarded children. In few other areas will the retarded have greater difficulty than in reading. The best combination of all reading methods should be employed in teaching the retarded. The same combination will not be satisfactory for every child because of children's unique patterns of weaknesses and strengths. Reading, therefore, demands that the teacher become an astute diagnostician, ready to alter and adjust practices whenever symptoms so indicate.

This section will discuss the spectrum of methodological practices which, to varying degrees, are appropriate for teaching the retarded to read. None of these techniques will be presented in complete detail; the principal objectives of this section are (1) to sequentially reveal those dimensions of reading which demand attention in teaching the retarded and (2) to familiarize the reader with the manner in which strategies of reading instruction can be combined and mixed according to the needs of each child. References which contain more comprehensive reports of the various methods will be provided in context.

Readiness instruction

Many of the areas of readiness which have been listed and discussed in preceding chapters have direct relevance to the reading program. Perceptual-motor development is one of the most basic areas required for learning to read (see Chapter 5). Other readiness factors are discussed in Chapter 6. These include auditory and visual memory and sequencing, auditory-vocal and visual-motor association, and the vocal and gestural expression of ideas. Techniques for directing the children's attention were suggested in Chapter 4. Since auditory and visual discrimination are important areas of reading readiness which have not been previously discussed, they will be considered in some depth in this section.

VISUAL DISCRIMINATION [1]   Research has suggested that perceptual-motor experiences are prerequisite to the development of the visual discrimination (Zaporozhets, 1965; Meier and McGee, 1958; Walk, 1958) and that success in discriminating flat shapes is preceded by the ability to discriminate among three-dimensional shapes wherein the individual can engage in motor manipulation of the objects (Hicks and Hunton, 1964; Walk, Gibson, Pick, and Tight, 1959). These and other studies by Russian psychologists (Pick, 1963) clearly show that the more manipulative experience a child has in the early stages of development, the more skilled he will become in complex perceptual activities, such as those involved in discrimination. Indeed, there is reason to believe that early sensory-motor experiences will facilitate skill development in areas involving sense modalities in addition to the visual. Pick (1963) has interpreted Soviet research as indicating that auditory discrimination will be facilitated by involvement in activities requiring motor mediation. Support of Piaget's position by these results is noteworthy.

Distinguishing among letters, and eventually between words, is important in the reading-readiness program. In order for children to develop this visual skill, the teacher must appropriately sequence activities so that skills learned earlier can be employed in subsequent activities. Moreover, a multisensory approach with particular emphasis on visual-motor experiences is indicated.

The work of Gibson (1963) is especially relevant to instruction in letter discrimination. She has identified four critical features of letters, viz., breaks and closes (o versus c), curves and corners (u versus v), rotations (M versus W), and reversals (d versus b). Her investigations have suggested that children must learn to discriminate differences in the unique characteristics within and between each of these pairs before being able to discriminate satisfactorily among letters per se. The following is an illustration of the sequence for teaching visual discrimination of letters which is suggested from this research.

SEQUENCE FOR TEACHING LETTER DISCRIMINATION

Level 1

At this level, activities should be designed to enable the child to distinguish the elementary features of shapes of letters, such as in breaks and closes, corners and curves, and lines and curves. They should be planned so that the manipulation of three-dimensional forms occurs in the early stages of instruction. The appropriate label-

[1] Appreciation is expressed to Mrs. Dina A. Deno for her substantial contribution to this section on visual discrimination.

ing of each form is also necessary. The two central components of this level are:

1 *Manipulating letters according to the unique features of each*
   a **Behavioral Objective:** The child can put all the three-dimensional objects (listed under materials) through the holes in the box (listed under materials) in any trial-and-error fashion.
   b **Materials:** Each child should have a set of three-dimensional objects of the following shapes: C (break), O (closed), I (line), u (curve), v (corner), and U, V, h, b (letters which contain only one or two of these features). These shapes should be approximately 3 by 3 by 3 inches and red. Each child should also have a light blue cardboard box that has holes outlined in black which correspond in size and shape to the set of objects.
   c **Procedure:** The children are told that they are going to work with certain letters and that they will learn to tell them apart. At first they should only learn to operate the C, O, I, u, and the v, because these are the elementary distinguishing features of letters. When the child can put all these forms through the holes, he can begin working with the remaining letters in the set. The teacher demonstrates putting the objects through the holes and makes clear that it is permissible to try different holes if the object does not fit in the first one.

2 *Visual discrimination of the distinguishing features of letters*
   a **Behavioral Objective:** When told to put an object through a specific hole (the teacher points), the child can pick up the correct object and put it through the hole without previously trying an incorrect object.
   b **Materials:** The same as in the above lesson.
   c **Procedure:** The procedure is the same as in the above lesson except that the teacher instructs the child to look from the hole to the object before picking the object up and trying it. The teacher works with the child until his glance automatically shifts from the hole to the object before he tries it. Studies have demonstrated the effectiveness of instructing the child to shift his glance in this way. After the child can perform this shift of glance, he is told to try to pick the correct one the first time.

Level 2

By the time the child has reached the second level, he should have developed stable associational patterns related to certain unique characteristics of letters and be ready to increase his present discrimination capabilities related to shape to include percepts of size and orientation. Discrimination in both these areas must be mastered. Two aspects of orientation are included at this level, rotation and reversal. Terms such as *smaller, larger, top, bottom, right,* and *left* should be presented and learned for subsequent communication to be effective. Tasks should proceed from sensory-motor experiences to purely visual. Up to this point, the materials used in the activities have been three dimensional.

3 *Manipulation of identical objects which vary in size*

    a Behavioral Objective: The child can put all the elements of a specific set (described under materials) inside one another in any trial-and-error fashion.

    b Materials: Each child must have sets of the following red, identically shaped elements which differ only in size: five bowls, five cardboard boxes, and five Chinese dolls all of which fit into one another.

    c Procedure: The children should be told that they are going to learn to put some objects inside other objects (they are not expected necessarily to know the meaning of "inside"). At first they should only work with the smallest and largest element of each set. The teacher should demonstrate and then have the child put one object into the other using trial and error. The teacher should name the objects as being smaller or larger and use these terms as the demonstration proceeds. The child, however, is not required to use them at this point. When the child can perform the task using two elements of each set, he can begin working with an additional element from each set until all the elements can be used with facility.

4 *Acquiring the concepts of smaller and larger*

    a Behavioral Objective: After the child has put any two elements of a set (as used in lesson 3) together, he can point to the smaller one and to the larger one upon request.

    b Materials: The same as used in lesson 3.

    c Procedure: Only two elements of any one set will be used at a time. The concept of "smaller" will be introduced first, since that seems to be easier to learn. The child is asked to put two objects together while the teacher simultaneously points to the smaller object. The child should repeat the same procedure with each set, labeling the smaller object along with the teacher. When the child can label independent of help, he should continue to use other elements in the set and place a red sticker on the smallest object. The same procedure is used for the presentation of the concept "larger."

5 *Visual discrimination between sizes*

    a Behavioral Objective: (1) The child can put all the elements within the sets (those used in lesson 3) together without trying one incorrect object. (2) The child is able to point out the larger and smaller object of any two combinations of elements within a particular set.

b **Materials:** The same as used in lesson 3.

c **Procedure:** The procedure is the same as lesson 4 except that the child should be given specific instructions to shift his glance between the two objects to be used. He should also be required to vocalize the words "smaller" and "larger," until he can vocalize the correct word before the object is manipulated. When this point is reached, the child should be asked to always label objects before manipulating them.

6 Acquiring an understanding of positional terms—right, left, top, and bottom

a **Behavioral Objective:** When asked to do so, the child can point to the left side, right side, top, and bottom of any paper placed on his desk.

b **Materials:** A marching record and the following items for each child: a piece of red material 12 inches long, a desk, and a stand-up calendar.

c **Procedure:** The first day the teacher introduces the concepts of "top" and "bottom" by showing the children where each position is relative to their own desks. A marching record should be played and the children asked to march around the room, touching the top and bottom of desks on a command. They should continue marching and extend their action of touching to any object near them. After they can do this, have them touch the top of a calendar which has been placed on each desk in an upright position. Next, have the students place their calendars in a flat position, keeping their hands on the top and continuing to refer to it as the top. After these concepts have been acquired, the children should be introduced to the concepts of "right" and "left" by attaching a piece of red material to each right arm and continuing to use the same types of activities.

7 Tracing reversed and rotated figures

a **Behavioral Objective:** After tracing two flat cutout figures, the child can correctly verbalize their likenesses and differences with respect to position.

b **Materials:** The following materials should be provided to each child: a yellow feltboard, two sets of orange cardboard figures with felt glued to the bottom side. These figures are as follows: (1) V, U, C; (2) M, T, P.

c **Procedure:** This program assumes that the child knows the meaning of "alike" and "different." It is the teacher's responsibility to be sure that the child knows these terms before proceeding. The teacher demonstrates tracing the figures from a set which has been placed on the feltboard. The child is assisted in tracing the figure. At the same time, the teacher should verbally emphasize the directions of the lines (such as from top to bottom) and position of the features (such as a corner on the right side). This procedure should be repeated with an identical figure with emphasis placed on the sameness of the directions. One of the figures should be rotated and the child helped to trace while the teacher emphasizes the differences in direction. The figure should subsequently be placed back in the original position. The child should trace and match shapes to identical positions until overlearning has occurred. After the performance is completed successfully on set 1, the child should continue the process with the more complex set 2. The child can then repeat the exercises working with reversed figures.

8 *Visually discriminating between rotated and reversed figures*
   a **Behavioral Objective:**   The child can name any pair of cutout figures (those used in lesson 7) as alike or different without handling them.
   b **Materials:**   The same as used in lesson 7.
   c **Procedure:**   The procedure is the same as in lesson 7, only the teacher should have the child shift his glance from one figure to the other and try to judge them before tracing.

Level 3

At this level, the tasks are designed to give the child experiences which will help to develop visual discrimination among complex written letters. These skills build on the previously developed competencies in discrimination among two-dimensional letters. This association with earlier learned material is fostered by giving the child tasks requiring the construction of letters from basic component parts. Three-dimensional lines and parts of circles of various sizes are used in the construction or modeling of letters. The child learns to match the concrete objects to the figures in terms of shape, size, and orientation. Initially, matching should be done along one dimension (e.g., shape) followed by various combinations of the above three components. At all times, the child should be asked to vocalize the characteristics of the elements being considered, such as "line" or "a smaller circle." Practice in constructing every letter should be given until the child can successfully discriminate among them.

9 *Concrete reconstruction*
   a **Behavioral Objectives:**   The child can construct every printed letter of the alphabet by matching three-dimensional cutouts of elements of letters to a graphic representation of each letter.
   b **Materials:**   A set of papers containing upper- and lowercase 3- by

3-inch letters of the alphabet, with one letter per page, and a set of cardboard cutouts of elements of these letters, such as:

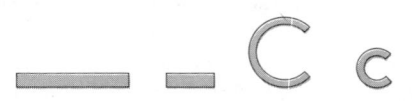

c Procedure: The teacher demonstrates and gives the child practice in matching first in terms of form, next size, and next orientation. He then matches along two of the former dimensions and finishes with matching along all three dimensions.

10 Visual discrimination between graphic letters
   a Behavioral Objectives: When presented with any two upper- or lowercase letters, the child can verbally indicate whether they are alike or different.
   b Materials: The same as those used in lesson 9, only one side of the paper must be folded under so that the letters can be presented in close proximity to one another.
   c Procedure: The child should continue with the preceding lesson modeling two letters successively and judging them as alike or different. The child is encouraged to make the discrimination decision as soon as possible, even before he is done modeling until discrimination can be made prior to modeling.

AUDITORY DISCRIMINATION [2] This research is not as comprehensive in this area as in visual discrimination; this is particularly true for investigations which have employed mentally retarded children as subjects. The research related to the auditory perception and acuity problems of the retarded, reviewed briefly in Chapter 6, has relevance to this section. Auditory discrimination is more than just the fact that a sound is audible to a listener; indeed, auditory discrimination requires that individual sounds and their components be accurately recognized.

Auditory experiences can be distinguished from each other in terms of intensity (loudness), pitch (frequency), and timbre (quality of tone). The ability to discriminate among sounds does not happen all at once. Wepman (1960), for example, has suggested that higher-level discrimination capabilities do not fully mature until a child reaches the age of eight. With the mentally retarded, optimum development in this area may not occur until the early teen-age years. Poor environmental backgrounds and/or organic difficulties of a peripheral or central nature often means that a child never reaches full maturity in auditory discrimination. Combinations of slow speech, language development, and problems of inattentiveness only further compound the situation.

As in other areas involving skills which are learned, when the child gets older, the difficulty in teaching the auditory discrimination increases because of the ineffective and inefficient habits already established. A planned program of early intervention should be initiated to encourage the development of auditory discrimination skills. This will require that a sequential program be used which requires the child to begin making discriminations among sounds which are very difficult but which gradually require finer and finer distinctions to be made. For skill development in reading readiness, a sequential program of auditory discrimination should consist of the following six levels: (1) sound discrimination, (2) rhyming, (3) initial-consonant discrimination, (4) final-consonant discrimination, (5) inital-blend discrimination, and (6) final-blend discrimination. The following suggests objectives and activities appropriate for fostering the development of auditory discrimination skills with the retarded.

SEQUENCE FOR TEACHING AUDITORY DISCRIMINATION [3]

I Sound Discrimination

    A Purpose: *to be able to differentiate between loud and soft sounds (volume), long and short sounds (duration), high and low sounds (pitch), sounds of different instruments and voices (timbre), and to follow directions*

    B Activities:

      1 Volume: Children can raise hands if sound is loud and leave hands down if sound is soft.

        a Tap on desk loudly and softly.

        b Clap two erasers or two pieces of wood together loudly and softly.

        c Ring a bell or beat on a drum loudly and softly.

        d Walk across room and then tiptoe across room.

        e Slam door and then open it gently.

        f Talk and whisper; talk and shout.

        g Drop a book and a pencil.

        h Listen to a clock and a watch ticking.

        i Use boxes filled with different objects and shake them.

      2 Duration: Children can raise hands if sound is long and leave hands down if sound is short. Almost any instrument can be used for this and the procedure would follow the same lines as that for differentiating between long and short sounds.

[3] Additional exercises and activities to develop auditory discrimination can be located in Betts (1946); Queen Anne's County Teachers Manual, 1954–1955; Russell and Kays (1951); Russell and Russell (1959); Smith, 1963.

3 *Pitch:* The same procedure can be followed as for volume and duration activities. The teacher can make use of the piano, a pitch pipe, or a whistle.

Responses to these activities can be varied by having children walk to sounds that are long, loud, or low; or tiptoe to sounds that are short, soft, or high. The students can clap their hands or stand up and down according to the earlier established criteria.

4 *Timbre*
  a Play "Who Is It?" or "Who Said it?" by blindfolding one child and having another pupil make a comment with the blindfolded child trying to identify the speaker.
  b Hit a triangle and a drum. Ask the children to name each instrument as you strike it. Any combination of instruments may be used.
  c Have children listen to and differentiate among sounds that are inside the room or outside the room or sounds that are near and far away.
  d After an animal noise is made, have the children identify the animal or pretend that they are animals.

Throughout all these activities, begin with gross discriminations. After the children master these, require them to make finer discriminations.

5 *Using music as children become more proficient in sound discrimination*
  a Children can be asked to identify simple tunes or songs.
  b Have the children skip, hop, jump, etc., to suitable music. Afterwards, have them stop when the music stops.
  c Beat on a drum a certain number of times, and have child clap back the identical number of beats. As a child is correct, he then becomes the next drummer. Instruments should be varied in this activity.
6 *Following directions*
  a Have them respond to simple individual directions such as, "Come here."
  b Present group commands to the class such as, "Stand up."
  c Require the children to do errands when asked.
  d Play games requiring commands such as "Simon Says" or "Bring me the _____ (e.g., book)."

II Rhymes
  A **Purpose:** to develop ability to hear rhymes, acquire a sense of rhythm, rhyme words, complete rhymes, compose rhymes, and pick out those words that rhyme in a group of words

B Activities:

1 Read nursery rhymes and other rhymes to children.

2 Engage them in choral speaking of nursery rhymes and other simple poems.

3 Read simple rhymes to the children, and have them fill in the last word, e.g., "We have fun when we _____."

4 When reading rhymes, have children clap hands on the rhyming words.

5 Have them think of pairs of rhyming words, such as "cat" and "hat."

6 Say a short rhyme leaving off the final rhyming word. Give the children two words from which to choose, and have them select the correct word.

7 Read a short rhyme leaving out the rhyming word. Show the children a picture which finishes the rhyme, and have them supply the missing word. Later, use two or more pictures.

8 Have them compose their own short rhymes.

9 Give the children three words, one of which does not rhyme with the others. Have them pick out the nonrhyming word.

III Initial Consonants

A Purpose: to develop ability to note the beginning sound of words, become aware that many words begin with the same sound, and develop recognition of like and unlike beginning consonants

B Activities:

1 Read short sentences that have a great deal of alliteration. Simple songs also can be used. Have the children pick out the words that are alike in their beginning sound.

2 After taking a trip, ask the children to think of all the things they saw. Point out the similarities in the beginnings of the words they choose to use.

3 In taking the class roll, point out that many of the children's names begin with the same sound, e.g., Jim, Joe, Judy.

4 Have them collect pictures of words that begin alike.

5 Present two words to the children, and vary the likenesses and differences in the beginning sounds. Have them tell if the words begin with the same sound.

6 Present three words to them, of which two are alike. Have the pupils pick out the two that begin with the same sound.

7 Encourage descriptive word activity. Say, "I have a book." Ask the students to think of adjectives, beginning like book, that could be used with the word, e.g., beautiful, big.

8 Show the children two pictures, and ask them if the pictures begin with the same sounds.

9 Have the children draw a picture, such as a ball, and ask them to think of other words beginning with the same sound.

Consonants should be learned in the following order (from easiest to the most difficult): b, p, m, w, h, d, t, n, g, k, ng, y, f, v, th (as in *then*), sh, zh, l, s, z, r, th (as in *thin*), wh, ch, and j (Wepman, 1960).

IV *Final Consonants*

V *Initial Blends*

VI *Final Blends*

The purposes for the activities related to these three levels of auditory discrimination are the same as for the initial consonants. Here, of course, final consonants, initial blends, and final blends are substituted for the initial consonant sounds.

Vowel discrimination should be introduced as the need arises within the program. The activities employed should be similar to those for the initial consonants. Generally long vowels are taught first, followed by instruction in short vowels.

Within each level, considerable time should be spent on each activity. No new level should be introduced until the previous level has been well mastered.

Developing a sight vocabulary and word-attack skills

The effective recognition of words in print hinges, to a large degree, on how well developed the retarded child is in those areas of readiness discussed above. Assuming these skills to be operating at a satisfactory level, the teacher is faced next with the need to assist in developing a sight vocabulary. Several considerations are paramount in selecting words for the sight vocabulary. Sampling words from previous experiences of the children or from areas of current interest will stimulate their desire to learn to read. Selecting words demands that the teacher be aware of the retarded child's speaking and listening vocabulary.

Of central importance is that these children be successful in their early experiences in reading. As is true in all areas involving initial learning, the retarded will become discouraged if their reading efforts fail. These children underachieve in reading too often because of having failed early in the process of learning to read. The teacher, then, must wisely select words and experiences of high stimulus value to the children.

Establishing a consistent and effective method for attacking words is equally important. Mentally retarded children should be instructed to employ a procedure for analyzing words on which they can depend and use with facility. Instruction dealing with procedures of word attack must be consistent within and between classrooms. Intellectually normal children are able to learn incidental relationships which exist between a visual and an auditory approach; mentally retarded children do not develop this facility for transferring from one approach to another so easily.

Developing a sight vocabulary and skill in word attack are interdependent on each other. Although word-attack skills may at first be underdeveloped, with the sight vocabulary being more extensive, as a systematic approach in word analysis develops, the child is able to simultaneously extend his sight vocabulary. There is, then, a solid relationship which exists between a child's skill in word attack and the comprehensiveness of his sight vocabulary. Controlling the possibility of failure is important and calls for attention being given to using all possible avenues of potential success. Various approaches to reading should be analyzed in terms of their unique potential for teaching the retarded.

APPROACHES TO BEGINNING READING INSTRUCTION   Making use of a printed primer series is one approach for introducing reading. In a series of this type, certain basic words are used in context with pictures. The children learn the words in association with the illustrations, gradually building a more extensive repertoire of sight words. Although these materials are carefully prepared, there are significant disadvantages in using this approach with the retarded. The inflexibility of the retarded often results in too great a reliance on relating the words on a specific page with the associated pictures. Dependence on specific page cues will result in rote recall of a particular selection and contribute little to the development of fine discriminations among the shapes of words and letters needed to develop adequate reading skills.

A spelling or alphabet approach illustrates another technique for introducing reading. Emphasis is placed on the analysis of single letters prior to being exposed to letter combinations and words. The sight vocabulary is gradually established using drill on words in isolation before exposure to a passage or story. The primary disadvantage in using this approach with the retarded is the danger of their becoming inclined toward word calling. In reading instruction with the retarded, there is need to emphasize the meaning of words in a variety of contexts. To teach the analysis of words, or their basic components, without considering meaning at the beginning of a child's reading program will restrict progress, convey a biased and narrow perspective of reasons for learning how to read, and hinder fluency.

Too much emphasis on phonetic elements is equally stifling during the initial stages in teaching the retarded child to read. In addition to all the disadvantages of the spelling method, early reliance on the phonics approach will often cause confusion between the names of the letters and what they should say at different times when they appear in various combinations. This potential for confusion cannot be allowed during the early stages of reading. It is important that words be learned in context, the child enjoy the process, experiences be successful for each child, use be made of the child's existing repertoire and background, and that the initial focus be global rather than emphasizing elements or basic parts of words.

The experience approach to reading minimizes the disadvantages in those techniques mentioned above for introducing reading to the retarded. Using the cooperative story and experience chart at the outset will enable the retarded to gain a clear picture of the reason for reading. Reading should become a basic part of communication. The children should be helped to see that it is possible to communicate not only vocally but also in reading and writing. The children's experiences should be used as a stimulus for wanting to learn to read and as a means for encouraging the development of a more flexible use of all the components of communication. There is no "lock-step" characteristic of the experience approach as is frequently the case of the primer series wherein stories and pictures are often inappropriate for various groups of retarded children. Moreover, the experience approach allows for complete integration with other subject areas in ways not easily possible with other procedures for reading instruction with the retarded.

STAGES IN TEACHING READING The teacher of the mentally retarded can present material in a progressively differentiated manner by using the experience approach. Three levels, or stages, of instruction characterize this technique. The mass stage is exemplified by the child reacting to the whole story, the differentiation level is characterized by emphasis on learning details, and the integration stage is typified by the child being able to read without awareness of details. These three levels constitute the core of the experience approach and will be treated in greater detail.

First in the developmental sequence is the need for the retarded to understand that reading is an extension of speaking. Emphasis should not be placed on details at this stage. The children should be encouraged to understand that reading results in meaning and that it is possible to record what has been spoken and later, by reading, gain understanding from what has formerly been said.

When the teacher elects to use the experience approach or cooperative story at the mass level, the children should be asked to help record a past, present, or future experience. The incident can be a direct or vicarious experience, but should ideally be reported by a group or by an individual. The short passage, of no longer than three or four lines, should be interesting to the children and reflect words from their own speaking vocabulary. The sentence structure should be the same for each sentence, and the words the children use most frequently should be repeated. The teacher should write each sentence on the blackboard or a large piece of tagboard as the story unfolds. Stories such as the following might be written.

We went for a walk.
We saw a bird.
We saw a dog.   or
The dog barked.

Snow is falling.
It is on the ground.
We can ride our sleds.
It will be fun.

After the story has been written, the teacher should repeat each sentence and follow along with a pointer. As the children remember the sentences, they should be asked to read with the teacher. The entire class should eventually be able to read in concert as well as individually. Emphasis should be placed on the notion that the entire story tells about something interesting that has or will take place. The idea of conveying a message should be stressed and no particular attention paid to any of the story components. Moreover, the configuration of the entire story should be emphasized and left-to-right progression clearly reinforced throughout all stages of reading instruction.

After the children understand that reading makes sense and that it conveys a message, they should be ready for instruction in the differentiation stage of reading. This second stage has several levels, each of which contains some characteristics of the massed stage of instruction. At this level, the children should be encouraged to see that the story components make sense in isolation.

The first step in this process is for the children to understand that each line says something different from the other lines, has a unique meaning, and looks different from the others. After they learn to differentiate among the sentences, the children should be asked questions which test their ability to discriminate, such as by the teacher saying, "Show me the sentence that tells us what the dog did." "Which line tells what we saw first on our walk?" "Which sentence tells us what we can do when snow is on the ground?" The chart can be cut into sentence strips and the children asked to replace them in order. The same general strategy can be used for sentences that can be employed for phrases.

After the child has developed ability to distinguish among words, several procedures can be initiated. An individual flash card for each word should be constructed so that each child can see how the printed word follows a unique configuration. The following illustrates this procedure:

| bird | dog | a | saw |

In a certain sense, this involves temporary movement back to the massed stage. A variety of drills and activities can be used to facilitate the learning and reassembling of the words in the proper sentence sequence. As examples, the child can be asked to locate any word that he knows on the chart, the teacher could pick a word by giving the child a position cue, a child could be asked to identify all the words that look alike, or the teacher could give an auditory cue and ask the child to identify the appropriate word, phrase, or sentence. The children should not be required to reconstruct more than one sentence at a time until the concept has been overlearned.

At this point the process of word analysis should be started. Some clinical sensitivity should be demonstrated by the teacher predicting which children tend to prefer an auditory-visualization ("look-and-say") approach or a kinesthetic approach for attacking words. The informal techniques suggested to assess factors of readiness of young children and the specific reading skills demonstrated by the older children will help to make such a determination.

The teacher can eventually reduce the configuration cues on each flash card. By this time, the children should be ready for instruction at the integration level. Plenty of drill is needed to help them reassemble sentences and place individual components in their proper order. As skill in these activities develop, the children should be able to assemble complete stories. It should be noted that differentiation and integration are not mutually exclusive but share certain areas of skill development. For example, during each of these stages, some effort should be given to the children developing a consistent means for word attack, left-to-right progression, skill in proper sequencing for clarity in the comprehension of ideas, and a more extensive sight vocabulary.

The experience approach can be as effective with older retarded children as with the younger if the following points are considered:

1 Each story should be simple, clearly express several main ideas, and reflect the vocabulary and interests of the children.

2 The story should be a cooperative venture, although the teacher should exert some control over the vocabulary according to the children's reading capabilities. To illustrate, in choosing a story with beginning readers, it would be important to emphasize initial consonant sounds and short vowels so that procedures for word attack can be systematically introduced.

3 Care should be given to reduce the tendency of the retarded to depend primarily on memorization and the use of context clues. This can be controlled by using new words in a variety of ways on several experience stories.

4 Each student should be asked to develop his own book of experience stories to which reference can be made. These will be of diagnostic value to the teacher.

5 Instruction during the early stages should adhere to the basic learning principles which were reviewed earlier. In no case should the child

be forced to discriminate or integrate before showing some competence at the massed level of instruction. The children should understand that meaning can be gained through reading even before one is required to analyze the components of the reading process.

6 Integration with other subject areas should characterize all instruction.

7 Continued development of auditory and visual discrimination, moving from left to right in reading, sequencing for meaning, and elaboration of the child's vocabulary should be considered an important part of the child's early reading activities.

ANALYSIS OF WORDS Systematically attacking words constitutes a vital component of reading instruction for the retarded. The teacher should be concerned about minimizing random behavior and guessing. In no other area will such behavior be manifested as extensively as when a child has not developed skill in the analysis of words.

There is no best single approach for instructing the retarded in word attack. Books on beginning reading emphasize different procedures. Because of their unique characteristics, certain children will learn to read best when an auditory approach is employed; whereas other children will acquire reading-analysis skills more effectively when emphasis is placed on a visualization procedure. Research in reading with the retarded has been more of an ex post facto type with only minimum systematic effort devoted to studying the reading process with retarded subjects. Suggestions in this area, therefore, are extrapolations from the literature on remedial-reading subjects.

The special-class teacher of the retarded will probably find greatest success in using an eclectic approach which combines the phonics, visualization, context, and kinesthetic methods. This procedure would seem to have greatest merit because of the frequent difficulties the retarded have in visual-perception development, auditory memory and discrimination, remembering and applying rules or principles, and in a host of other skills. The wide spectrum of difficulties in these necessary-skill areas forces the teacher to employ components from many methods, placing particular emphasis on those procedural techniques appropriate to each child's pattern of strengths and weaknesses. For example, children who show weakness in using the visual but not the auditory channel would probably learn best by emphasizing a phonics approach with a gradual introduction of the appropriately associated visual components. Differential emphasis, therefore, is needed according to any significant characteristic of each child.

Comprehensive coverage has been given to each type of procedure for teaching word-attack skills. The procedures described by Kirk in 1940 have been reiterated in more recent volumes devoted to reading (Anderson, 1965; Otto and McMenemy, 1966; Spache, 1964).

Their treatment of the principal characteristics of each word-attack method differs little from the early proponents of these different methods. The reader who is unfamiliar with these techniques will find coherent discussions of each method in these sources. Although it is important that the teacher have a firm grasp of these procedures, the need for parsimony here will not allow for the reiteration of the basic tenets of each technique. Instead, the generalizations and principal teaching considerations listed below illustrate the relationship which should exist among these methods of word attack in teaching reading to the retarded.

1 Two important advantages for using a combination of several word-attack methods are that:

    a The teacher can quickly see on which method emphasis should be placed by observing how effective each child performs when different means of presentation are emphasized. This procedure, then, has diagnostic value and will readily show which method or combination of techniques should work best with each child.

    b Provision is made for more opportunity for association of stimuli received from the different receptors. This will have a direct influence on the level of initial learning, recall, association, and general skill development through the establishment of more comprehensive associational networks.

2 In word attack, children should not be obliged to learn rules. Such an expectation will prove disappointing because of the retarded child's weakness for applying and generalizing rules to various situations. In addition, there are many problems inherent in the frequent exceptions to rules, such as those exemplified in the unique phonetic structure of the English language.

3 Primary use should be made of words learned in the cooperative stories and experience charts. In this beginning stage of reading, the children should be made aware of the entire spectrum of auditory and visual clues related to words and their combinations. Attention should be given to the use of context clues, the configuration of letters and words, and the sounds of words, letters, and letter combinations. Each child should be encouraged to engage in kinesthetic experiences during this stage of reading development by systematically tracing and writing words contained in the stories. Full use should be made of each sense modality during these early stages of reading.

4 New words should be said, traced, and written. Early in the process the new word should be written by the teacher on a card and made available to the child for tracing and for reference as he learns to write the word. This provision will allow for the quick comparison of a child's performance with that of the model. The use of some type of translucent material as a medium for response which, after

the child has written or constructed a word, is placed on top of a model response, will allow for an immediate check on errors of omission and commission.[4] This provides immediate knowledge of results.

5 At first, whole words should be presented instead of emphasizing parts of words. When too much emphasis is placed on details, children often have trouble with comprehension. When details are stressed in phonics training, sound-blending problems frequently occur.

6 Similarities between old and new words in sound, appearance, and meaning should be explicitly pointed out. The closeness between this concept and the desirability of employing minimal change in learning new words is worthy of note. For example, after the child has learned c-a-n, by changing only the initial consonant to r-a-n or t-a-n, a basis for new instruction from previously successful experiences will be provided.

7 Attention should be directed to identifying and responding to all areas of significance in which the retarded children are particularly weak. For example, blending small units or words, discriminating among b, d, g, and p, or reversing letters in words are areas of weaknesses with the retarded.

8 Children should move naturally and as rapidly as possible from total use of the cooperative story and experience chart to books of high interest and low vocabulary. This is a gradual weaning process and one which should not take place before word-analysis skills have developed in connection with the first formal reading activities associated with the experience chart.

Developing skill in comprehension of what is read

Reading is essentially useless exercise if the reader does not understand the meaning of the words he calls. Comprehension cannot occur unless the individual has the necessary skills to expand his sight vocabulary and attack words in a systematic manner. It is reasonable, therefore, that the teacher of the retarded devote attention to assisting the youngsters in developing reading comprehension skills.

The importance of stressing accuracy instead of speed in all aspects of reading cannot be overemphasized. It is natural for children to want to rush ahead in reading after having achieved some competence in basic skills. The competition engendered by such achievements is quickly kindled between students in terms of the number of pages each is able to read or the speed with which a child is able to complete an assignment passage. Every attempt should be made to reduce this tendency and to encourage accurate reading. Pronounced focus on speed will result in the development of sloppy and inadequate word-analysis skills which, in turn, will reduce com-

4 Suggested by Dr. George Brabner through personal communication.

prehension. Gradually, as these basic skills develop, the children will be able to gain speed in reading without sacrificing their understanding of what appears on the printed page.

In teaching for comprehension, the teacher needs to give attention to the vital role of the feedback and monitoring systems. As children read selections of various lengths, gaining meaning will depend on their remembering what has been visually and/or auditorially read. If words are being called and the child is not alert to the meaning contained in each passage, comprehension will be reduced. A central aim of the reading program is for each child to eventually move from overattending to the process of attacking words to focusing on their meaning and content. Often it will be necessary for the teacher to act as a monitor during the reading process by stopping the child at the end of a sentence and questioning him concerning the meaning of what was just read. In more difficult cases, it will help for the teacher to read short passages in concert with the child so that feedback and memory are emphasized more dramatically. Gradually, the child will develop a "style" which is characterized by greater attention being given to thoughts contained in passages.

Comprehension can be encouraged by the teacher closely relating other activities to the material being read. Activities that are of high interest will often provide the impetus for children focusing on the meaning of what is being read. For example, if a child is interested in sewing, it would be proper for the teacher to capitalize on this interest by rewriting the directions for constructing a garment according to the child's reading level. This type of integration with other areas of the school program will help direct the child's attention to reading for meaning.

For the retarded, reading comprehension should center on instruction which will allow the children to (1) understand thoughts contained in sentences, (2) comprehend the meaning contained in paragraphs, and (3) grasp the meaning and implications of entire selections. For some children, these objectives are reasonable; for other children, intellectual limitations will decrease the possibility of their satisfactorily achieving these three aims. Otto and McMenemy (1966) have suggested certain informal diagnostic techniques for assessing comprehension skills in each of these areas and have outlined procedures for remediating weaknesses in these types of comprehension.

SELECTED REFERENCES

Anderson, P. S.: *Language Skills in Elementary Education,* The Macmillan Company, New York, 1965.

Betts, E. A.: *Foundations of Reading Instruction,* American Book Company, New York, 1946.

————: "Informal Inventories," in A. J. Harris (ed.), *Readings on Reading Instruction,* David McKay Company, Inc., New York, 1963, pp. 121–125.

Bond, G. L. and Tinker, M. A.: *Reading Difficulties, Their Diagnosis and Correction,* Appleton-Century-Crofts, Inc., New York, 1957.

Cleland, E. J.: "Development of Perception: Discrimination of Depth Compared with Discrimination of Graphic Symbols," *Monographs of the Society for Research in Child Development,* vol. 28, 1963, pp. 5–23.

Hicks, L. and Hunton, V.: "The Relative Dominance of Form and Orientation in Discrimination Learning by Monkeys and Children," *Psychonomic Science,* vol. 1, pp. 411–412.

Johnson, M. S. and Kress, R. A.: *Informal Reading Inventories,* International Reading Association, Newark, Del., 1965.

Kirk, S. A.: *Teaching Reading to Slow-Learning Children,* Houghton Mifflin Company, Boston, 1940.

Meier, G. W. and McGee, R. K.: "Re-evaluation of the Effect of Early Perceptual Experience on Discrimination Performed During Adulthood," *Journal of Comparative and Physiological Psychology,* vol. 51, 1958, pp. 785–787.

Otto, W. and McMenemy, R. A.: *Corrective and Remedial Teaching,* Houghton Mifflin Company, Boston, 1966, pp. 181–186.

Pick, H. L.: "Some Soviet Research on Learning and Perception in Children," *Monographs of the Society for Research in Child Development,* vol. 28, 1963, pp. 185–190.

Queen Anne's County Teachers Manual: *First Steps in Word Recognition,* Queen Anne's County, Maryland, pp. 1954–1955.

Russell, David H. and Karp, Etta E.: *Reading Aids Through the Grades,* Teachers College Press, Columbia University, New York, 1951.

———— and Russell, Elizabeth F.: *Listening Aids Through the Grades,* Teachers College Press, Columbia University, New York, 1959.

Smith, Nila Banton: *Reading Instruction for Today's Children,* Prentice-Hall, Inc., Englewood Cliffs, N.J., 1963.

Spache, G. D.: *Reading in the Elementary School,* Allyn and Bacon, Inc., Boston, 1964.

Strang, R.: *Diagnostic Teaching of Reading,* McGraw-Hill Book Company, New York, 1964, pp. 62–63, 199.

Walk, R. D.: "Visual and Visual-Motor Experience: A Replication," *Journal of Comparative and Physiological Psychology,* vol. 51, 1958, pp. 785–787.

————, Gibson, E. J., Pick, H. C., and Tight, T. J.: "The Effectiveness of Prolonged Exposure to Cutouts vs. Painted Patterns for Facilitation of Discrimination," *Journal of Comparative and Physiological Psychology,* vol. 52, 1959, pp. 519–521.

Wepman, Joseph: "Auditory Discrimination, Speech and Reading," *Elementary School Journal,* vol. 60, 1960.

Zaporozhets, A. V.: "The Development of Perception in the Preschool Child," *Monographs of the Society for Research in Child Development,* vol. 30, 1965, pp. 82–101.

instructing in arithmetic

Among those studies conducted in subject areas, relatively little attention has been directed toward investigating factors of arithmetic performance among the mentally retarded. Cruickshank's research has been most comprehensively descriptive in this area (1946, 1948a, 1948b). He reports that, compared with the intellectually normal of the same mental age, the retarded (1) are reasonably alike in areas of computation, although they are more careless than the normal and exhibit a greater incidence of "primitive habits" such as making marks and counting on their fingers, (2) have greater difficulty in understanding and identifying which process should be used in solving a problem even when presented verbally, (3) lack the skill to separate irrelevant facts from the significant dimensions of a problem, and (4) have greater difficulty with the reading and language peculiar to arithmetic. The literature agrees that the retarded tend to achieve at a level consistent with their mental age in arithmetic computation but often significantly below that level in arithmetic reasoning (Dunn, 1954; Bensberg, 1953).

Studies seeking to identify a relationship between etiology and arithmetic achievement have been contradictory and inconclusive (Strauss and Werner, 1938; Fouracre, 1958; Capobianco, 1954). Teaching methodology has been studied by only a few investigators (Burns, 1961; Costello, 1941). These investigations suggest the relative value in emphasizing an experience approach in teaching arithmetic to the retarded.

Although lacking in empirical documentation on mentally retarded subjects, several authors have suggested the potential value in applying the work of Piaget to the arithmetic problems of the retarded (Clarke and Clarke, 1965; Woodward, 1961, 1962a, 1962b). Their position is that traditional teaching strategies do not allow the retarded to develop an understanding of number concepts which, in turn, relates directly to reasoning ability. Teaching computational skills solely through "devices" is to be eschewed according to this school of thought, since it results in a level of skill in arithmetic reasoning similar to "word calling" in reading. Bereiter and Engelmann (1966) have assumed a closely allied position by suggesting that arithmetic skills can be effectively taught to disadvantaged preschool children by focusing on the numerical concepts embodied in the language of arithmetic and by deemphasizing specific computational facts.

BASIC ARITHMETIC OBJECTIVES

In no other areas are the implications of ignorance more severe or longlasting than those concerned with personal finances. A person who is unconcerned about or unable to manage his monetary affairs is a ready target for unscrupulous members of society, whose primary goal is to make an easy dollar without concern for the difficulties this precipitates for others. A great many areas of personal and social interaction depend on an understanding of fundamental arithmetic skills involving both computation and reasoning. Since most educable retarded will become part of the social and occupational world, their success in this environment will depend on their performance level in these important areas. By the time they leave the school program, the retarded should be skilled enough to handle affairs which require a minimum level of arithmetic skill and understanding.

The basic objectives of the arithmetic program for educable retarded children differ significantly from those for intellectually normal children in terms of breadth and depth of treatment. As was true in other subject areas, great variation will be observed between the children in ability and performance. The most dramatic differences occur between arithmetic computation and arithmetic reasoning. In order to delineate the specific emphasis of an arithmetic program for retarded children, the following objectives should be focused upon:

1 *Development of an understanding of numbers and the processes involved in arithmetic computation*

2 *Seeing relationships between various computational processes and the manner in which these tools can be used for solving various types of problems*

3 *Development of a more structured and organized response repertoire emanating from an understanding of the logical structure of arithmetic*

4 *Development of more dependence on and comfort in using abstractions as points of references instead of total dependence on concrete reference points*

5 *Movement toward greater dependence in using a consistent method for solving problems in place of random, impulsive behavior*

The first two of these objectives focus on the developing of basic understanding and skills in computation and in using these skills to solve everyday arithmetic problems. The latter three objectives are broader and suggest the important potential role arithmetic instruction can play in helping the retarded to develop a general conceptual style of thinking. This competence has implications for solving problems in nonarithmetic areas of life.

EVALUATING ARITHMETIC SKILLS

Comprehensively diagnosing a retarded child's arithmetic difficulties involves the employment of testing and assessment at four levels. The techniques used are similar to those discussed in the preceding chapter on reading. The child's capacity for dealing with arithmetic skills, level of readiness for such activities, present achievement level, and specific arithmetic weaknesses with any faulty habits of process should be evaluated. A specific program of instruction in arithmetic for each child can be formulated from the data collected in these areas. Without such information, the special-class teacher will have an inadequate basis for determining the nature and level the arithmetic program should take. Earlier emphasis was placed on the notion that effective clinical teaching must be based on specific information which emanates from this testing and assessment process.

Estimating potential for arithmetic

The suggestions given earlier for formally and informally assessing an individual's predicted capacity for reading (see pages 131–132) are equally appropriate in arithmetic. The use of formal individual or group intelligence tests, if correctly administered and scored, will provide an indication of the child's predicted potential for doing arithmetic. Informal estimates can be based on the child's progress in other subject areas or by calculating each individual's rate of learning to be somewhere between 50 and 75 percent that of an intellectually normal child of the same chronological age. Translating these data into mental age equivalents will provide a fairly good estimate of the level at which each child *should* be able to perform in arithmetic.

Assessing levels of readiness

The concept of readiness has emerged as being vital to subsequent success in reading. In arithmetic, readiness is of equal importance, although this area usually receives less attention in most special-education arithmetic programs.

Readiness for arithmetic can be viewed from two perspectives. First, adequate arithmetic achievement is fundamentally dependent on the student's ability to discriminate among and remember auditory and visual stimuli, attend to a task, accurately perceive spatial orientation and translate these phenomena into temporal sequences, associate stimuli, and express himself. For rote counting alone, a very elementary arithmetic skill, students must listen carefully, perceive accurately, discriminate among sounds, remember the components and their appropriate sequence, and vocally or gesturally express the numerical chain. This simple task requires a certain minimum level of achievement in each of these basic areas. As computational and reasoning problems increase in complexity, the fundamental readiness skills become increasingly significant.

Techniques for assessing various factors of readiness were reviewed in the previous chapter. Formal techniques mentioned included using tests such as the Illinois Test of Psycholinguistic Abilities, the Lee-Clark Reading Readiness Test, and the Purdue Perceptual-Motor Survey. Informal procedures suggested included a description of various tasks and activities in which children can be engaged to evaluate the total spectrum of foundation skills.

The second way for viewing readiness for arithmetic is in terms of how far into the logical arithmetic sequence the student has proceeded with satisfactory achievement. To illustrate, the student would not be able to satisfactorily perform a two-digit addition problem involving carrying before understanding concepts of grouping; addition is based on this fundamental understanding. From this perspective, then, readiness to do arithmetic requires the developmental and sequential ordering of arithmetic skills. The evaluation of each retarded child should be made in terms of the degree to which prerequisite skills are understood and accomplished before the child is allowed to move to the next level of instruction.

The importance of language development as a precursor to formal arithmetic instruction should be recognized. The students must understand the significance of what is being said and exhibit some facility for using the language of arithmetic. If any of the children show weaknesses in language, problems in computation and reasoning will be more frequently manifested.

Establishing the general instructional level for arithmetic

FORMAL PROCEDURES   Many of the survey tests which are part of any general achievement battery, such as those reviewed in the preceding chapter, contain a group of subtests designed to assess levels

TABLE 8-1 *Survey Tests which Assess Factors of Arithmetic Achievement*

Name of test	Dimensions evaluated	Grade level
California Arithmetic Tests	Fundamentals Reasoning	1–9
Coordinated Scale of Attainments in Arithmetic	Arithmetic experiences Number skills Computation Reasoning	1–8
Lee-Clark Fundamentals Survey Tests		
Metropolitan Achievement Tests	Computation Problem solving	1–9
Stanford Achievement Tests	Computation Reasoning	2–9
Wide Range Achievement Test	Computation	K–College
SRA Achievement Series	Concepts Reasoning Computation	1–9

of achievement in a variety of arithmetic factors. These tests can be administered individually or in a group situation. A more accurate estimate of an individual's level of achievement can be obtained through individual administration of an instrument since the examiner has greater control over the student's behavior. In this way the assumed, standardized procedures for administering an instrument can be followed more closely. Table 8-1 provides a sample of instruments frequently used to measure arithmetic factors.

INFORMAL PROCEDURES As in reading, a teacher may wish to evaluate arithmetic achievement infrequently during the school year by making use of one of the formal standardized procedures. This strategy will allow for systematic comparisons over time. There is the added advantage of achievement test typically not requiring a specially trained examiner for administration. It is inadvisable to use formal achievement survey techniques too frequently. Students become test wise, and consequently, instruments lose their meaningfulness.

To circumvent this problem, the teacher will find it beneficial to frequently check on a retarded child's progress using informal means of evaluation. Appraising the value of a different method of instruction, the instructional regrouping of students, and the placement of new children in an appropriate arithmetic group all require the frequent evaluation of achievement. The purpose of this assessment procedure must be understood before an informal arithmetic survey is constructed. If computational skills are to be studied, tasks should be developed so that reasoning skills are controlled. The assessment of a child's computational performance should not be contaminated by poor reasoning abilities. If, on the other hand, the teacher is interested in sampling arithmetic reasoning skills, it would be wise to control any reading requirements needed to solve arithmetic reasoning problems. Being aware of this differentiation will provide a more accurate estimate of achievement, strengths, or weaknesses which require special attention.

The assessment of arithmetic achievement is closely associated with the identification of specific arithmetic difficulties. The latter typically involves a more intensive analysis, usually individual testing of some type. Informal group checks of achievement do not provide a situation which allows for the accurate observation of processes or habits a child might exhibit in attacking a specific arithmetic problem. Informal individual checks of achievement, however, will provide general indications of specific weaknesses, such as difficulties in carrying, borrowing, grouping, combinations, or counting problems.

In sampling computation and reasoning performance, tasks should be designed to include a variety of arithmetic processes and skills. Adequate samples of these various arithmetic skills should be included in an informal survey. To this end, specific items can be gathered from arithmetic workbooks or texts. The following illustrates items which might be included in an informal computational survey designed to sample achievement in those areas of particular relevance to the retarded.

**Examples of items appropriate
for an informal test
of computational achievement**

Addition

6	3	4	10	8	11
+ 2	+ 5	+ 0	+ 5	+ 3	+ 4

17	33	67	11 12	42	523
+ 5	+ 15	+ 71	+ 9	+ 9	+ 162

692
+ 349

Subtraction

6	3	4	17	98	47
− 4	− 3	− 0	− 3	− 4	− 32

10	14	27	7 − 5 = _____
− 3	− 6	− 24	

17 − 12 = _____   18 − 9 = _____   462
                                                       − 321

176	253
− 36	− 89

Multiplication

3	2	2	6	33	22	3
× 2	× 2	× 8	× 0	× 1	× 4	× 22

232	204	8 × 6 = _____	7 × 7 = _____
× 3	× 2		

1403	105	2675	1760	22	17
× 2	× 3	× 3	× 5	× 33	× 12

46	60	328	6023
× 32	× 16	× 21	× 34

Division

3) 3   2) 4   3) 963   6) 18   5) 155   2) 1864

3) 10   4) 1208   7) 56714   7) 1500   22) 484

36) 864   15) 3666

In this suggested informal schedule, a general sequence was followed wherein each subsequent task requires an additional skill not necessary for a correct response on any of the preceding items. This sequencing allows for a quick check on the approximate level of achievement each child exhibits in the various arithmetic processes. Moreover, if the teacher observes that a youngster consistently misses problems involving certain skills, a more intense follow-up assessment can be made by presenting additional tasks which require a further demonstration of skill in those areas of particular weakness. Without difficulty, a tally can be made of the types of errors each child manifests in the informal computational tests during the entire year. Data from these informal surveys can then be related to the performance of the retarded on standardized achievement tests which are usually administered at the beginning and end of each school year. The comparison of these data will help the teacher to get some indication of the validity of the informal techniques.

Reasoning skills, controlling for the possible influence of reading difficulties, can be informally assessed by having the teacher read to the children a problem which requires the use of one or more of the arithmetic processes. At the most elementary level, these problems should contain no irrelevant information and should be sequenced according to the computational level attained by each child. The computational requirements of the reasoning problems should move from problems demanding the application of very simple skills to those requiring greater sophistication in the application of arithmetic fundamentals.

Reasoning capabilities of retarded children can be further analyzed by introducing irrelevant information into the problem and determining the facility of a child for identifying those facts essential for a correct solution. Reading the word problem will further complicate this task for the retarded student. As the results of the word problems are analyzed, specific difficulties of computation should be separated from those problems related to reasoning and problem solving. This procedure is needed to check for process, or computational, difficulties which the child may exhibit. As errors in computation and reasoning are delineated, the arithmetic program should be adjusted according to each student's needs. In some instances, this may simply mean that a child is placed in another group. For other children, a totally different methodological attack or curriculum revision may be necessary.

In addition to using teacher-constructed achievement surveys, a review of the previous arithmetic work done by students will be revealing. This material will provide clues to the general achievement level and progress each child has made during the course of formal instruction in arithmetic. Further, each child's record should be compared with his present daily performance. Some attention must be given to daily activities and awareness shown of any errors the child makes or poor habits acquired during the course of instruction. A daily check of workbooks and seatwork will help to maintain control over these potential difficulties.

Diagnosis of specific arithmetic deficits

A child may be achieving poorly in arithmetic for any of a variety of specific reasons, which if allowed to go unremediated will result in the accumulation of deficits which deleteriously influence other areas of arithmetic performance. For example, lack of understanding of the concept of zero could influence each of the fundamental computational processes in addition to reasoning. The potential influence of this type of problem could be even more widespread and possibly result in guessing, impulsivity, lack of cooperation, antisocial responses, or a general dislike for anything dealing with a particularly difficult subject or even the entire school program. The illustration is by no means overstated; lack of success will characteristically result in atypical behavior. It is significant, indeed, that difficulty in a very specific component of a process, if unremediated, has the potential for mushrooming into negative attitudes and poor behavior.

The point has been emphasized that the teacher must be alert to diagnostic clues and formulate the total program accordingly. Factors related to successful performance in arithmetic computation and reasoning will require evaluation in order to identify any specific disabilities. The process of identifying possible difficulties should be combined with the formal and informal assessment of arithmetic achievement, assuming that these instruments have been administered individually to the students. With arithmetic, as well as in reading, the teacher's interests should be focused on the *types of errors* made by each child and also on the *process* each student uses in solving problems.

FORMAL PROCEDURES   Less recent attention has been given to the construction of diagnostic instruments in arithmetic than in reading. However, some effort has been given recently to techniques for teaching "modern math," and interest has been shown by many for applying the observations of Piaget to arithmetic instruction. This has resulted in academicians reconsidering the traditional approaches for arithmetic assessment and instruction (Stephens, 1966).

The formal procedures available to check on specific arithmetic defects do not usually require the formal instruction and experience for administration characteristic of most reading diagnostic tests. Teachers will find it helpful to have samples of these tests available. It is not always necessary to administer the entire test to a child each time it is given. The teacher may wish to select items only from those areas of relevance to a particular child. Table 8-2 summarizes a sample of the formal tests available to diagnose various arithmetic deficits.

TABLE 8-2 *Instruments for Identifying Specific Arithmetic Weaknesses*

Name of test	Dimensions evaluated	Grade level
Brueckner Diagnostic Arithmetic Tests	Addition Subtraction Multiplication Division	4–8
Diagnostic Arithmetic Tests	Addition Subtraction Multiplication Division Weights and measures Fractions Decimals Percentages	2–5
Los Angeles Diagnostic Tests: Fundamentals of Arithmetic	Addition Subtraction Multiplication Division	2–8
Los Angeles Diagnostic Tests: Reasoning in Arithmetic	Reasoning	3–9

TABLE 8-2 (Continued)

Name of test	Dimensions evaluated	Grade level
Diagnostic Chart for Fundamental Processes in Arithmetic	Habits Procedures Types of errors made in computation	2–8
Diagnostic Tests in Arithmetic Fundamentals	Addition Subtraction Multiplication Division Fractions Decimals	2–8
Diagnostic Tests and Self-Helps in Arithmetic	Twenty-three computational tests, each of which deals with a different operation, arranged in a carefully graded sequence. All areas of fundamental operations are covered.	3–7
Easy Steps in Arithmetic	Addition Subtraction Simple multiplication Simple division Money computation	2–6
Essential Arithmetic Tests	Several computational areas Arithmetic problem solving	2–7

INFORMAL PROCEDURES   Errors of computation can be identified and recorded at any time in the arithmetic program and in a variety of situations. Use can be made of workbooks, seatwork, and informal or formal tests to gather such data. The types of errors made by the children and their habits used in arriving at incorrect answers to problems should be surveyed. When a certain type of mistake is revealed, the reliability of this observation and the consistency of its occurrence should be studied by giving the child more problems of the same type.

Computational errors in addition, subtraction, multiplication, and division are often the result of (1) the use of incorrect procedures or sloppy work habits, (2) problems in counting and in combinations, (3) difficulties in carrying, borrowing, and in the use of remainders, (4) guessing or the need to use crutches, or (5) an inability to understand what type of solution is needed from the language of arithmetic. The formal diagnostic tests mentioned earlier provide a comprehensive list of possible atypical habits and types of errors. This list can be used to check on the retarded child's arithmetic progress.

To survey errors in arithmetic reasoning requires that the teacher consider possible difficulties in (1) reading, (2) attention and listening, (3) understanding the nature of the problem, (4) extracting the significant elements from the problem and selecting an appropriate computational procedure, (5) translating the word problem into a proper medium for computation, (6) correctly computing the answer, and (7) using the computed answer in adequately responding to the problem. Arithmetic reasoning is a complex process which involves the use of a variety of high-level intellectual skills. The more mechanical components of arithmetic computation are much easier for the retarded to learn than the more complex skills required for a child to reason through an arithmetic problem which is presented either visually or vocally. Care must be exercised in the evaluation process to differentiate between the factors involved in these two components of arithmetic.

PROCEDURES FOR ARITHMETIC INSTRUCTION

Experiments in arithmetic using retarded subjects have been descriptive in the past and not designed to provide evidence concerning the efficacy of various methods, materials, or curricula. Those studies which have been designed to shed light in these areas have been inadequate in terms of program duration, research questions asked, subjects used, and alternative control procedures employed. Hence, specific direction from research for instructing the retarded in arithmetic is relatively nonexistent.

Special educators are in agreement on several points concerning the teaching of arithmetic to the retarded. First, instruction must be practical and utilitarian with especial emphasis on a social and vocational orientation. Second, the retarded must be instructed in a manner which will facilitate the development of a conceptual understanding of arithmetic processes instead of the rote manipulation and application of figures. Teachers of the retarded should ask questions such as the following about the arithmetic program:

1 *Is the material under consideration potentially important to the retarded child's future success?*

2 What procedures can be employed to teach the important components of the topic under consideration in the most efficacious and practical way?

3 What procedures can be used to foster a conceptual understanding of the material by the youngsters, and how can they be encouraged to generalize and apply these understandings?

Mathematicians view success in understanding arithmetic to be basically dependent on the establishment of a firm understanding of numerical concepts. This skill encompasses more than the simple recitation of numbers; indeed, many believe that arithmetic instruction designed to help children develop a conceptual understanding of numbers should not begin with tasks involving rote or rational counting. Their point is that practice of this type encourages number calling and limits the possibility of children developing an appreciation of the full meaning of numbers.

Various authors have suggested different approaches for teaching arithmetic to the retarded. Kirk and Johnson (1951) suggest a mechanistic approach with emphasis placed on counting in the early stages of instruction. Bereiter and Engelmann (1966) stress a language approach for disadvantaged preschool youngsters, many of whom find their way into a special-education class without some type of early intervention. The procedures suggested here are somewhat different from either of these and, as is true with approaches suggested by others, lack the extensive experimental evidence on retarded children desirable to provide indisputable conclusions.

If the retarded are to develop a conceptual understanding of arithmetic which will allow for the flexible and practical application of the arithmetic processes in social and vocational situations, great care and attention must be given to the early basic instruction in numbers. Because the understanding of basic number concepts is so crucial to subsequent arithmetic performance by a child, substantial emphasis should be placed on early instruction in this important area. After this basic conceptual foundation has developed and as the retarded youngster increases in age, a more utilitarian application of the principles and skills should be provided. Throughout the process of instruction, the principles of learning, reviewed earlier, should assume a central position in all pedagogical practices. Factors such as active participation, overlearning, reinforcement of success, and reducing various types of cognitive inhibitions must be considered.

Teaching number concepts

The most promising suggestions of Piaget (1952), with interpretation by others (Lovell, 1961; Churchill, 1961; Hood, 1962; Mannix, 1960) seem to have relevance to the problems of early arithmetic instruction for the mentally retarded. Piaget indicates that numerical concepts do not develop from the use of symbols, mechanical procedures, or verbalization by the child or teacher. Instead, he suggests that the manipulation of objects and active participation during the stage of *concrete operations* provide the necessary and most desirable circumstances for the establishment of two important concepts which, in turn, form the foundation for understanding numbers. These two central concepts are *classification* and *seriation*.

CLASSIFICATION   The grouping of objects according to some common property is basic to understanding other arithmetic processes. In order to be successful in classification activities, a retarded child must be able to perceive the unique characteristics of and differences between objects. Discrimination, then, is a sequential precursor to classification. Additionally, a certain level of language capability will enhance the development of skill in classifying.

Learning how to group according to a common characteristic must be acquired first in the process of developing the concept of number. This initial skill may take a long time for the retarded children to understand well at a conceptual level. Briefly, the steps of instruction are the following:

1 *An object with obvious, but somewhat limited, characteristics could be shown to the class. The object should be named or labeled, discussed, and the children encouraged to attend to its outstanding characteristics. By using a simple object, such as a spoon or a ball, the number of possible characteristics is controlled allowing the class to quickly see what is wanted and decide on the most unique characteristics of the object.*

2 *The children might be presented with several small objects which have common characteristics. They should be asked to describe the one or two most outstanding features of each. For example, the spoon and ball each have a unique shape and are used in certain types of activities. Through the use of a variety of similar experiences, some with variations, the retarded will gradually develop skill in grouping objects into classes. Eventually they will begin to understand that most sets of objects can be subsumed under progressively large classification sytems.*

As many sense modalities as possible should be employed in helping the retarded to form concepts of classification. To this end, opportunities to manipulate objects in gamelike situations should be provided. A stable understanding will not become established if the teacher hurries through this stage of instruction by too quickly requiring children to respond to seatwork which has been duplicated on paper. Exercise of this type should come only after each young-ster has demonstrated some capacity for organizing objects by characteristics. This suggestion is consistent with the perspectives of Hebb and Piaget. It has especial relevance for the retarded.

3 Gradually the teacher should require that more abstract objects and pictures be classified. For example, Cuisenaire Rods are excellent materials to use at this level. These rods, which are of ten different colors, vary in length from 1 to 10 centimeters and are 1 centimeter in cross length. Rods of the same length have similar colors. The rods offer an excellent instructional medium for classifying and grouping. In addition, pictures of various objects requiring grouping can be presented; those shown the children initially should be meaningful and have limited and very obvious characteristics. The more difficult tasks requiring classification might involve more inclusive criteria, e.g., color, size, and shape, or use of objects which are abstract or without meaning.

CORRESPONDENCE   Moving to the next prenumber stage, the understanding of correspondence, requires that the retarded have previously attained an understanding of the concept of class. This concept will need to be reinforced frequently during the instruction. Relating a unit in one group or set to a unit in another group or set, regardless of the possible dissimilarity in the characteristics of the groups, requires that the children understand one-to-one correspondence. There are many subtleties involved in the notion of correspondence which may prove to be very difficult for the retarded unless the teacher is especially aware of potential areas for misunderstanding or misinterpretation.

Correspondence is vital for the subsequent teaching and learning of addition and subtraction. Instruction can be initiated at this stage by the teacher placing two sets of three-dimensional objects, each of which contains the same number of objects, in front of a retarded child. The child is asked to match an object from one set with an object from the other set, thusly.

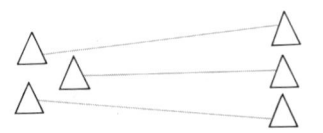

As in the earlier level of arithmetic, after the children have gained an understanding of the concept, the materials of instruction can gradually become more obtuse and remote in contrast to the first presentation which involved three-dimensional objects having meaning. For example, in asking a child to associate one object in a set with another object in a set, during the early stages of teaching one-to-one correspondence, the relationships of the units between the two sets should be logically realistic. The children might be asked to relate a piece of candy with a coin or a picture of a mustache with a picture of a man's face.

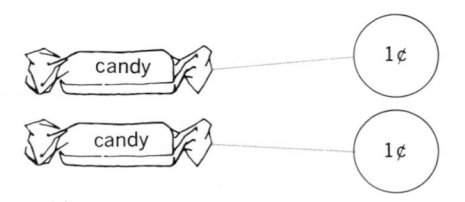

Practical activities for developing this notion of equivalence between sets might include playing a game of musical chairs, setting a table for the members of the class or for a family, or checking to see if enough cups or glasses of milk are available for the class members.

As they begin to see that any time two groups contain an equal number of units the sets are equivalent, the teacher can move to exercises which involve some type of variation, such as differences between elements of sets whose members vary in terms of size, shape, color, or purpose.

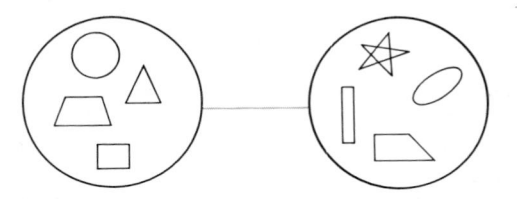

Exercises should evolve gradually from the manipulation of three-dimensional objects to responses by the children on paper. Those students who have a firm understanding of classification and equivalence should be able to relate members of sets on more than one criterion. For the children to perform well in this skill, the teacher should present material sequentially so that the retarded can proceed from working at a concrete manipulating level to a more abstract level of response.

The activities of one-to-one correspondence, which follow instruction in classification, should always include elements from sets having the same number of objects. The number of objects presented in teaching correspondence should include sets with no more than two members. This number should gradually increase, but never exceed nine. Movement to the higher numbers should be based on a criterion of success exhibited by a child during the course of instruction.

In activities of correspondence, children should first be asked to pair elements of sets whose members, although grossly different in certain unique characteristics, are equivalent in number. After this concept is understood, they should be asked to pair sets in which one set contains more members than the others. To illustrate:

from

to

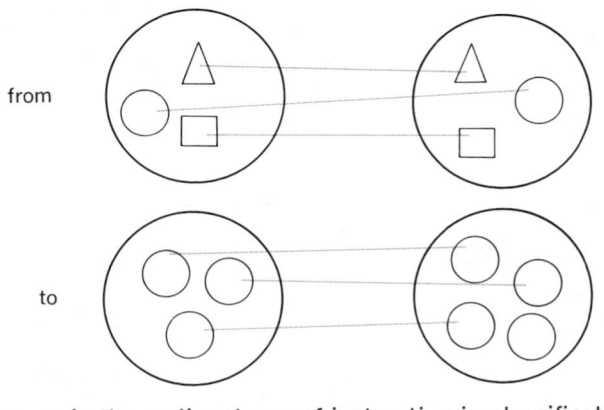

Here, as in the earlier stages of instruction in classification and correspondence, the objects presented for pairing should have an obvious relationship. In fact, the principles of obviousness and concreteness should always be followed whenever a new activity or experience is introduced to these children. In this case, one set might contain four units with pictures of birds; the other set might contain three units of pictures of birdhouses. The children are asked to associate a bird with the birdhouse and to mark the set containing more elements than the other set. As in the earlier exercises of this sort, using three-dimensional objects which the children can manipulate is recommended. Employing paper and pencil exercises should occur only after success with the concrete objects has been observed.

CONSERVATION AND REVERSIBILITY Two additional concepts should be taught at this point in the arithmetic program. The first is conservation, i.e., that the number of units within sets remains the same irrespective of any changes made in the arrangement of the units contained in each set. The second concept is reversibility, i.e., the idea that it is always possible to restore units to their original positions without changing their nature or relationship with other sets. The teacher will find the Cuisenaire Rods to be a valuable instructional device in teaching these concepts. By altering the position of groups of rods, the teacher can demonstrate that the number of rods and the characteristics of each remain the same irrespective of their location or position relative to other sets. The children will gradually realize that the space between members of a set and the relative position of each unit is totally irrelevant and in no way alters the number of elements or the relationship existing among groups. These concepts will be difficult for many retarded children to acquire without a great amount of practice and repetition. Children below the mental age of eight will find it most difficult to separate all the irrelevant perceptual components related to shifting element positions within groups. Most children at this age perceive that a set changes in number simply by virtue of the elements having been rearranged. The concepts of conservation or equivalence and reversibility are necessary for later instruction in addition and subtraction. Opportunities, therefore, should be provided for overlearning to occur.

To reinforce the earlier notions of conservation and reversibility, members of sets, which at this stage should be unequal, should be altered by moving the units into various positions in order to further reinforce the notion that change in number does not occur simply because elements are rearranged. As the children relate elements from one set to those of a second set, they should be asked to describe exactly what they see and what they are doing. This will help to encourage overlearning, provide immediate knowledge of results, facilitate feedback, and be of diagnostic value to the teacher. By observing and listening to the students, the teacher can identify specific areas or concepts which are not clearly understood.

By the time the child has reached this stage of arithmetic development, the language of arithmetic begins to become commonplace. The children will be able to react to situations involving the use of words such as "more than," "as much as," "less than," "large," and "small." Much of arithmetic language deals with qualitative differences such as the dichotomies between hard and soft, light and heavy, or large and small. The language of arithmetic, therefore, can be viewed as the result of perceptual outgrowth and develops basically because of the active interaction an individual has with the environment. To estimate qualitative dimensions accurately requires that an individual be able to compare an object with himself. The relationship existing between certain factors of the language of arithmetic and perceptual-motor development is worth considering. The basic rationale for this position was developed in some detail in Chapter 5.

ORDERING The ability to order sets into a series according to the number of members contained in each is another major concept the retarded must understand in order to grasp the idea of number. The notion of relations or seriation is as important as classification and one-to-one correspondence. Indeed, the number system is based on a blend of the operations of classification and ordering. The idea of five, for example, requires the child to classify in his mind five objects and to place five between four and six in the proper order. When able to deal with these operations in combination, the student will simultaneously see the cardinal and ordinal meanings of number; that is, the number five is both understood conceptually and correctly located between the fourth and sixth position.

Seriation must be taught to the retarded by using concrete objects. This is required for two reasons: (1) Research employing Piaget's concepts reports that seriation of objects can be accomplished by children by the age of seven or eight; whereas seriation of verbal abstractions rarely occurs at an appropriate level of competence before the age of eleven or twelve, and (2) mentally retarded youngsters are relatively stronger in nonverbal than in verbal areas of performance. The teacher, then, should make use of the retarded child's relative strengths in nonverbal areas to help develop the concept of ordering. At the same time, these children should be required to verbalize their observations during the process of ordering.

The Cuisenaire Rods are ideal for beginning instruction in seriation. By providing each child with three or four rods of different lengths and requiring the ordering of these rods according to size, seriation skills can be facilitated. Materials other than those produced commercially can be used for this activity. For example, the teacher could cut cardboard strips which vary in length from 1 to 10 inches. Each 1-inch interval can be identified and the children asked to tell the number of smaller strips of cardboard required to make one of the larger strips. Both ordination and cardination can be taught using this approach.

It is interesting that although a great amount of formal instruction in arithmetic has taken place up to this point, little has been said about numbers either by the child or the teacher. The classification and seriation exercises used with the retarded do not explicitly have the development of rote or rational counting as a primary objective. As the children work with various combinations and groups, however, they will begin to realize the concept of "twoness," "threeness," "fourness," and so on. Association with a specific numeral, however, should not be formally introduced prior to the presentation of seriation activities. It is particularly interesting and signficant that understanding the concept of number does not depend on ability for rote and rational counting prior to classification and grouping instruction. In many respects this is the reverse position presently held by many teachers of the mentally retarded. Although rote counting and rational counting can be taught relatively quickly to the mentally retarded, this procedure does not allow for development of concept of number which, in turn, forms the basis for understanding and correctly applying concepts concerned with simple addition and subtraction.

ASSOCIATING NUMBERS WITH NUMERALS After the children have demonstrated skill in ordering sets of objects in terms of their relationship to other sets, they are ready to focus their attention on the association of numerals with the number of elements contained in appropriate sets. By this time the notions of oneness, twoness, and threeness will have been introduced, and the children will know that sets containing a like number of elements exhibit a common property which differentiates them from other sets. The common property of sets having a similar number of elements can be associated with a certain name and symbol.

The following procedure might be employed in teaching the retarded to make this association. First, identify for the children a variety of three-dimensional sets each of which contains a different number of elements. Place the sets around the perimeter of a large table, allow the children to manipulate them and rearrange the position of the objects within an individual set in any way they wish. After they have had a chance to study the various sets, choose a set which contains one element; and explain that whenever we have a set with this many members, holding the set out so that all the children can see, we think of the number 1. At this point, the teacher should place a large cutout of the numeral 1 in the center of the table which contains the various sets of objects. After the relationship between the numeral 1 and the appropriate set has been established, the children should be asked to select from all the sets on the table those which can be described by the numeral 1. The children might be allowed to work in groups at first. The teacher must be careful to give clear directions and provide numerous examples concerning the association of sets with the number 1. Emphasis should be given to the common characteristic of all the sets which have been selected as being descriptive of oneness and described by the numeral 1.

This same type of exercise can be used for sequential presentations through number nine. Similar types of activities can be given which make use of paper and pencil tasks, but only after they have had plenty of opportunity to work with three-dimensional objects. As they are required to move beyond sets containing more than four members, it may become difficult for them to identify the correct sets at a glance without counting the elements of each set. At this point, rational counting should be encouraged. The advantage of emphasizing rational counting here is to make the point that "Whenever we need to know how many, we should count." The additional advantage of having the children count the members of sets is the clear vocal feedback provided to them. This exercise will also be of diagnostic value to the teacher.

In teaching the relationship between a numerical symbol and the appropriate set, the teacher will find it helpful to proceed from one through nine in an ordinal fashion. Objects can be arranged to contain two elements, three elements, four elements, and five elements, as a means for reviewing and reinforcing earlier concepts prior to introducing the relationship between the numeral 6 and sets containing six members. Following this review, the teacher can introduce the numeral 6 by saying that by adding one member to the set which has five members we no longer can think of the set as five, but we must now think of it as six. Have the children count the elements of the set.

The concept of cardinal numbers from one through nine must be constantly reinforced. The child's ability to recognize the standard numerals and to associate the numeral with the correct number of elements is important. Exercises such as presenting them with the numeral 6 and asking them to draw six balls or make six X's will help to reinforce the idea and provide a means for evaluating the degree to which the concept becomes overlearned. Numerous variations from this activity are possible. For example, the teacher could reverse the procedure and supply the children with a certain number of circles or X's and ask the students to indicate how many objects were in each row by writing the appropriate numeral. Ordinal positioning should not be overlooked in these activities.

Teaching concepts related to number are basic for children to develop flexibility in understanding and correctly applying even the most elementary arithmetic process. Substantial attention should be given to these fundamental arithmetic matters in special classes for the retarded. The teacher should not be overly concerned if the children spend a great amount of time with these basic concepts. The advantage of establishing a firm understanding of the prenumber concepts will become visible as they move toward the more difficult aspects of the arithmetic program.

The special-education teacher will find that many of the contemporary arithmetic workbooks and texts used with children from the kindergarten to second or third grade will help to design and sequence arithmetic activities for the retarded. Some selection of arithmetic exercises and activities will need to be made with the principal criterion being their potential value for the future social and occupational skills required of the retarded. Revision of workbook activities may be necessary. It should be emphasized that the child must spend time manipulating three-dimensional objects. For this reason, materials such as the Cuisenaire Rods are particularly useful for instruction in combinations, classifications, and seriation. Not only will these materials help in presenting concepts, but the children can work individually with these materials at their own desks.

Teaching simple addition

Although it is true that the teacher will view the operations of simple addition and subtraction as being closely related, they should be taught separately to the mentally retarded so that the retarded do not become confused in using and applying these processes. Eventually, they will begin to see that addition involves combining groups into a new, larger group.

The initial introduction of simple addition should emerge from the earlier study of classification and grouping. The children should move from a consideration of the characteristics of a group, to more than one group (involving the study of correspondence), to activities involving combining two separate groups into a new group. The first activities in addition should be very concrete and involve dramatization; for example, having two small groups of children join to form a single line. Subsequent activities might involve the use of inanimate three-dimensional objects. Verbal statements should be made which describe the process of combining groups. These will help the retarded pupils become familiar with the language of addition. For example, at this first stage the command, "Mary and John, go and join Herb for lunch," will gradually evolve into the more precise statement, "Two people and one person make a group of three."

When the teacher feels that the children understand conservation and reversibility, the instructional program should move into the use of pictorial materials. Although the appropriate numerical terms should be used to verbally describe the quantity in each set or group, the instruction should be broken into basic sequential steps. The printed numeral should not be used at this point for instruction in addition. This is recommended in spite of the fact that the retarded will have already developed an awareness of the association between the numeral used to describe how many are contained in each set. The retarded should not be required to perform too many operations at once, particularly at this point, where the emphasis should be placed on understanding the process of combining, or adding, groups of things. The terms *and* and *make* can be used to describe the process of addition. The following illustrates the type of exercise appropriate at this level:

two cents and three cents make five cents

Whenever the students want to know how many are in a group, they should be encouraged to count. It is quite proper for the youngsters to do rational counting at this point.

The next step in the process is to focus on developing association among the figures, appropriate verbal statements, and numerals. To illustrate:

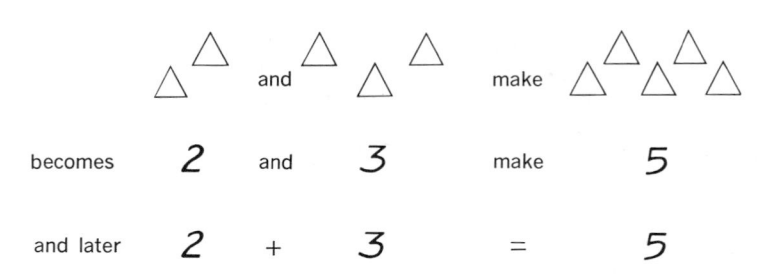

becomes	2	and	3	make	5
and later	2	+	3	=	5

At the same time, a transition should take place from the less precise verbal statement, "Two tents and three tents make five tents" to, "Two plus three equal five." The more generalized statement will be understood and used only after presenting many concrete examples of making combinations in a variety of situations. The children's achievement at this stage will be slow since they must adjust their thinking, principally in terms of seeing relationships between sets and among symbols involved in addition.

It should be realized that placing an algorithm in a horizontal position instead of in a vertical arrangement during the first stages of simple addition will help to reinforce the left-to-right progression necessary in reading. Moreover, this type of placement is more consistent with the earlier arithmetic activities involving the use of concrete objects and pictures. In order to aid the retarded child to know where to start in the process, an arrow could be drawn below each algorithm.

$$2 + 3 = 5$$
$$\longrightarrow$$

If the retarded child has developed an understanding of conservation, reversibility, and correspondence, it will be relatively easy for a transition to be made to a vertical arrangement of the algorithm. This conversion should be made before instruction is given in carrying and borrowing. In teaching simple addition, the teacher should concentrate on helping the children to use their newly developed skill for solving problems which have been presented verbally. This will help them to relate arithmetic computation skills to arithmetic reasoning situations early in the sequence of instruction and thus emphasize the utilitarian value of arithmetic. Exercises of this type can be given before the children develop a comparable level of achievement in reading.

The use of zero in simple addition is introduced after the children have had many opportunities to work with combining sets up to nine. Zero can best be introduced by indicating that it represents an empty set or group. There is nothing in the group to add to the other set, and, therefore, the total is the same as the number of members found in the nonempty group. The teacher will find it best to return to a more concrete stage of instruction by using people or three-dimensional inanimate objects to illustrate the point.

A variety of exercises should be used with the retarded in order that they firmly understand the addition process, know when it can be appropriately used, and are able to use the process in a flexible way.

Teaching simple subtraction

The procedures used in teaching simple subtraction are basically similar to those employed in simple addition instruction. The concept of groups is used to begin teaching subtraction. Instruction should proceed from total use of concrete objects to abstract forms. Verbal statements will help to emphasize the process at all stages; the utilitarian theme should be stressed. The terms *take away* and *leaves* instead of *minus* and *equals* can be used when the children engage in subtraction activities initially.

Subtraction instruction can be started by illustration or through some type of dramatization. For example, start with a group of four children, and ask one child to leave the group. Ask the class how many children are left in the original group. Emphasize that the large group was divided in some way and two smaller groups formed. Even at this stage, the use of language of subtraction should begin.

The same types of activities suggested for addition are applicable in teaching subtraction. Moreover, the same sequences can be followed. The children should manipulate objects first and gradually be introduced to more abstract stimuli including the use of the signs and symbols of subtraction. Making the transition from descriptive statements to the more precise language of subtraction must be done gradually. Placement of the algorithm in a horizontal position will provide a helpful reference point from the child's earlier experiences with addition. Eventually the students will become familiar with the vertical arrangement.

The use of zero in simple subtraction should emerge in the same relative sequence as it did in addition. Constant focus on the use of groups and the concept of an empty set will help the notion of zero to develop.

Certain students may eventually see that subtraction is the opposite of addition. *The important point is that the retarded understand when the process of addition is applicable and when subtraction is to be used.* If they are skilled in the computational aspects alone, and have no understanding of when to use the various processes, the objectives of the arithmetic program will not be met. For this reason, therefore, early experiences in addition and subtraction should be combined with activities which will help the students develop a firm understanding of number. If each of these skills develops in isolation without the other being considered, arithmetic instruction will be rendered relatively useless.

Teaching carrying and borrowing through place value

Understanding place value is necessary for the accurate execution of two- and three-place addition and subtraction, particularly when it involves carrying and borrowing. Place value should be introduced as part of instruction in simple addition and subtraction. As children engage in arithmetic activities involving two- and three-place addition and subtraction without carrying and borrowing, the teacher should use the place-value box. This is a small plywood box with three equal-sized compartments into which sticks, such as tongue depressors, can be inserted. The compartments are labeled "Ones," "Tens," and "Hundreds" appropriately.

As the children add and subtract, they can simultaneously add to or remove from the groups located in the various compartments. This introduction to the place-value box, using number combinations that do not exceed nine in any column, will help the students become familiar with using the device. Moreover, the concept and habit of correct column positioning will be developed; this is vital in the process of carrying and borrowing. Throughout the introductory stage, arithmetic activities should focus on experiences with manipulating objects (such as the place-value sticks), writing the appropriate algorithm, and using the child's computational skills to solve practical problems.

The next stage in the teaching of place value follows logically from the earlier instruction involving combinations and grouping. At this point, the retarded must understand that whenever the "Ones" compartment reaches ten, the group of objects is to be bundled together (with a rubber band to emphasize) and placed in the "Tens" compartment. The principle of "overcrowding" should lead to the realization that each bundled group now represents one group of ten. A great deal of practice should be given in making and taking apart bundles of ten so that the children realize that 1 ten is the same as 10 ones. The concepts of conservation and reversibility are inherently a part of place-value manipulation at this stage.

As the children make numbers and experiment with the use of the place-value box, the close association between this activity and the appropriate written and oral numerical symbols should be emphasized. As they manipulate the materials, the children should discuss, with the teacher or another student, what they are doing and the proper numeral which describes how many are contained in each compartment. To emphasize accuracy in this calculation operation, paper with vertical lines should be used to help impress on the children the need to execute accurately this important task.

Zero should be introduced during this early stage of experimenting. Some controversy exists as to whether zero should be explicitly called a "place holder." Since there is always the possibility that an additional rule or new concept will confuse the retarded child in beginning arithmetic, the concept of zero might best be introduced by pointing to an empty "Ones" compartment and asking the children, "How many ones are here?" A response by the children such as, "None," or "I don't see any," will lead to the teacher simply saying, "Correct. When we have none, we call that zero." This concept can be further reinforced by asking questions such as, "How many cats are with us today?" By continuing this line of questioning, with infrequent nonzero questions inserted, the retarded will soon gain a more realistic understanding of the concept of zero.

At the appropriate time the symbol zero should be introduced and the statement made that whenever there are none, the figure 0 is used. This point can be reinforced by having the children first write numbers which contain zeros when there are no sticks in any of the compartments in the place-value box; the same procedure can eventually be used in simple addition and subtraction with algorithms containing zeros. The teacher must not move too rapidly during this stage of instruction, nor should the logical sequences involving minimal change be ignored. Throughout this process, the retarded must be given plenty of practice in number building by relating numbers in the place-value box to written numerals.

By the time the children have developed reasonable level of competence in the skills outlined above, they will be ready to begin learning the process of carrying in addition. Carrying can be introduced best by using the place-value box. In demonstrating, ask a child to place sixteen sticks (1 ten and 6 ones) in the appropriate compartments. The number should be recorded on the blackboard. Ask another child to add six more sticks. With twelve sticks in the "Ones" compartment, the previous experiences of the students in building should alert them to the "overcrowding" in the "Ones" compartment. The solution to group 10 ones and "carry" them to the "Tens" compartment should come from the students.

Throughout the process, the teacher should construct the algorithm as the students do the grouping and carrying. With the retarded, it is particularly advisable that the number of tens being carried to the next column be recorded at the top of the algorithm. The process for this sequence is shown on page 189.

Developed in this fashion, carrying is initially mechanical and greatly dependent on the use and manipulation of concrete materials and the concepts learned earlier. The retarded youngster will need to continue using these devices until practice has led to overlearning and the concept of carrying is understood by the child at an abstract level. This development may take a great amount of time, and, indeed,

First

~~/////// ~~	/////
Tens	Ones

1   6

Adding 6 more

~~//////// ~~	///// /////
Tens	Ones

1   6

+   6

Bundling 10 ones and carrying 1 ten to the tens side of the box

~~////// ~~ ~~//////// ~~	//
Tens	Ones

① 1   6

+   6

22

or   ①

   1 ten 6 ones
+   6 ones
  2 tens 2 ones

some retarded youngsters may continue to need concrete crutches even into the high school program. If these devices are needed, the students should be allowed to use them by all means. As the children learn how to do simple carrying, the teacher should introduce addition which requires the carrying of two-digit numbers and, eventually, introduce instruction using the hundreds column.

The fundamental principles employed in borrowing are no different from those used in carrying; thus, these two operations should be taught in close contiguity. Most teachers will elect to use the decomposition method in connection with the place-value box. This process is the opposite of grouping in addition and involves breaking down a bundle of ten into ones and relocating them in the "Ones" compartment. For example, in the preliminary stages of instruction in borrowing, the students would break down 31 (or 3 tens and 1 one) into 2 tens and 11 ones. At first the children may argue that the "Ones" compartment should contain no more than 10 ones. The teacher must quickly indicate that this situation involves only a temporary grouping which is necessary in certain types of subtraction.

The retarded should make use of the place-value box with the algorithm during the subtraction process. As the minuend undergoes decomposition, appropriate changes should be made in the written numerals. The sequence is as follows:

First

~~/////////~~ ~~/////////~~	
Tens	Ones

2   1

Subtracting 5 requires breaking down 1 ten and relocating the 10 ones into the "ones" slot

~~//////~~ ~~/////////~~	/
Tens	Ones

2   1

−   5

This results in

~~/////////~~	////////// /
Tens	Ones

1   11
2̶   1̶
−   5

Remove 5 from the "ones" compartment

~~/////////~~	/////
Tens	Ones

1   11
2̶   1̶
−   5
1   6

or

2 tens 1 one
−   5 ones
1 ten 6 ones

Again, as in carrying, the use of the place-value box or any other similar device should not be denied the retarded. They must be given plenty of practice in manipulating the objects and associating the changes in the grouping with the numerical alterations required in the algorithm. The students should understand that they can check on the accuracy of their subtraction by adding the subtrahend and difference to see if the sum equals the minuend. Their earlier developed understanding of conservation and reversibility again comes into focus as being an important basic concept to be emphasized in early arithmetic instruction.

Throughout the instruction in borrowing and carrying, the retarded should be given opportunities to employ their developing skills in a practical and realistic way. The early introduction of problems involving reasoning should constitute an important segment of the arithmetic period. A utilitarian theme must characterize the problems presented to the students.

Multiplication and division

Retarded children who have developed a firm understanding of addition and subtraction and who can use each of these processes with flexibility in proper situations will be able to solve most problems involving arithmetic computation. For this reason, therefore, great emphasis should be placed on teaching these fundamental skills. Multiplication is a shortcut for addition and essentially a more parsimonious procedure for adding equal-sized groups to form a new group. Division is a shortcut for performing successive subtractions. Certain retarded children will be capable of learning the more elementary skills involved in each of these areas, frequently depending on crutches for successful achievement. Many other retarded youngsters will find multiplication and division too difficult. The teacher must make a decision as to whether further, more comprehensive instruction or tutoring in multiplication or division constitutes the most efficient use of time. The decision will differ for each child within a classroom and should be primarily based on the diagnostic clues each student exhibits. When the teacher judges that multiplication or division either confuses or has the potential for not being adequately understood by a youngster, greater emphasis should be placed on the further development of skills in addition and subtraction.

Those children who show some promise for being able to learn simple multiplication can be introduced to the process by first adding three numbers, e.g., $2 + 2 + 2 = $ ____. The next step is to introduce the notion that this algorithm can be viewed as 3 twos or, more technically, two times three. The children should realize that multiplication is a shortcut way to do addition and that a check can be made on the accuracy of their multiplication by repeated addition.

Multiplication will save time for the children, and, if they can develop an understanding of the computational procedures as well as accurately apply the process, eventually it should become part of the retarded students' arithmetic program. To be sure, they will need to commit some of the multiplication tables to memory or use a multiplication chart during the initial stages of instruction. A chart such as the following will often be helpful.

NUMBER TO BE MULTIPLIED

	1	2	3	4	5	6	7	8	9	10
	2	4	6	8	10	12	14	16	18	20
	3	6	9	12	15	18	21	24	27	30
	4	8	12	16	20	24	28	32	36	40
X	5	10	15	20	25	30	35	40	45	50
(TIMES)	6	12	18	24	30	36	42	48	54	60
	7	14	21	28	35	42	49	56	63	70
	8	16	24	32	40	48	56	64	72	80
	9	18	27	36	45	54	63	72	81	90
	10	20	30	40	50	60	70	80	90	100

The use of a mnemonic device or a chart, such as the one illustrated above, is valuable to the retarded because it provides immediate knowledge of results, fosters an emphasis on accuracy, reinforces the correct response through the use of a variety of sense modalities, and gives the students opportunities for active participation. The teacher should not be hesitant to allow the retarded to use these devices.

Two-place multiplication is more difficult than simple multiplication and would be appropriate for only selected children in the special class. The combination of multiplication, addition, and the proper placement of numerals is often too difficult an operation for retarded children. Those students with the potential for satisfactorily performing this relatively complex task should be instructed in a fashion which prevents errors being practiced. Weaknesses in using the process must be identified quickly and properly remediated. Teaching two-place multiplication to the retarded is different from instruction with the intellectually normal. In the former case, the special-class teacher must allow for the extended use of concrete devices and crutches, pace the instruction at a very low rate, adhere to principles of learning, and not push the children beyond reasonable expectations.

Learning the process of division is a major stumbling block for many intellectually normal children, but it is especially difficult for the retarded. In reality, the retarded will find relatively few social or occupational opportunities for which knowledge of division is required. The teacher, therefore, should give some thought to the value of spending time teaching division to the retarded.

It would be wise to go back to the earlier stage of instruction in combinations to dramatize the meaning of division. Emphasis should be placed on the notion that division is the process of successively subtracting subgroups, each of which contains a certain restricted number of members, from a larger group of objects. For example, present a group of six blocks to the students and ask them to break down the group into subgroups, each of which contains two blocks. The question to be answered is, "How many groups of two are contained in six?"

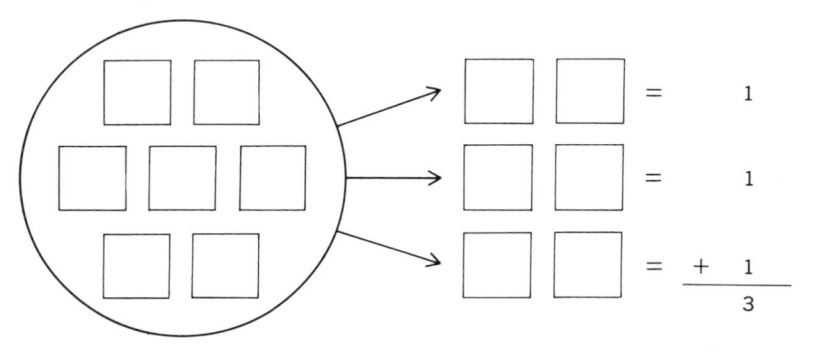

The problem can be written in another way using successive subtraction.

Problem: How many twos are in six?

$$2 \overline{)\ 6}$$

(1
$$\frac{-\ 2}{4}$$
(1
$$\frac{-\ 2}{2}$$
(1
$$\frac{-\ 2}{0}\quad \overline{3}$$

There are 3 twos in six.

Or

$$2 \overline{)\ 6} \atop {-\ 6}$$ (with 3 above)

In every division problem, the retarded should be taught to use the long-division approach which requires that the divisor and quotient be multiplied as a check of the dividend. Some children will be able to estimate the quotient when there is a one-figure divisor; most of the retarded will find it too difficult to learn the technique of estimating the quotient with a two-figure divisor.

As in other areas of arithmetic, the children should have plenty of practice using division by applying the process to practical problems. A great deal of manipulation of concrete objects which allows the child to return to the earlier stage of combinations should characterize early instruction in division. If a retarded child has not developed the basic concepts of reversibility and conservation, division, as well as other computational processes, will at best be done in a rote fashion. This situation will make the correct application of the appropriate arithmetic process to practical problems all the more difficult for the child. The assumption is that an understanding of the concept of number will reduce the incidence of random application of the appropriate process to a problem situation. Indeed, it could be suggested that reasoning skills will be substantially increased after a child has developed an understanding of these basic concepts.

Fractions

Certain fundamental notions concerning fractions should be part of the retarded child's arithmetic program. The instruction, however, must have a decided practical flavor. A number of commercially developed visual aids are available to supplement the teaching of fractions. Charts such as the one below and on page 195 will help the retarded see relationships of fractional parts to a whole.

The teacher should emphasize that (1) the bottom numeral of a fraction tells into how many pieces an object was equally divided, (2) the top numeral tells the number of pieces we have or are talking about, and (3) that the larger the bottom numeral, the smaller will be the pieces. Instruction in fractions should be varied and related directly to areas in which the children will need to make use of this information or skill. They should understand what is meant by one-half loaf of bread, one-third cup of flour, or one-quarter spoon of

1							
$\frac{1}{2}$				$\frac{1}{2}$			
$\frac{1}{4}$		$\frac{1}{4}$		$\frac{1}{4}$		$\frac{1}{4}$	
$\frac{1}{8}$	$\frac{1}{8}$	$\frac{1}{8}$	$\frac{1}{8}$	$\frac{1}{8}$	$\frac{1}{8}$	$\frac{1}{8}$	$\frac{1}{8}$

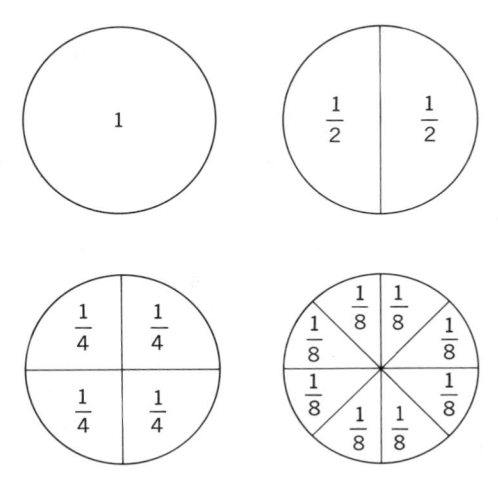

medicine every half hour. Activities of this type, which require a basic understanding of fractions, should be stressed.

Measurement

The mentally retarded will need to understand and accurately use several types of measurement. Their depth of understanding will be totally dependent on each child's demonstrated ability and achievement along with some general prediction of future occupational expectations. Higher-level competence in specific areas of measurement which are required of certain occupations should be stressed during the work-study program. Instruction in basic skills in measurement, however, should begin much earlier in the school program.

MONEY   Beginning instruction with money must be concrete and allow children to manipulate the real thing. Fundamental operations of changing a coin into an equivalent sum using other coins, purchasing objects, making change, recording the amount of a purchase and calculating the amount of money to be returned, and understanding reasons for saving money should be introduced and practiced in a variety of ways throughout the instructional program. The more practical and real the situation, the greater assurance the retarded child will have in engaging in experiences with money.

TIME   Its abstract nature and the minimum number of ways available for children to manipulate objects related to time often make teaching this concept to the retarded a long, arduous task. Empirical data describing a preferred strategy for teaching time are not available. Because of the more obvious switches between days of the week, the teacher can introduce time using days of the week instead of discussing relationships between minutes and hours. In the initial stages of teaching, no attempt should be made to use anything other than the names of each day. Gradually, dates, months, and years can be introduced. Activities should be provided to help them remember the ordinal position of the days.

The relationship between hours and minutes can be introduced by the teacher adhering to a certain time schedule during each day. This schedule should become part of each child's activities. They will eventually begin to see relationships between the position of the hands on the clock and the activities typical of a particular time period in the day. Gradually, the children will show readiness for more systematic instruction in telling time. A variety of visual aids are available, or can be constructed by the teacher, to aid in this instruction. Each child can make his own model of a clock from tagboard for use at his desk.

DISTANCE   The inch, foot, and yard are the concepts of distance on which emphasis should be placed in the special-class program for the retarded. At a more advanced instructional level, the concept of mile can be introduced. Special attention should be given to techniques for making conversions from one dimension to another. The need for accuracy in measurement must be stressed, with practice in measuring and converting to another dimension included in all phases of the program. A variety of situations which occur during the day offer opportunities for the students to measure distance.

WEIGHT   This subject can best be introduced by each student weighing himself and maintaining a weekly record. Attention should be focused primarily on the concepts of pound and ounce. The students should gain skill in converting ounces to pounds and vice versa. Activities of various types which involve measuring the weight of flour, sand, sugar, wood, or any other commodity, using a kitchen scale will allow for concrete experiences in this area of measurement. Experiences in the home economics and industrial arts classroom are particularly important in this regard.

VOLUME   The use of half-pint, pint, quart, half-gallon, and gallon containers will help develop an understanding of relationships among the various measures of volume. It will be conceptually helpful for the children to understand the significance of conservation of matter, i.e., when two containers of equal size are filled with fluid and the fluid in one vessel poured into a smaller but taller container, the amount of fluid is altered in no way. Understanding this principle will help the retarded to conceptually see relationships among measurements of volume. The notion of conservation of matter in many ways is similar to conservation of number which was discussed earlier.

SELECTED REFERENCES

Bensberg, G. J.: "The Relationship of Academic Achievement of Mental Defectives to Mental Age, Sex, Institutionalization, and Etiology," *American Journal of Mental Deficiency,* vol. 58, 1953, pp. 327–330.

Bereiter, C. and Engelmann, S.: *Teaching Disadvantaged Children in the Preschool,* Prentice-Hall, Inc., Englewood Cliffs, N.J., 1966.

Burns, P. C.: "Arithmetic Fundamentals for the Educable Mentally Retarded," *American Journal of Mental Deficiency,* vol. 66, 1961, pp. 57–61.

Capobianco, R. J.: "Quantitative and Qualitative Analysis of Endogenous and Exogenous Boys on Arithmetic Achievement," in L. M. Dunn and R. J. Capobianco, "Studies of Reading and Arithmetic in Mentally Retarded Boys," *Monographs of the Society for Research in Child Development,* 1954, pp. 101–142.

Churchill, E. M.: *Counting and Measuring,* University of Toronto Press, Toronto, 1961.

Clarke, A. M. and Clarke, A. D. B.: *Mental Deficiency: The Changing Outlook,* The Free Press of Glencoe, New York, 1965.

Costello, H. M.: *The Responses of Mentally Retarded Children to Specialized Learning Experiences in Arithmetic,* unpublished doctoral dissertation, University of Pennsylvania, Philadelphia, 1941.

Cruickshank, W. M.: "Arithmetic Vocabulary of Mentally Retarded Boys," *Exceptional Children,* vol. 13, 1946, pp. 65–69.

————: "Arithmetic Work Habits of Mentally Retarded Boys," *American Journal of Mental Deficiency,* vol. 52, 1948a, pp. 318–330.

————: "Arithmetic Ability of Mentally Retarded Children: I. Ability to Differentiate Extraneous Material from Needed Arithmetic Facts; II. Understanding Arithmetic Processes," *Journal of Education Research,* vol. 42, 1948b, pp. 161–170, 279–288.

Dunn, L. M.: "A Comparison of the Reading Processes of Mentally Retarded Boys of the Same Mental Age," in L. M. Dunn and R. J. Capobianco, "Studies of Reading and Arithmetic in Mentally Retarded Boys," *Monographs of the Society for Research in Child Development,* vol. 1, 1954, pp. 7–99.

Fouracre, M. H.: "Learning Characteristics of Brain-Injured Children," *Exceptional Children,* vol. 24, 1958, pp. 210–212.

Hood, H. B.: "An Experimental Study of Piaget's Theory of the Development of Number in Children," *British Journal of Psychology,* vol. 53, 1962, pp. 273–286.

Kirk, S. A. and Johnson, G. O.: *Educating the Retarded Child,* Houghton Mifflin Company, Boston, 1951.

Lovell, K.: *The Growth of Basic Mathematical and Scientific Concepts in Children,* University of London Press, London, 1961.

Mannix, J. B.: "The Number Concepts of a Group of ESN Children," *British Journal of Education Psychology,* vol. 30, 1960, pp. 180–181.

Piaget, J.: *The Child's Conception of Number,* Routledge and Kegan Paul, Ltd., London, 1952.

Stephens, W. B.: "Piaget and Inhelder—Application of Theory and Diagnostic Techniques to the Area of Mental Retardation," *Education and Training of the Mentally Retarded,* vol. 1, 1966, pp. 75–86.

Strauss, A. A. and Werner, H.: "Deficiency in the Finger Schema in Relation to Arithmetic Disability," *American Journal of Orthopsychiatry,* vol. 8, 1938, pp. 719–725.

Woodward, M.: "Concepts of Number in the Mentally Subnormal Studied by Piaget's Method," *Journal of Child Psychology and Psychiatry,* vol. 2, 1961, pp. 249–259.

————: "Concepts of Space in the Mentally Subnormal Studied by Piaget's Method," *British Journal of Social and Clinical Psychology,* vol. 1, 1962a, pp. 25–37.

————: "The Application of Piaget's Theory of the Training of the Subnormal," *Journal of Mental Subnormality,* vol. 8, 1962b, pp. 17–25.

developing personal and social skills

Compared with the research effort related to learning, relatively little attention has been directed toward studying the social and emotional characteristics of the educable mentally retarded or investigating the impact of programs specifically designed to develop desired social and personal skills. Nonetheless, it is the unanimous opinion of the professional community and, indeed, of society that the educable mentally retarded should take their places as members of the community and contribute to its stability and enhancement. Without appropriate experiences leading to the achievement of this aim, the probability of the retarded being skilled enough to react appropriately to social demands will be minimal. It is necessary, therefore, that a great deal of attention be given to developing and directing the behavior of the educable child early and continuously during the course of the school program.

In order to be effective in social interchange, an individual must be sensitive to the requirements of his environment and responsive to appropriate ways for dealing with these social demands. Evidence suggests that the retarded are weak in these requirements, particularly when placed in situations in which interaction is required with the intellectually normal. Goldstein (1964), in reviewing the literature, has noted the difficulty frequently characteristic of the retarded in adhering to social demands and the difficulty others often experience in tolerating their behavior. These findings are particularly relevant to the employment situation in which the mentally retarded commonly have more difficulty with the social and personal requirements of a position than with the occupational and manipulative demands. The need for special-education programs to give more comprehensive and continuous attention to the social development of the retarded has been clearly demonstrated.

Additional support for placing greater emphasis on the development of socialization skills in programs for the retarded comes from the research which has examined delinquency among this group. Although the evidence suggests that a marked relationship does not exist between intelligence and delinquency, there is reason to conclude that mental retardation is a complicating factor of particular significance when combined in some as yet unidentified mix with other environmental elements. Substantial effort has been given to studying reasons for criminal behavior among the retarded; included among the suggested causes are the difficulties the retarded have in telling right from wrong (Harrington, 1935), problems in controlling their impulses (Gregg, 1948), their frequent lack of association with an appropriate school situation (Kvaraceus, 1944; Wallin, 1929), and their typical association with a deprived social and cultural milieu (Poucher, 1952; Gregg, 1948). The retarded tend to commit relatively more minor than major crimes, and, of those committed, the great majority seem to be the results of impulsive and momentary acts and not of planned aggression (Gregg, 1948). This finding underscores the possibility of a lack of social awareness on their part in those areas typically learned incidentally by intellectually normal children who are often associated with a relatively more stable family situation.

Allied to these social difficulties are the emotional and personal problems often observed in the retarded. For a variety of complex reasons, but, with a few exceptions, the retarded view themselves generally as being inadequate (Heber, 1964). Certainly a frequent history of failure will be generalized and serve to reduce the child's eagerness to participate in activities wherein success has not earlier been experienced. Developing friendships and a satisfying association with others are areas in which the retarded often fail. The possibility of increased emotional disturbances among this group exists because of (1) their inflexibility in behavior and tendency to perseverate on a goal even when it is out of reach, (2) their restricted background of experiences which delimits the possibility of an appropriate response and reduces insulation against personal degradation, and (3) their difficulty in interpreting personal and social situations.

DIMENSIONS OF PERSONAL, EMOTIONAL, AND SOCIAL GROWTH

Physical health and personal attractiveness

Chapter 5 emphasized the relationships that exist between early perceptual-motor development and subsequent achievement in school-related activities. The need for the teacher to give attention to the early perceptual-motor development of the retarded and the desirability for providing the children with activities designed to increase skill in these areas was emphasized. An equally significant reason for an early emphasis on motor activities is to give the retarded opportunities for consistent and vigorous exercise. This is particularly important for those children from a depressed environment, frequently characterized by overcrowding with a lack of space in the surrounding neighborhood for sustained physical activity. For reasons of health, therefore, it is advisable that the teacher establish a reasonable amount of time each day, twenty to forty minutes at the very least, for vigorous physical activity. This should extend beyond the typical recess and lunch periods of free play and have more organization and structure so that everyone can participate. Many of the children will need to be shown how to exert themselves actively. Often a collaborative effort between the special-education teacher and the school's physical education department will allow for the provision of a perceptual-motor and physical education program which satisfies the health aims as well as the development of certain basic perceptual skills.

The work of Cureton (1965) is exemplary in this respect. This noted authority on physical fitness has tested and trained thousands of individuals at the University of Illinois Physical Fitness Research Center. From his research effort, Cureton has described certain procedures for testing one's physical condition. In addition, he has a practical program designed to enhance one's general physical status. Exercises have been recommended to develop balance, flexibility, agility, strength, and endurance. Not only is this physical fitness program of great potential value to the retarded students, but the teacher may find it advantageous to participate along with the students.

The teacher of the retarded should attempt to exercise some control over the diet of the students. This is a particularly difficult goal, for to have any lasting effect, control of nutrition must begin in each child's home. A parent education program is one approach for exerting influence in the home. Within the school program, the children should be instructed about reasons for eating carefully. Most teachers of educable retarded children who live in a depressed environment are aware of the need to devote time during the instructional program to considering proper nutrition. In the early stages of their education, the mentally retarded should develop some awareness of the reasons for eating certain kinds of food and the advantage in using various dietary supplements as frequently as possible. For example, being aware that a small amount of meat included in a large pot of beans will substantially increase the protein value of the food is an important fact of which few deprived families are aware. One can always hope that by presenting young children with a systematic program aimed at informing them about nutrition some of these ideas will be communicated to their parents. The older retarded children should come to realize the significance of appropriate nutrition. Many of these children will find themselves in situations in which they will be forced to decide on the kind of food to purchase for their families. The teacher can dramatize the impact of poor nutrition by using a variety of experiments with different types of plants which receive or are denied a certain type of nutritional supplement. In connection with the experience, films or slides can be shown to illustrate the relationship between the experiments with plants and problems resulting from nutritional deprivation among people.

A logical relationship exists between physical fitness, nutritional considerations, and the need for the children to learn more about bodily functions. The teacher should capitalize on the youngster's natural curiosity about his own body by systematically presenting units on the primary functions of the various bodily systems. A detailed explanation of the functioning of each system is beyond their capacity; however, the major bodily processes should be considered. The degree to which they understand these processes will be related to their motivation to care for themselves physically. For example, teaching the children about the process of elimination will help them conceptually understand the reasons for eating certain foods in moderation and keeping their bodies clean and make them aware of other types of difficulties that might result from not caring for themselves. In considering the respiratory system, a desired goal should be that they become aware of the disadvantages of smoking and of being near toxic vapors. Understanding the functions of the reproductive system, for example, provides a basis for an awareness of the physiological concerns of reproduction and the moral and social considerations as well.

Personal grooming and appropriate dress are other important areas for instructional concern. These are not only of social significance but have some direct relevance to physical health. Students should learn about the relationship between health, good grooming, and appropriate dress. For example, a clear difference can be shown between a person with hair which was recently washed and another with dirty hair. A strand of hair can be taken from each student and placed under a microscope. Differences in cleanliness between the strands will be quickly seen. This will be very revealing to most students and have the potential effect of altering the behavior of the child with dirty hair. Further, the level of motivation of the class may increase because this type of activity uses equipment which is often used by students in other classrooms.

It is much easier to work with older mentally retarded children in the areas of grooming and dress since peer pressure to be accepted is often so firmly established. The teacher should use this situation by continually reminding the students about the danger of offending others by not maintaining good grooming. By the time the retarded have reached the secondary school special classes, they should have developed some understanding of the health reasons for cleanliness and good dress. The importance of spending enough time in this area is amplified when one realizes that it is easier to detect a dirty and untidy person at a glance than to identify an academic problem in the retarded. One is often classified by others as a result of this type of evaluation.

Emotional growth and mental health

Emotional development and interest in promoting good mental health among the retarded are other areas of concern to the special-education teacher. Systematic attempts at studying personality factors among the educable retarded located in the community have been predominately clinical and not based on empirical research. This situation is not unusual because of the great difficulty one experiences in adequately identifying and controlling the many influential, active variables which affect personality development. Heber (1964) has summarized the results of a number of the investigations in which some control has been exercised. His summary suggests that (1) the retarded are poorly motivated after having once acquired a generalized expectancy of failure, (2) being located in a regular class is associated with more personality maladjustment than placement in a special class, (3) educable individuals located in the community show susceptibility for personal maladjustment, (4) the retarded tend to have a more unrealistic picture of their own abilities, and (5) the retarded seem to respond well to social reinforcement.

An individual's view of his own capabilities is founded to a large degree on his history of success and failure. If a child has not had an opportunity to succeed in school activities and has constantly failed, for example, a complex network of antagonisms will develop with the result that the youngster will eventually exhibit a general dislike for anything associated with school, begin to view himself as inadequate, and develop some hostility toward authority figures such as school teachers.

Factors which have particular relevance to the special-education teacher as attempts are made to foster good emotional development and mental health include:

1 *Helping the retarded to develop a positive, realistic view of themselves*
2 *Assisting them in understanding how to employ healthy adjustive mechanisms in various situations*
3 *Providing experiences which will allow for the development and acceptance of reasonable goals and objectives*
4 *Assisting them to develop the capabilities for controlling impulsive behavior*

Figure 9-1 illustrates the interrelationship that can occur between these factors, shows the type of behavior which often results from a person not being able to satisfy his needs, and suggests possible procedures for dealing with potential difficulties which, in turn, have direct implications for fostering mental health.

This figure indicates that behavior is goal-directed and the result of a desire to satisfy needs. Certain goals are highly positive, and the need for achieving them is high. Other goals do not have as positive a valence. For example, because of peer pressure a child may have an intense desire to learn how to ride a bicycle; whereas he may not view learning long division with the same degree of positiveness. Each of us is often frustrated in achieving goals because the necessary repertoire of skills has not been developed, and, therefore, we do not have the requirements needed to circumvent or penetrate obstacles which often arise and make the achievement of these goals difficult or impossible. The mentally retarded are constantly faced with this problem. Most frequently the obstacle or barrier of intellectual subnormality prohibits their satisfying goals which, unwittingly, they often consider to be highly realistic in terms of their abilities.

The diagram also suggests that each of us has a certain level of tolerance for frustration and tension. When this level is reached or exceeded, excessive frustration will result in the need for tension to be released through some type of adjustive or defensive behavior. In a sense, then, the organism decides to use any of a variety of mechanisms as a means for protecting the integrity of self because the original and desired goal could not be satisfied. Aggression, substitution, withdrawal, projection, suppression, and reaction formation

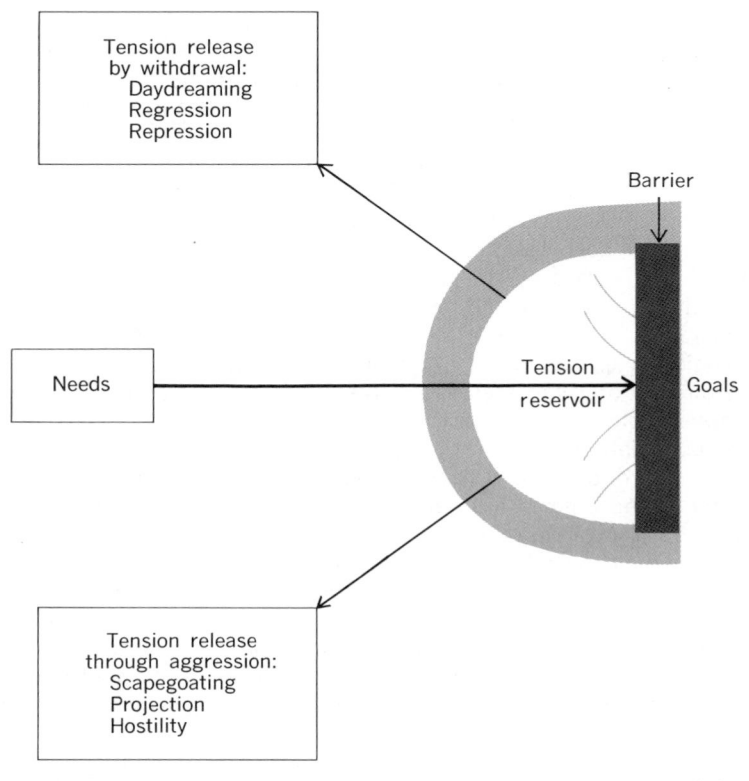

FIGURE 9-1 *Examples of behavior resulting from tension produced by frustrated needs. (From: G. M. Blair, R. S. Jones, and R. H. Simpson, Educational Psychology. New York: The Macmillan Company, 1962, p. 170. Used with permission by the publishers.)*

illustrate some of the types of adjustive mechanisms people employ to relieve this tension.

The components of the behavioral network diagrammed in Figure 9-1 have important educational implications. Although the system is a dynamic one, constantly changing and undergoing alteration, the special-class teacher will find it helpful to consider the factors of this system and their relationship to instructional methodology in classes for the retarded.

NEEDS AND GOALS   The types of needs which the mentally retarded have are basically no different from those of the intellectually normal. Attention, affection, activity, acceptance, and success illustrate only some of the needs characteristic of all populations of children. Among the strongest of these needs, the mentally retarded feel an intense desire to blend into the social matrix and not stand out as being different. This wish is clear and obvious among high school educable children. These youngsters usually show extreme concern over the possibility of making a social *faux pas* and, because of their apprehension, do all in their power to avoid situations in which a "social goof" might occur. At the same time, the retarded have the same need as the normal to be accepted by their chronological age peer group. These needs are strong, although the motivation for achieving them often becomes diminished after repeated failure.

Goals held by the mentally retarded for themselves are commonly unreasonable and more consistent with the types of objectives characteristic of their intellectually normal peers of the same chronological age. It is not at all atypical for older retarded youngsters to desire for and consider themselves capable of eventually becoming lawyers, physicians, or teachers. When unrealistic goals are held for an extended period of time, even under optimum circumstances, the influence of a program designed specifically to help them reconsider altering these goals will have little impact and most often meet with increased perseveration and rigidity. This is a common problem among the older educable population.

To illustrate this point, the author worked with a teen-age boy whose primary occupational desire was to become a concert drummer. This lad, who was also legally blind, had held this ambition for a number of years. The teacher of the class considered attempting to alter this unrealistic goal held by the child as a worthwhile objective. A program was designed to assist him in restructuring his occupational aims so that they were more consistent with his capabilities. The reading period was devoted to reading about occupations which were more consistent with his potential; the occupational education period included activities that would help him learn about possible positions for which he could qualify, and the individual and group counseling sessions held with this boy were designed to stimulate him to reconsider his occupational objectives.

At the end of the school year, a summarization session was held. The boy volunteered to have himself used as an illustration in the final class on occupational education. The class decided to make three lists. The first list contained all those skills that were needed by a concert drummer; the second list contained all the problems which would make it impossible for this boy to ever realize his occupational goal; and the third list was made up of all the skills that he had which would assist him in becoming a concert performer. As the lists developed, members of the class spontaneously decided that their close friend should reconsider his occupational objectives. As this opinion was expressed throughout the class, the boy listened intently to the suggestions of his classmates. At the appropriate time, the teacher decided that the boy seemed to be grasping the message and asked him to summarize his feelings on the matter. With great delight, he acknowledged the thoughtfulness of his fellow classmates in considering his problem and, in the face of overwhelming data to the contrary, indicated that their deliberations had provided the stimulation that he needed. He ended by saying that he now was determined and would devote all his efforts to become the best concert drummer in the country.

This situation, although humorous and somewhat unfortunate, is not atypical among retarded children. Their long-term goals are often extremely unreasonable, and they usually have no accurate perception of the short-term, intermediate goals on which an individual needs to focus in order to satisfy the more long-range objectives.

BARRIERS The mentally retarded face a variety of barriers which provide obstructions to the achievement of their goals. Perhaps the most obvious barrier is intellectual subnormality along with any associated physical and health problems. These might be considered primary difficulties. There are, however, a constellation of secondary barriers that also impede the satisfaction of goals. These barriers, mostly social and psychological, result from the conflict which exists between the child's capabilities and society's expectations of him. The educable mentally retarded typically do not stand out in the community, and because they meet minimum demands of cultural acceptability, most people expect them to achieve and behave in a manner characteristic of the general population. Being located in such an environment, wherein society expects one to achieve as others although not aware of any intellectual or physical weakness, could cause any number of psychosocial difficulties. Factors such as self-derogation, reduced tolerance for frustration, antisocial behavior, regression to earlier and more satisfying stages of development, and overdependence on family members are often observed in the retarded who are associated with such a situation. Each of these factors could be considered a barrier to the successful completion of goals.

To speak in unscientific terms, the capacity of a child's tension reservoir is important and directly related to his emotional development and mental health. The amount of tension each of us is able to tolerate varies every day and is directly related to specific idiosyncratic circumstances. At times one can be extremely tolerant of frustrating situations; on other days it might be more difficult to deal effectively with tension-provoking situations. The retarded seem to have a lower tolerance for frustration and tension. The reason for this can be related directly to their frequent history of failure in all areas. When people are unsuccessful in a task, there is a tendency to avoid future experiences with such activities; and, in fact, many people feel so strongly about their lack of success that they are openly aggressive or hostile and wish never again to engage in that type of activity. Because the barriers are often so substantial with the mentally retarded, it is reasonable that they are often less tolerant of frustration and tension.

BEHAVIOR RESULTING FROM FRUSTRATION When thwarted toward successfully completing a goal, an individual can either make another frontal attack, attempting to penetrate or circumvent the barriers, or, after repeated failures, he can search for a reasonable substitute for the goals which he finds unattainable. Mentally retarded children should be encouraged to attempt goals which are reasonable. Tension can be released, however, by engaging in some type of adaptive behavior. Withdrawal and aggression of some variety constitute the two major types of adjustive mechanisms. It is often necessary for each of us to make use of mechanisms of this sort in certain situations. There is nothing inappropriate or unhealthy about their use so long as the adjustive strategies are not employed more frequently than the goal-satisfying behavior. Psychological equilibrium within the organism will result as tension is released through the judicious employment of adjustive mechanisms of behavior.

IMPLICATIONS FOR EDUCATION Some of the implications for teaching that emerge from this discussion include the following:

1 *The teacher should assess the types and extent of each child's specific desires and identify those which seem to be in most urgent need of attention.*
2 *Some attempt should be given to surveying the goals of each child. In many instances their long-term goals will be unrealistic. The teacher should minimize long-term goal striving and place emphasis on a series of well-defined short-term goals which are reasonable and which, predictably, will allow each child to be successful. As the youngsters achieve each successive short-term goal, they will gain some ability to see the direction in which these goals lead.*
3 *Attempts should be made to minimize the influence of the barriers. The intellectual and physical barriers can be reduced only in part, and any impact that the teacher can make in these areas will be minimal. Some attempt, however, can be made in the school program to reduce secondary barriers. The teacher's influence can be substantial if she judiciously manipulates a child's environment to reduce the influence of those barriers resulting from differences between his ability and the expectations of society. The child can be shielded from discouraging and disappointing situations until a tolerance for and capability in handling dissonant situations has been developed. The child will begin to see himself as a more capable*

person, able to handle difficult situations in a more appropriate, systematic, and healthy way.

4 The teacher needs to be aware of the nature of each child's tension reservoir. Some general predictions concerning the potential level of frustration each child will be able to tolerate under various kinds of circumstances are required by the teacher each day. This frequent informal assessment of the level of frustration should be combined with some general prediction of how far to allow each child to go in potentially frustrating situations before the teacher decides to intervene. For example, if a child seems to be having some difficulty in using scissors to cut paper, some judgment has to be made by the teacher as to how far the child should be allowed to go.

To reduce tension, an individual must either achieve the goal being sought or engage in some type of socially accepted and situationally appropriate adjustive behavior. The retarded must learn that aggressive behavior and hostility are inappropriate responses to frustrating situations. Similarly, certain types of withdrawal, used in the extreme and continuously, are not mentally healthy ways of reducing frustration and tension. The teacher, therefore, will need to provide the children with experiences which will help them understand other possible socially appropriate behaviors which can be used in various situations. For example, when someone teases the children, they need to be able to determine if striking out at the individual, cursing, worrying about what has been said, verbally attacking, or leaving the scene are appropriate reactions to the situation. For mental health reasons, and to support emotional development, the teacher cannot consider the task one of satisfying the child's immediate needs. Instead, the job is one of manipulating the social and physical environment in such a way that the child builds up certain optimum levels of tension, desires, and anticipations. These are subsequently channeled in the direction of the child's learning skills and aimed at solving those problems which will lead to a reduction in tension. The teacher should strive for tension reduction in those socially appropriate ways which are consistent with good mental health principles and which lead to the child enhancing his response repertoire so that problems can be solved in an effective and efficient way.

Social awareness and behavior

Many of the educable mentally retarded children in the public schools come from lower socioeconomic situations in which standards of acceptance in social interaction are often at variance with the general mores and folkways of society. Lying, cheating, stealing, and the use of profane language are often considered acceptable behavior in the more depressed environments. Children in these surroundings are frequent observers of various immoral acts by adults with whom they have direct association. It is not surprising, therefore, that the middle-class teacher of the retarded is often shocked at the pronouncements and demonstrations of behavior of these young, deprived educable children. It is difficult for many classroom teachers to understand and accept this type of behavior.

Without pursuing the philosophical arguments concerning whether the special-class teacher has a responsibility for attempting to change the cultural patterns of the educable retarded children from a deprived environment, most everyone would agree that some attempt should be made to help the children become aware of two interrelated facets of our social order: (1) the mores and folkways of our society, including the legal, moral, and social expectations of the citizenry, and (2) the reasons for and the need to become sensitive to the feelings of others. Each of these factors is an important interacting component of social awareness and should be given attention in all subject areas and at each level in the instructional program for the retarded.

Specific focus in the socialization program for the mentally retarded is suggested in the following areas. Procedures and practices for implementing their understanding by the children will be detailed later.

1 The students must develop an understanding of reasons for laws and rules in our society and the implications of breaking or violating these established standards.

2 The retarded child must develop an awareness of the need to be alert to the attitudes, feelings, and opinions of others and learn to respect these opinions as sources of possible additional information which could be of direct value to them personally. This type of awareness can be developed most easily by engaging the child in various activities within a very restricted social circumstance. For example, it would be inappropriate to expect the child to gain an understanding of these concepts by engaging in experiences with a large group of people before having had the opportunity to interact with smaller groups. We must first be interested in each child's understanding and respecting the feelings and attitudes of the one sitting next to him in the class, tentatively understanding the mores associated with effective social interaction with this person, and then finally generalizing this principle to others around him within a large social context. It is advisable, therefore, that the children be given initial experiences in a rather restricted milieu, gradually enlarging their sphere of contacts to include more complex associations among people.

3 Concepts associated with personal care and good grooming need to be stressed throughout the school program. The children should

learn to care for their personal needs so that they are viewed as attractive and better accepted as compatriots and models of appropriate behavior by their fellow students.

4 *The value in the children's showing mannerly behavior, honesty, and truthfulness needs to be stressed. One approach to encouraging this type of behavior is to place particular emphasis on the personal advantages of such behavior. Children at all ages are sensitive to what their peers think of them. By judiciously manipulating the classroom environment, the teacher can place certain children in direct contact with other children who will often be able to serve as models and, in fact, idols for the one who is socially unsophisticated. Through propinquity and with appropriate rewards provided by the teacher to those exhibiting model behavior, the more social child will continue appropriate behavior; the asocial child will begin to see the value in modeling his behavior after the child being reinforced.*

Perhaps in no other area is the teacher more of a manipulator of the environment than in the area of social development. It is important that the teacher learn to accept the often repulsive social and personal characteristics of some retarded children and begin to provide a sequential and systematic program aimed at shaping more desirable behavior. As a side benefit, by example there is always the possibility that the child will communicate some of these social skills to other members of his family. The first responsibility of the schools is to the children. Nevertheless, it is entirely proper to use each child's developing skills as a wedge into the family in an effort to begin the arduous process of altering family patterns of behavior.

METHODS FOR TEACHING SOCIAL, PERSONAL, AND EMOTIONAL SKILLS

Behavior is the result of a person interacting with his environment. Its continued occurrence is dependent on the individual's expectation that the environment will in some way reinforce the behavior and that the reinforcing agent is of some value to the individual. In studying this complex process, psychologists have attempted to alter, manipulate, or control the environment in various ways in an effort to modify an individual's behavior. The term *behavior modification* has been used to describe this approach. The studies conducted in this area with retarded youngsters have been promising and have caused educators to reconsider the direction of teaching methodology. Much of the research in this area has been reviewed by Krasner and Ullmann (1965). The following discussion presents certain broad tenets of behavior modification as applicable to the retarded.

Reinforcement and reward are methodological components required to modify social, personal, and emotional behavior. Long-term modification toward desired behavior requires shaping by rewarding successive approximations which are directed toward the desired goal. The teacher will have certain long- and short-term goals in mind for each child as well as for the total class. As the children closely approximate this desired behavior, it should be strengthened by reward. The child's behavior at first may be quite random and not intentionally directed toward the goal established by the teacher. Whenever this behavior approximates the goal, it should be rewarded. Gradually, the children will begin to realize the advantages of behaving in a certain way because of the rewards. It should be pointed out that rewards are most effective if scheduled intermittently as the child moves toward the goal. Rewarding or reinforcing successive approximations leads to shaping of desired behavior. Rewarding appropriate behavior by providing the children with tangible objects such as candy or trinkets is not necessary. It was pointed out earlier that social rewards, such as verbal statements of praise, are highly valued by the mentally retarded.

Caution should be exercised so that undesirable behavior is not rewarded. This occurs frequently, particularly in cases involving discipline. Many children, whether intellectually retarded or not, seek attention by misbehaving. All too frequently teachers, as well as parents, reward misbehavior by calling attention to it. Children seeking attention are reinforced in this behavior, and, in fact, the behavior is strengthened by acknowledging its presence. In most instances, the preferred technique for handling a social or behavior problem is to ignore the person misbehaving. Certain reprehensible circumstances require that the teacher remove the child from the environment or administer some type of punishment. Punishment should always be administered in ways which have some significance to the child. Every attempt should be made to control the possibility that the child is being rewarded for misbehavior.

To illustrate this latter point, on one occasion when dinner guests were visiting the author's home, the youngest child in the family began to misbehave at the table. The crying and undesirable behavior became offensive enough that another member of the family went to the cookie jar, withdrew a chocolate frosted cookie, and handed it to the crying child. After the cookie had been consumed, the child immediately resorted to the same type of misbehavior previously exhibited. The effect was to reward the unwanted behavior in a way that was quite satisfying to the young child. Fortunately, other observers present at dinner held their composure long enough to point out the fallacy in strengthening this behavior pattern, and, although the dinner was completed with substantial background noise, the unwanted behavior was soon obliterated by withholding attention and reward.

Procedures for helping retarded children understand and develop satisfactory social, personal, and emotional behavior are often characterized by the teacher telling or lecturing the children about how and why they are to behave in a certain fashion. Even with the best intentions in mind, this method of instruction will have only minimal impact for several reasons. First, lecturing assumes that the children have developed the language and conceptual skills needed to understand abstract notions. Moreover, lecturing is a poor strategy since opportunities are not provided for the children to look at themselves and evaluate their own performance. The importance of each child to be given opportunities to engage in activities which will demonstrate reasons for and against behaving in a certain fashion in various circumstances cannot be overstated.

Acceptable patterns of behavior will be most rapidly and effectively acquired by using the dual influence of models and differential reinforcement. Children will value and reflect the behavior of models whom they consider to be of high prestige. Moreover, they will react more favorably to the reinforcement provided by these "high-prestige" individuals than to those dispensed by a "low-prestige" person. In contrast to the less effective teaching strategy of lecturing, the teacher will find that the behavior of children can be dramatically changed and subsequently controlled when models are used in ways which allow for imitation by the youngsters. For example, if a high-prestige person begins to clean up the classroom, within a short time those students who value the model will begin to conform, and they, in turn, will serve as models for their other classmates. When this behavior is differentially rewarded by the model, the acquisition of the new behavior patterns is facilitated. There is, then, a clear teaching advantage in making use of imitation in concert with reward to modify general or specific behavioral patterns.

Developing procedures for presenting concepts related to social, personal, and emotional development is difficult because of the abstract nature of the material to be covered and the lack of effectiveness that the retarded have for operating at a level other than the concrete. It is also of significance that effective social, personal, and emotional development requires that the individual be flexible and have the ability to understand and apply principles in various situations. The important point here is that the teacher should not be satisfied with developing an automaton who can mechanically apply *the* correct solution to the appropriate problem. These situations demand an individual who understands principles, morals, and the variety of appropriate behaviors that are suitable for a particular situation at one specific moment. For example, if a child learns to withdraw whenever he encounters conflict with another individual, he will have difficulty satisfying certain requirements of employment when faced with a questioning foreman. If a retarded child is "programmed" to respond with, "Good morning," in a robotlike fashion any time greeted before noon, he may find himself in an embarrassing position when another type of response might be more appropriate. Such errors quickly alert others to weaknesses and are emphasized out of proportion and used by insensitive associates for their own amusement and advantage.

Instructional activities in these areas should provide the retarded with ample opportunities for success. Implicit in what has been said is the need to structure activities so that each child's predicted weaknesses will not be manifested, but that some obvious demonstration of success will be observed and appropriately rewarded. It is important, then, that activities be chosen with care and for short duration initially so that opportunities for failure are minimized.

The types of activities in which retarded children can be engaged should emanate directly from the diagnostic hunches of the teacher. As was true in the academic areas, certain children will show weaknesses or strengths in specific areas of social, personal, and emotional development. For example, one child may be particularly weak in interacting with authority figures and in accepting their directions; whereas the same child may interact very effectively with people his own age. Another child when facing a particularly difficult personal situation might respond by striking out at an individual; whereas the child sitting next to him may withdraw when facing the same situation. These patterns of variation between and within children under different circumstances will eventually become obvious to the teacher. The learning situation must be structured to allow the children to gain value in considering a range of possible responses, each of which should be dramatized in some fashion. Most teachers will not have psychometric data available to give direction concerning the areas in which each child is strong or weak. It is necessary, therefore, that the teacher become an astute observer of behavior in order to provide each child with proper experiences which are aimed at their developing understanding and manifesting a more acceptable performance in areas of particular weakness.

Commonality exists among the areas of personal, social, and emotional development. The teaching procedures appropriate for developing social skills are equally appropriate in fostering personal and emotional development. The following describes specific methods teachers might use to work with the educable retarded in these areas.

Sociodrama

To produce appropriate social behavior, the best method would be to set up actual social situations and systematically reward desired responses, ignoring undesired response patterns. Obviously, the teacher does not have the resources available to provide an actual social situation in all the areas in which the retarded require development and training. It is possible, however, to duplicate these situations to some degree in the classroom through the use of sociodrama. This technique will allow the teacher to call on the full array of reinforcement and imitation procedures that characterize behavior modification techniques. Because of the relative realism of this approach, sociodrama would seem to offer a particularly promising approach in classes for the retarded; therefore, the technique will be discussed in some detail.

Follow-up studies done with the retarded suggest that their most pronounced weaknesses lie in areas of social adjustment and not in how well they handle the mechanics of employment. The retarded seem to consistently have difficulty in all employee-employee, employee-employer relationships, but especially in relationships with authority figures. Systematic attempts have not been made to pinpoint those areas of the school curriculum which are not reflecting the need for greater devotion being given to problems of social adjustment during the school experiences of the retarded. It legitimately can be hypothesized that an obvious weakness of most secondary programs is that the retarded are not given opportunities to practice responding in situations similar to those with which they will eventually find themselves associated in the community. Apparently, characteristics of actual community situations are either totally foreign to the young retarded adult or the youngsters are unable to transfer understandings presented during classroom instruction periods into practice. Because of this apparent weakness in the typical school experience of the retarded, sociodrama has been suggested as a technique to facilitate the acquisition of social concepts and skills under more practical circumstances (Kirk and Johnson, 1951; Blackhurst, 1966).

Sociodrama, also called role playing, is the dramatization of some social situation with individuals assuming certain roles of the characters involved in the situation. The process involves four steps: (1) identifying a specific problem; (2) delineation of the roles to be played, description of the specific problem situation to be enacted, and selection of the participants to play various roles; (3) dramatization of the problem and alternative solutions; and (4) a comprehensive discussion with a reenactment of other possible solutions if necessary.

IDENTIFYING THE PROBLEM AND DELINEATING THE ROLES In the beginning when the students are becoming familiar with this technique, it is necessary that dramatizations involve relatively simple, specific problems. Since the procedure will be new to the students, they should select a precise topic from their own experiences which could be easily dramatized. Using this process of selection at the beginning will encourage more spontaneity from the students and cause less embarrassment. As experience is gained in using the technique, problems for dramatization at a later time will evolve in a variety of ways. A student may have had a certain experience at home which is found to be particularly perplexing. Other problems could arise as a result of group discussions in or out of school, from the teacher making certain suggestions, or emanating out of the reading done by the students in other subject areas. In every case the teacher should have the specific goals for each session clearly formulated. The overall aim is to assist the retarded in developing greater social awareness and more healthy emotional stability as a result of being engaged in the actual experience of the process of solving problems.

After a specific problem has been defined, the group should identify characteristics of the various personalities to be involved in the plot. Clarification and simplification on this point should be encouraged by the teacher asking questions such as, "What is this person like?" or "How could we describe this individual?" Gradually, the problem will come more clearly into focus for the students, the characters and the nature of their roles will be clearly defined and understood, and certain students should be selected or volunteer to participate in the dramatization of the roles previously defined.

After selection, the students involved in the various roles should get together with the teacher to discuss their parts and plan the manner in which they intend to enact their role. At this point the teacher should impose any limits felt necessary. These limits are imposed to help the students focus on the specific problem and not run too far afield. Encouraging the role players to maintain the intended direction can be aided by using only one scene or a single situation such as might occur in a living room, lunchroom, or during a coffee break at work. Choosing such a scene or situation will help to establish more circumscribed components for the dramatization. At the same time, the teacher should discuss with the nonparticipants in the class how to observe and what they should look for in the dramatization. Before the role players begin, the players and observers will find it helpful to describe the setting in detail and elaborate on any specifics of the problem which they intend to emphasize.

THE DRAMATIZATION The sociodrama can begin most easily by one of the players asking a question or making a declarative statement to another player. Such a statement might express an opinion which has the potential for stimulating discussion more easily than if the statement is neutral. To get the dramatization moving initially, it may be necessary for the teacher to feed lines to the students or coach them when the enactment loses its value or tapers off. The behavior of the participants and their conversation should be allowed to flow freely from their own experiences, and the dialogue should not have been previously practiced nor memorized. Members presenting the characterizations should feel free to express their thoughts and feelings frankly during the enactments and in the discussions which follow. No pressure should be imposed on the members to respond in any certain manner. When such pressure is brought to bear, the value of sociodrama is reduced.

The major objective of this technique is to clarify issues concerning a certain problem and to help the students consider various types of behavior resulting from the dramatizations. Clearly, the role playing should not concentrate on "play acting"; instead, focus should be on the kinds of behavior exhibited by members playing the roles. The players should gradually begin to realize that problems can be appropriately handled in a variety of possible ways.

POSTDRAMATIZATION DISCUSSION After a situation has been dramatized, members of the group should discuss the enactment and consider all the ramifications of the solution presented. These should include a discussion of the interpersonal behavior accompanying the solution, the potential effectiveness of the solution, and the reactions of the observers. Criticisms by the class or the teacher should be directed at the role which was played and not at the acting qualities of the role players. The teacher should act as a friendly supervisor and one who reflects attitudes as the students discuss the earlier dramatization among themselves. All the players and observers should be given a chance to make suggestions of alternative ways to solve the problem. This discussion should be followed by another enactment which either redramatizes the former solution or develops an alternative explanation to the situation. Members of the group should switch roles in order to obtain a better understanding of the types of situations others were in, situations which might have been misunderstood by fellow participants and observers. The spontaneity encouraged by this procedure will help the students gain experience in meeting new problem situations and encourage behavioral flexibility.

Following the final enactment of a problem for the day, the teacher should summarize what has been learned from the dramatization and generalize the solution to other similar situations. The relevance of the various solutions for solving any problems the students might encounter should be indicated. Any similarity among solutions should be focused upon in order to help the students develop an appropriate generalized style of behavior.

DIAGNOSTIC VALUE As the students develop skill in using this technique, more complex and sensitive topics can be considered. With the advantage of a comfortable and nonthreatening environment which has the support of the teacher, the retarded children will begin to show less hesitation in expressing their real attitudes and feelings.

Each student should have the opportunity to assume a variety of roles. Here again, however, the teacher will need to consider each child's strengths and weaknesses and place those youngsters who need to develop skills in certain areas into roles which will allow them to experience solving problems in these less well developed areas. Sociodrama, therefore, is as much a diagnostic procedure as a technique for developing social and emotional maturity among the participants. Through careful observation, the teacher can reliably identify any unique response patterns of the children to certain situations. This information will provide for subsequent manipulations of the child's environment in an intelligent fashion and according to each child's needs.

Dramatization of problems should eventually include individuals other than the students and classmates. As the youngsters engage in sociodrama, they tend to become familiar with the techniques used by their classmates. This behavior sensitivity allows them to predict the responses of other players. Spontaneity is lost because of this awareness, and the value of the technique is reduced. To make situations realistic, other students and adults should be invited to participate in the dramatizations. The object is for the retarded to gain experience by interacting with all segments of society. The teacher, therefore, must make a conscious effort to sequence the order of activities to be encountered by the students and intelligently select other people to cooperate in these activities. It is important, of course, that outside participants be fully aware of the goals and procedures of the dramatization. Eventually, the more experienced mentally retarded child might find himself alone in a dramatization with several intellectually normal or intellectually superior children or adults. The degree to which the child is able to handle everyday situations is the appropriate criterion for evaluating the technique.

SOCIODRAMA WITH THE RETARDED Since the educable mentally retarded will be expected to interact satisfactorily in the community setting, they must have a breadth of experience with others. Cloistering them in a special class during their *entire* schooling experience will work to their disadvantage by not providing them with chances to experience the problems and appropriate behavior which emanates from social and emotional integration into society. Educable children at all levels should be allowed to move beyond the walls of the special class, into a more socially realistic setting, for a portion of the day. This can be effected by locating the retarded in small groups, or as a total class, with teachers whose subject areas do not particularly engender intense competition among students. Teachers of art, music, industrial arts, home economics, and physical education are in a position to substantially assist the mentally retarded in personal and social development.

The special-education teacher has a responsibility to encourage other teachers to include educable retarded children in their programs as much as realistically possible. Sociodrama is a particularly useful approach for the retarded when used in connection with activities in subject areas. A valuable interrelationship between other school areas and the special-education program is possible when other teachers include the retarded in their program. This united effort combines the best of both situations—the practical environment of the regular class and the unique tools and techniques characteristic of the special class. This is particularly true in the case of home economics and industrial arts classes. The unique physical facilities characteristic of these classes provide a realistic setting for the dramatization of problems that eventually will have direct relevance to the retarded child's social or occupational life. In these classrooms, numerous problems can be staged which are particularly unique to the home situation or the industrial situation. The teacher of these subject areas, in consultation with the special-education teacher, has the best situation available to provide a program which will aid the retarded in synthesizing the many facts and concepts to which he has been exposed throughout his school years. This experience, which can be made very practical, will provide another means for evaluating each child's readiness to move toward occupational training or into a specific job situation.

The following list describes certain specific problems about which the mentally retarded often exhibit some confusion. Each of these problems offers a situation which is specific enough to be dramatized, yet each is broad enough to allow for generalization to other situations. The advantage of dramatizing these problems within the industrial arts or home economics laboratory is one of providing as realistic setting as possible.

1 *"My friend Charley says that I don't have to report to the foreman that I broke the bandsaw."*

2 *"If that fellow keeps talking behind my back, I'm going to meet him in the back alley."*

3 *"Bill said that we could take an extra fifteen minutes for lunch without anyone knowing that we were late."*

4 *"When I get tired on the night shift, I go into the bathroom, lock the door, and try to get a few winks of sleep."*

5 *"The best way to find out what you are supposed to do is ask old Bert; he's a good guy and doesn't mind being bothered."*

6 *"What shall I say tomorrow when I'm interviewed for the welding job?"*

7 *"He's making me do the dirty work because I'm an apprentice."*

8 "Herb says that if I don't know how to run a machine not to worry about it because he'll teach me before the foreman finds out."

9 "The reason I'm slower doing my job on the production line is because I have more work to do than the others."

10 "If I get laid off, I'll get back at the boss either by breaking a machine or breaking the windows in his car."

11 "I wonder what would happen if I put a down payment on a new car this month instead of paying the rent?"

12 "If Charley is going to be cross with me when he leaves for work in the morning, I'll get back at him by not giving him a good supper."

13 "I think that I will ignore the baby today and maybe he won't cry so much."

14 "Should I tell the grocer that he made an error in counting my bill? It was in my favor."

15 "I don't know whether to go and get a job because the baby is only six months old."

16 "How can I tell my next door neighbor that I simply don't have time to come over each morning for coffee? I don't want to offend her."

Each of these problems is commonly experienced by the mentally retarded. By using sociodrama in the industrial arts or home economics classroom, the retarded will more realistically experience the variety of problems often characteristic of their situation. Using role playing in these settings provides an opportunity for the retarded to use skills acquired in other classrooms for solving actual problems. Transfer of understandings from one subject-matter area to another, therefore, does not need to be assumed. Moreover, incidental learning does not need to be assumed. This results in the retarded developing a greater understanding of concepts which are often unclear to them and frequently communicated incidentally or by way of a lecture.

Counseling in the classroom

Offering counseling and guidance to children is typically considered to be totally within the domain of the professional counselor. Although people are generally aware of the problems of the retarded, most counselors find that they do not have enough time to work with the retarded in as comprehensive a way as is needed by the youngsters. The guidance counselor in most school systems is most often completely inundated with other responsibilities which involve other members of the school's population. The counseling and guidance needs of the mentally retarded typically are left up to the special-education teacher, unless certain hard-core cases exceed the teacher's professional training and require highly professional advice.

In one sense it is reasonable that the special-education teacher work with the retarded in responding to their counseling and guidance needs; the special-education teachers in all likelihood know the children best. Moreover, most training programs designed to prepare teachers to work with these youngsters include units on counseling the retarded in their programs. Teachers must realize, however, that it is outside their professional responsibility and authority to provide anything other than informal counseling to the retarded. The teacher's knowledge of each child's weaknesses, needs, ambitions, attitudes, and general environment situation in no way suggests that the proper qualifications are held to offer diagnostic or other psychological assistance. In the following discussion, therefore, informal counseling and guidance should be viewed more as an informal discussion period than as a formal counseling session. Those retarded children who are seriously disturbed should be referred for proper psychological or psychiatric assistance.

Informal counseling sessions with the educable mentally retarded will work best when they occur spontaneously and are not contrived. The sessions can be conducted with an entire class, small groups within the class, or with an individual. The topic for discussion should emanate from the students and may frequently occur during the course of instruction in some other area. If the teacher views the problem or topic as important, placing the scheduled lesson aside and moving logically into a more comprehensive discussion of the topic or issue which has been raised should certainly be done. To schedule a certain portion of each day or week for sessions of this type will be relatively unproductive because of a lack of spontaneity and the consideration of problems out of context.

The types of issues discussed in these sessions are similar to those considered in the sociodrama section of this chapter. When all the basic facts of a situation are understood by the group, they should be given ample opportunity to discuss the facts, relate them to existing concepts, and consider possible appropriate alternative responses to the situation. Reactions to the expressions of others should be encouraged. Whenever possible, information and concepts used to solve previously discussed social or personal experiences should be directly related to the current problem or issue.

The teacher should realize that these sessions will be most beneficial when their structure and direction is flexible. This is particularly true when some authority figure is present. Since the major objective of the counseling sessions is to have the children gain a better perception of themselves, help resolve their own difficulties, and strengthen their weaknesses, the teacher does more harm than good by lecturing or giving an opinion at inappropriate times. The suggested role for the teacher in these sessions should be one of providing the necessary reflection or clarification on points expressed by the students as well as subtly manipulating the discussion through the judicious use of leading questions. This manipulation of the conversation will help the youngsters to see relationships between points discussed and the problem. In addition, this strategy will help the children gain experience in generating alternative ways for reacting to problems. Only when asked directly should the teacher express an opinion; even in these situations alternative suggestions should be provided. The teacher, thus, should never be placed in a position of making a decision for a child concerning a social, personal, or emotional problem. Instead, the children should be instructed to generate a variety of solutions to problems and evaluate each alternative in terms of its relevance and appropriateness.

As was true with sociodrama, counseling sessions in the classroom require that certain ground rules be understood and accepted by all the participants. Regulations such as not interrupting someone else who is talking, not being critical of an opinion or point of view, being accepting of the behavior of others, and recognizing that there is often more than one correct answer to a problem, illustrate basic ground rules necessary for a successful group discussion.

Because of the informal and spontaneous nature of these sessions, the teacher should be prepared and willing to abandon her prepared lesson when an issue seems important enough. Although this approach may seem most valuable with older mentally retarded children, a modified version of this technique will work effectively with primary- and intermediate-age retarded children. The types of problems discussed by the younger children should be narrowly described and involve concrete problems and illustrations. Further, the number of possible interactions within a group should be kept as small as possible for the young children. The author has observed upper-level primary and intermediate children participating in group discussions of this sort and considering with eagerness topics such as, "How should we act during our free time?," "What should I do when someone says that I am dumb or look funny?," and "Should I learn how to smoke like my friends?" Older retarded children at the upper intermediate and secondary levels will profit by considering topics such as, "What should I do when a boy makes advances toward me?," "How can I get my mother to allow me to wear cosmetics?," "Why can't I quit school and go get a job even though I don't know how to read?"

Counseling in the classroom is an effective method for helping the retarded to develop social, personal, and emotional awareness and stability. The teacher must capitalize on the specific and immediate concerns of the children and allow them to initiate and engage in this type of discussion when beneficial. In no case should the teacher be considered the leader and dictate the direction of the discussion. It is true, however, that some manipulation, through the use of appropriate questions, must be done so that focus is maintained and the results of the discussion are profitable to the children. The solutions decided upon by the children can be reinforced by introducing them as topics for sociodrama at a later date. In this way the children can check on the validity of their deliberations. If viewed by them as constituting a suitable response to the issue or problem, the retarded will gain increased confidence and be eager to continue participating in the information discussion sessions. There is not only habilitative potential in these discussions, but the nature of the issues and problems raised by the children has diagnostic value because it allows the teacher to appraise any specific concerns or interests of the children at a certain moment in time.

Other teaching considerations

The following points have a direct bearing on the effectiveness of instruction in social, personal, and emotional development of the mentally retarded:

1 *Liberal use should be made of films and other audio-visual aids. These aids will allow a child to experience a variety of typical and atypical personal, social, and emotional situations on repeated occasions and, by stabilizing stimuli, allow each child to analyze and reanalyze faulty behavior. Moreover, use of audio equipment gives each child a chance to monitor his own responses and reflect on their appropriateness.*

2 *Throughout instruction in these areas, emphasis should be placed on appropriate behavior, with inappropriate behavior deemphasized. The mentally retarded tend to remember best what not to do instead of what constitutes a correct response. Whenever appropriate, the teacher should use models, idols, and authority figures to emphasize important points or correct behavior.*

3 *The older mentally retarded children should see a clear association between vocational requirements and appropriate social and emotional behavior. Correct behavior should both be understood and satisfactorily applied to various situations.*

4 *Each child's experiences and activities should be based on what the teacher predicts will constitute the child's future social and occupational situation. The program, therefore, may differ substantially for each child.*

5 *Professional advice from school psychologists, guidance counselors, clergymen, local health officers, and other experts should be sought by the teacher whenever needed.*

6 *Opportunities to interact in practical situations with children and adults who are intellectually normal should be provided the retarded.*

7 *For the more mature, some variety of self-government within the classroom will help to demonstrate the various dimensions and ad-*

vantages of government. This practical involvement will serve to encourage students to participate in social and community affairs.

SELECTED REFERENCES

Blackhurst, A. E.: "Sociodrama for the Adolescent Retarded," *Training School Bulletin,* vol. 63, no. 3, 1966, pp. 136–142.

Cureton, T. K.: *Physical Fitness and Dynamic Health,* The Dial Press, Inc., New York, 1965.

Goldstein, H.: "Social and Occupational Adjustment," in H. A. Stevens and R. Heber (eds.), *Mental Retardation: A Review of Research,* The University of Chicago Press, Chicago, 1964, pp. 214–258.

Gregg, A. E.: "Criminal Behavior of Mentally Retarded Adults," *American Journal of Mental Deficiency,* vol. 52, 1948, pp. 370–374.

Harrington, M.: "The Problem of the Defective Delinquent," *Mental Hygiene,* vol. 19, 1935, pp. 429–438.

Heber, Rick: "Personality," in H. A. Stevens and R. Heber (eds.), *Mental Retardation: A Review of Research,* The University of Chicago Press, Chicago, 1964, pp. 143–174.

Kirk, S. A. and Johnson, G. O.: *Educating the Retarded Child,* Houghton Mifflin Company, Boston, 1951, pp. 336–341.

Krasner, L. and Ullmann, L. P.: *Research in Behavior Modification: New Developments and Implications,* Holt, Rinehart and Winston, Inc., New York, 1965.

Kvaraceus, W. C.: "Delinquency: A By-Product of the Schools?" *School and Society,* vol. 59, 1944, pp. 350–351.

Poucher, G. E.: "The Role of a Juvenile Court Psychiatric Clinic in the Management of the Defective Delinquent," *American Journal of Mental Deficiency,* vol. 56, 1952, pp. 275–282.

Ullmann, L. P. and Krasner, L.: *Case Studies in Behavior Modification,* Holt, Rinehart and Winston, Inc., New York, 1965.

Wallin, J. E. W.: *The Education of Handicapped Children,* Houghton Mifflin Company, Boston, 1924.

preparation for gainful employment

The complete introduction of the educable mentally retarded into the community as active participants must be given serious consideration by the public schools. The increased emphasis by institutions for accepting only the most severely retarded and disallowing placement for those persons less retarded, unless extenuating circumstances are present, dramatizes this need. It is not enough that the educable retarded simply fade into the ranks of the unskilled and semiskilled workers; it is important that they become socially and occupationally prepared to function as contributors within the community setting. Social and personal considerations were focused upon in the preceding chapter; the material discussed in this section will be devoted to those components of independent living related to occupational development.

The relative instability of the labor market due to increased production efficiency and the many demands imposed upon workers is substantial enough to restrict the occupational flexibility of even the intellectually normal. Now that specific training is required for even the most elementary task, employers are hesitant to employ those whose work careers are checkered or who show a restricted potential for maximum efficiency. The escalation in production and automation of most industries has reduced the wide spectrum of unskilled and semiskilled positions heretofore available to those less well endowed intellectually. The parallel increases in service occupations have been filled by individuals brighter than the educable mentally retarded. Such persons demonstrate a greater ability to understand and deal with the semitechnical requirements of the service professions. These employment trends have resulted in fewer positions being available to the educable mentally retarded and a higher incidence of competitive failure and job skipping among these individuals.

PRAGMATIC CONSIDERATIONS FOR OCCUPATIONAL EDUCATION

The initial thrust for preparing the retarded for gainful employment should not occur suddenly, just as the youngster reaches the high school work-study program. Instead, throughout the child's special-class experience the subtle flavor of occupational skill development required for mastery of appropriate work situations should permeate the program's activities. The child should be encouraged to first participate in parallel play with others and develop those perceptual-motor skills required to learn the tool subjects. All of these experiences should be geared to the youngster's eventually becoming firmly situated in a rational occupational setting; throughout the program, the prime goal should be on successful job placement and community living. Whereas in the primary and intermediate grades the emphasis was on developing skills in subject matter areas, the work-study program during the late junior high and senior high years should make practical use of these academic skills in a more vocationally oriented program. The diagram on page 227 illustrates the relative amount of emphasis that the tool subjects and the occupational skills should receive at various stages of the special-education program.

Most of the classroom time during the primary years is devoted to helping the retarded gain skill in the basic tool subjects. Instructional emphasis should be on reading, arithmetic, perceptual-motor development, communication, and social and personal adjustment. At the same time, during these early school years, some attention should be given to those specific work skills which are vital for subsequent successful employment. To help the young to develop sensitivity and skill in this area, for example, the teacher should expect

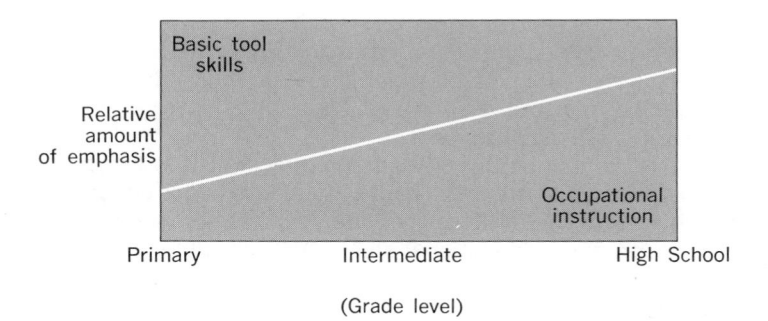

FIGURE 10-1 *Relationship between emphasis in basic tool subjects and occupational instruction.*

class members to assume a major responsibility for maintaining the classroom. Specific jobs should be assigned to the youngsters, and all the ramifications of conducting the jobs should be discussed during the instructional periods. Even during the early school years, the children must become aware of proper job behavior. It is at this time, therefore, that they develop attitudes and concepts concerning proper care, completing a job, respect for others, satisfying responsibilities, and appropriate responses to authority figures. All this instruction should be aimed at the children developing foundation skills which can be further elaborated as the special-class program unfolds.

During the intermediate grades, after certain elementary tool skills have been developed, relatively more attention should be devoted to occupational instruction than was in the early primary grades. At this stage of instruction, the children should be exposed to a more realistic occupational environment characteristic of the industrial arts laboratory and the home economics classroom. In these classrooms the children have opportunities to make use of the tool skills which have constituted the core of the instruction in the special-class program. Perhaps at no other time than during the intermediate grades is there so crucial a need for the teacher to blend components of the special class into other aspects of the school program. At this very time, the children begin to "try their wings" and are at a propitious period for learning about the practical application of the tool skills. Children in intermediate classes often raise the question, "Why do I have to learn this stuff?" Precisely at this point, the teacher must clearly demonstrate the practical application of and need for developing skills such as word attack, learning how to carry in addition and borrow in subtraction, communicating with adults, or being able to write legibly.

As the retarded move through the school program and are

placed in a work-study situation at the high school level, ostensibly they should be at a point at which the basic tool skills have developed to the eleven- or twelve-year level. General achievement should be at the level of grades five or six.

The impact of an earlier assumption which is felt at this point is that the children have had a sequential instructional program designed to develop those tool subjects which are relevant to their predicted future occupational and social circumstance. If somewhere in the child's prior instruction too much time was devoted to the development of a skill which has relatively little importance to his future, or too little time was spent on concerns of greater urgency, the child and teacher will find themselves faced with a very difficult problem. It is during the high school program that the educable mentally retarded have an opportunity to use the previously developed skills in a practical way outside the cloistered environment of the special classroom. If they have not developed the skills required for reading, for example, the opportunity for becoming integrated into the community is substantially reduced. If, on the other hand, skills have been mastered at a level adequate enough for a satisfactory performance in the demands required of occupational and social situations, the child will have a more promising chance for complete integration into everyday society.

The high school program, therefore, is in sharp contrast to the emphasis given in the primary school special class. It must emphasize practical occupational considerations. Some time, however, should be devoted to remediating any specific weaknesses in the basic skill armamentarium of the educable children. At this point, directed attempts should be made to diagnose and remediate those weaknesses in the children's performance which might predictably impair effective interaction in the community.

Although personal and social development should have been emphasized throughout the school program, children in the secondary-level program need especially to learn appropriate techniques for interacting with others and procedures by which they can eliminate any obnoxious personal or social habits. Sociodrama has been suggested as a technique whereby the children can learn appropriate social and personal skills in practical situations. In the late junior high and early senior high school years, this tactic is most beneficial. As the older retarded child gains experience, he should be placed in social situations which require interaction with members of the community other than classmates for extended periods of time. When experiences of this sort are provided early in a child's program, a diagnosis can be made of any major "cracks" in the child's social and personal development. As specific difficulties are identified, proper remedial procedures can be developed and implemented.

In practical terms, it is much more difficult for the mentally retarded to develop satisfactory skills in the tool subjects and achieve healthy and adequate emotional and social adjustment than to perform the manipulative requirements of a position in a competent way. Not only do these academic areas demand greater conceptual skill for a satisfactory performance, but educable retarded children simply are less responsive to instruction in areas of minimal development (such as in verbalization areas) and show greater responsiveness and eagerness to participate in those activities in which they have been more successful. As a group then, the retarded are more responsive to nonverbal stimuli and enjoy becoming involved in manual and manipulative activities. From the perspective of clinical teaching, therefore, it makes sense for the teacher to use the retarded child's relative strengths, typically in nonverbal areas, to strengthen the relative weaknesses in verbal and conceptualization skills. In the face of this consistent finding, it is puzzling, indeed, that teachers of the retarded tend to eschew the use of laboratory experiments as the major basis for teaching, applying, and extending the academic skills of the retarded.

The high school work-study program should provide opportunities for the retarded to develop skill in those specific manipulative tasks which may be required in various occupations. Whereas before the retarded were engaged in more general nonverbal activity, during the high school years it is important that instruction in the manipulative activities become job specific. The child can no longer assume the casual, cavalier approach often characteristic of the early school years in finishing a task. The high school teacher must require that each individual learn to complete the requirements of a job in the shortest time and in the most effective way. If these types of skills and attitudes are not encouraged, the retarded youngster will find himself in the tenuous position of producing less than a reasonable level of expectation. Although a youngster may have all the personal and social expertise needed to effectively participate in a job, if the required level of manipulative skill is lacking, the young person will be a likely candidate for dismissal.

Society expects educable mentally retarded children to interact effectively within the community. This requirement will not be met if the youngsters are not given frequent opportunities to associate with others around them. To cloister the retarded in a special class for an entire school career may have certain academic advantages, but this strategy is bought at a price which will probably exceed any academic advantage. Children who are not integrated into other components of the school program will be viewed as defective by other members of society. A legitimate aim of special-education programs should be to reduce any social stigma associated with atypical conditions. Moreover, the retarded must learn how to deal with teasing and personal insults made by insensitive members of society. If these youngsters are not offered an opportunity to be exposed to problems of this type throughout their school career, but are secluded from the world in a special class or school, they will lack the necessary skills for facing these problems after moving into the community. The newness of the situation will be so dramatic that the unthinking responses of aggressively striking out or withdrawing into a safe environment will become predominant. It is the author's position, therefore, that every attempt should be made to integrate the special-class program with other school components.

In high school, the retarded should be integrated into the industrial arts and home economics program, physical education, art, music, and extracurricular activities. Competition between students in each of these areas does not have to be as intense as in the more academic areas. Further, by their very character, each of these areas mixes well with the main focus in the high school special class.

BASIS FOR A SUCCESSFUL WORK–STUDY PROGRAM

An effective work-study program requires the coordination among various in- and out-of-school agencies and the expertise of any number of specialists. Developing a close relationship with other agencies occurs at every level of the special-class program; this combined effort, however, becomes more intense as the youngsters move closer toward complete integration into the community. The tools required for preparing the retarded for gainful employment far exceed the available resources within most school communities. For example, many work experiences cannot be duplicated in the schools even under the most astutely contrived conditions. Moreover, the kind of information required by the retarded prior to entering an occupation will often exceed the training and experience of the classroom teacher. A great deal of mutual understanding needs to be established between labor unions, employers, and school work-study coordinators concerning the relationship that should exist between these groups and the retarded employee. To illustrate a potential source of difficulty, it is reasonable to anticipate that a mentally retarded worker could qualify for promotion to a supervisory level simply because of having worked longer in the shop than other workers. Most labor unions would demand that this individual be promoted. A promotion of this sort probably would not be wise for all concerned. A clear understanding of the dimensions of the situation must be agreed upon by all groups involved with the program.

The coordinator of the work-study program for the mentally retarded should establish a close relationship with the local division of vocational rehabilitation. Vocational rehabilitation provides a variety of services and training opportunities for all types of handicapped people. Retarded adolescents, in most cases, qualify for these services. A variety of diagnostic, remedial, and occupational placement services are available from vocational rehabilitation. The extensiveness of the services typically exceeds the resources available from the public school's work-study program. The work-study coordinator should register each student with this agency as soon as he enrolls in the work-study program. It is the coordinator's responsibility to maintain liaison with vocational rehabilitation and to keep the assigned rehabilitation counselor informed of each student's progress in the work-study program, noting any change of status or special problems the student encounters during the course of the program.

In many respects, the success of a secondary program is based on the level of skills each student has mastered in the specific subject areas. The high school teacher must spend a large amount of time on the application of the basic skills; therefore, only minimal time will be available for extensive subject matter instruction. The retarded child in a high school program should have developed academic skills at a level which will allow the teacher to emphasize their social and vocational use.

In a great number of school systems, retarded high school students have not developed a satisfactory level of understanding and skill in academic areas. This unfortunate situation is frequently the result of the youngsters having been socially promoted prior to being placed in a special classroom. Social promotion, frequently the result of administrative expediency, only pacifies temporarily. When the youngsters are later placed in a special class, they will not be able to demonstrate the required degree of proficiency in all the precursive skills required for dealing with academic material. The result is that the child will be able to operate less efficiently and effectively in an occupational setting. Under these circumstances, the only recourse the high school teacher has is to initiate a large scale "crash program" designed to program the students with certain kinds of responses for specific situations. The foolishness of this procedure was stressed in previous discussion. Logically, then, school systems must provide the retarded with a systematically designed special program from the early school years through post high school and in doing so, provide the retarded with opportunities to sequentially develop their capabilities in a total fashion.

The need for the special program to be sequential, wherein skills are built on earlier skills, has been stressed throughout this book. The degree to which instruction has been ordered will be felt most directly in the work-study program. Criteria which one might use to judge the appropriateness of the sequence employed in previous instruction include (1) the number of remedial cases in reading, arithmetic, and language at the high school level, (2) the attitudes of the children toward engaging in activities related to academic skills, (3) the incidence of specific types of learning difficulties such as borrowing or carrying in arithmetic, and (4) the degree to which the children have developed an understanding of the employment of various processes to solve problems, such as, in learning to pronounce unfamiliar words.

Clinical teaching in the high school work-study program for the retarded implies that an analysis has been made of the social and occupational components of a job and that the position has been matched with an individual whose background and areas of competence are congruent with the demands of the job.

The requirements and components of each job under consideration should be analyzed and related to the students in the work-study program. The major factors to be considered in this job analysis include

1 The specific type of job, level of competence required, and amount of previous experience necessary
2 The employment procedures, types of certificates needed, and degree of involvement required with labor unions
3 The extent to which the employee is required to interact with fellow workers and members of the public
4 The types of working conditions prevalent and the potential for being relocated or moved to a different shift
5 The specific types of requirements needed for job success, the amount of training provided by the employer, and the type of supervision given to the employee
6 The types of educational skills and background necessary to satisfactorily perform on the job including the amount of reading required, the type of arithmetic skills needed, the demands for handling money, and the level of communication skills required for satisfactory employment

Locating jobs for the students is an important component of occupational education. Equally significant is that placement be decided according to the degree of congruence between the job requirements and the characteristics of the job candidates. Locating jobs is only the first step of the process and must be followed by skillfully relating the right job situation with the most appropriate student.

The evidence suggests that the retarded rarely remain established in their first or second positions. In the first few years of employment, they show a history of movement among jobs, with little or no locomotion to positions requiring higher-level skills. The reasons for this movement seem to be directly related to their frequent inability to get along with others.

It is probably unreasonable to assume that educable retarded children will remain in the original job in which they were located during the work-study program. The instructional component of the work-study program, therefore, must be of great enough breadth to allow each child to generalize understandings to other occupations easily. The individual must be prepared to perform satisfactorily in a variety of settings and not in a circumscribed, narrowly defined occupation. The coordinator should realize that movement to a more skilled position will not occur readily and that large-scale retraining of the retarded would and should not be possible. Instructional success will be accomplished when all the experiences allow the retarded to formulate a pattern of acceptable behaviors which are easily transferred to other occupations requiring similar levels of accomplishment.

The degree of student success in the work-study program is related to the degree to which they become actively involved in all aspects of the program. Showing and telling these high school youngsters what and when to act will be ineffective. They must be given a chance to try out their responses in a realistic setting.

TEACHING CONSIDERATIONS

Preliminary classroom experiences

The high school program for the retarded must vary enough to allow for training and placement according to each child's capabilities and promise for success. Some children may be unable to operate within a competitive situation because of temperament or ability problems. Other retarded high school students will be successful in occupational training and placement. The former group requires a more sheltered and restricted environment, the latter group a more normal vocational situation which allows for interaction among other members of society.

Suitable placement and success on the job demands a certain level of academic skill as well as a common sense understanding of practical matters. These practical matters which are related to vocational employment include (1) social awareness and a sensitivity by the child for the needs of others, (2) realization of the dimensions of good citizenship and reasons for adhering to the principles contained therein (3) skill in the rudimentary manipulative requirements of a job, and (4) an understanding of the manner in which facts learned in subject areas are applicable to practical day-to-day problems. To some degree, overlap exists among these five areas in terms of the teaching units that might be developed within the work-study program. The common threads characterizing these principles include (1) factors related to personal problems and (2) factors specifically concerned with occupational placement and effective participation on the job.

PERSONAL FACTORS   Techniques for emphasizing good grooming, good health, and care of personal belongings and clothing were previously considered. These factors require special emphasis because of the potentially deleterious effects poor personal appearance will have on an employer and fellow employees. Lack of concern for one's personal appearance will result in the individual being labeled as retarded even before the opportunity is presented to demonstrate academic or occupational capabilities. Some attention in the work-study program must be given to the children developing a sensitivity to these important factors.

During the first few years of the work-study program, time and effort should be devoted to considering factors of personal finance. The public school program offers the most logical place for controlling the tendency of the retarded to engage in impulsive behavior. The risks of the educable retarded handling their personal finances in an unfortunate manner are high, unless some systematic attempt is made to encourage intelligent management of these affairs. One of the important dimensions in this regard is the need to give particular stress to intelligent budgeting of their salaries. The students should actively practice the process involved in saving in order that stable patterns of behavior be established. Lecturing or demonstrating the process will not suffice.

Employment for the first time often results in the new employee being deluged by various dealers interested in selling their services and products. These offers range from providing management of personal finances to a lifetime guarantee for a picture each month of every child born into the family. The retarded are especially vulnerable to accepting these deals without considering all the implications. The factors involved in wise purchasing must be realized by the retarded so that they do not find themselves in situations which are irreversible. To illustrate, even the normal have some difficulty justifying the amount of insurance coverage carried after being exposed to the magic of a loquacious and mesmerizing insurance salesman. Certain guidelines or criteria, therefore, must be presented to the retarded very early in the work-study program concerning, for example, what is a reasonable amount of health, accident, and life insurance coverage.

In almost every employment situation, a variety of elective and nonelective programs are available to the employees. If uninformed, the mentally retarded employee will have difficulty understanding the nature of and reasons for the many payroll deductions. The high school program, therefore, should include experiences which emphasize the employer and employee responsibilities concerning income tax, social security, pension plans, and health and accident coverage. A good deal of instruction and activity should go into those units which consider the employee's responsibilities concerning income tax. Instructional materials from the Federal government are available to illustrate and practice the procedures required for submitting annual returns. A "one shot" program in this area is not enough; these matters need continual reinforcement throughout the work-study program.

The many goods and services available in our society make it difficult for most people not to succumb to acquiring the symbols of status and comfort even at the expense of going into debt. The sharpened skills of salesmen, who are totally informed about the advantages of their product as well as the products of others, tend to reduce the resistance of prospective buyers. The combination of the retarded child's lack of perspective with his difficulty in perceiving the implications of present actions for the future, and the ease with which goods can be purchased on time and money borrowed beyond all rational suitability, makes for a particularly difficult situation. These factors denote areas with which the high school program must give comprehensive and systematic attention. If the retarded are to understand the problems of installment buying, borrowing, and lending money, the dangers of impulsivity must be dramatically pointed out. The technique of sociodrama and the evolutionary process of the work-study program, extending from total in-class participation to final placement on the job, will provide opportunities for the children to "box themselves in" within a somewhat restricted and safe environment under supervision. This period of practice provides a circumstance whereby the results of their behavior can be demonstrated and in which failure will not have too severe an effect on the students.

OCCUPATIONAL PLACEMENT FACTORS Preliminary to actual job placement, the work-study students should have some experience finding jobs which are consistent with their own capabilities, interviewing for occupational placement, and in making application for a position. A great deal hinges on the first impression made on the personnel officer dealing with the youth's application. Considerations concerning pay, working conditions, advancement possibilities, fringe benefits, in-service training programs, and other important factors are often deliberated and conclusions reached when the initial application is made. By the time the retarded are ready for employment outside of the relatively restricted environment of the school, each youngster should understand the procedures employed in applying for employment. It is highly important that youngsters develop an attitude of self-assurance in making such applications. This attitude cannot be completely achieved unless the students have experiences of this type outside of the confines of the special-education class. The activities in which the children are engaged must not be perceived by them as contrived. At the same time, the students must be placed in situations in which success will be forthcoming in order that the desired attitude concerning abilities develop.

The potential difficulties inherent in the aspects of employment which precede the actual work experience must be considered during the work-study program. For example, the issue of solving transportation problems, getting to work on time, or the relationship the workers should establish with the union should be discussed with the students and considered by the entire class. Alternatives to purchasing an automobile should be clearly delineated. The retarded youngster just entering the occupational scene will feel pressures to minimize transportation problems by purchasing an automobile. The retarded adolescent should have a complete understanding of the problems which will be encountered after making such a purchase.

Two components of employment which are relevant to all occupations and which require constant attention include (1) the need to maintain an appropriate standard of excellence in terms of the accuracy and quality of each child's performance and (2) the requirement that principles of safety be maintained on the job. It is the coordinator's responsibility to continually focus on each of these factors and to remind students of their importance by rewarding behavior which exemplifies these tenets. If sloppy or unsafe work is tolerated, the child's potential for subsequent employment is reduced. Because of poor work habits, rapport between the work-study program and potential employers could be seriously damaged.

Finally, each retarded student must be given opportunities to develop appropriate response patterns to the often antagonistic and disrespectful behavior of fellow employees. The retarded employee must learn how to handle these situations gingerly, but effectively. These potential workers, therefore, should have certain experiences prior to placement on a job which will help them understand the need to respect authority. They should realize that employers and others may often appear antagonistic and that this is not because of any personal vendetta but for reasons of maintaining the effective use of workers and maximizing production. As members of the production team, the retarded worker should understand his responsibility for constantly giving his best performance.

Relationship between work and study

Kolstoe and Frey (1965) have suggested a three-level sequence for the work-study program, each level of which allows the retarded child to gradually assume more responsibility and exercise greater independence within an occupational setting. These levels are defined as:

> 1 *Prevocational: students able to participate in sheltered, supervised, and semi-competitive work environments for a portion of each*

school day, but who by nature of their handicap or age are not eligible for vocational adjustment placement

2 **Vocational adjustment or work try-out:** students who have demonstrated a sufficient degree of work and social and personal skills to become eligible for part-time competitive work placement on selected jobs in the community

3 **Placement:** students who are capable of performing work at a minimum competitive level and who have completed the general academic requirements for graduation from the work study program. (pp. 95–96)

This program, which is evolutionary, allows the retarded child to move from total in-class involvement to full-time placement in a position, with ample opportunities for counseling and guidance on a follow-up basis from one to three years after leaving the school program. Because of the variation in characteristics of the retarded, the work-study program must be flexible enough to allow students to move from one level to another and, perhaps, return to an earlier level on the basis of the demonstrated ability each child exhibits in solving problems. It is difficult, therefore, to structure a program rigidly so that certain experiences occur only during a school year and never again. Moreover, some of the retarded children in the work-study program will not be able to operate effectively within an unstructured occupational environment. The determination of the location of each child within the total spectrum of work-study activities and his graduation into full-time employment require careful assessment of every student's characteristics in relation to the demands of each specific occupational situation.

The following sequence is an elaboration and extension of the levels of the work-study program as suggested by Kolstoe and Frey.

In-class activities (exclusively): During the first year of the work-study program, the children should be given a heavy concentration of prevocational information. Some of the specific content of this first stage of instruction was discussed in the preceding section. Emphasis should be placed on the personal and social demands of employment with substantial time devoted to such job prerequisites as interviewing for a position, filling out all the required forms of application, developing those manipulative skills required of unskilled and semiskilled workers, and making practical use of the academic skills developed during the primary and intermediate school years.

During this preliminary stage, the teacher should begin to formulate some general impression as to how well each child will be able to accept responsibility and handle the requirements of a job. Some broad estimate of suitable placement should be made at this point.

This judgment should be based on each youngster's ability to use and apply skills in the academic subjects and how well he comprehends occupational information demanded for employment success. At the same time, an estimate should be made of each child's personal and social development and maturity.

A work situation which is as realistic as possible should be replicated in the special-education classroom in order to make the activities, situations, and experiences very meaningful to the children. This can be done methodologically by using sociodrama. During this period, the younger students will find it informative to hear about the experiences of the older retarded children who have some familiarity with the demands of employment. These older youngsters, by introspecting a bit on the difficulties encountered in employment, can help to alert the younger, more naïve child to some of the possible areas of difficulty. At this level of the children's development, the teacher should use peer pressures and models to aid in the formation of proper attitudes. In certain instances, the more experienced students will be able to make a greater impact on the young retarded children by describing the need for learning the skills and information required for a successful employment experience.

In-class activities with supervised work of a short-term duration within the school building, gradually becoming more extensive as experience is gained: At this second level, the retarded child should be encouraged to relate classwork to practical problems within an environment in which certain controls are maintained. This propinquity allows for the close observation of each child and at the same time, provides a certain sense of security during each child's first experience at work. By working in the school building, the children find themselves in a familiar environment in which the regulations for appropriate behavior are well known. The adults with whom the children will be associated or supervised during the period of work should know about the objectives characteristic of this stage of the program and what constitutes reasonable expectations for the children. This relatively structured environment and work situation gives the work-study student a chance to try out an actual job situation.

It is important that the work experience at this level of instruction not be so contrived as to detract from the program objectives. If the students develop a feeling that their performance level is unimportant and their best effort not required, work performance at subsequent levels will be manifestly ineffective. Attitudes of the adult supervisors must be such that the children realize that a serious, concentrated effort is required of them during the work-study program. It should be made clear to each student that subsequent opportunities and job positions will be jeopardized if they view their responsibilities in too casual or cavalier a fashion.

In order to replicate the work situation as closely as possible, the children involved at this program level might be given a series of realistic incentives and rewards. Financial remuneration should be provided for work done. These rewards should be given *only* after work has been accomplished at a satisfactory level. Control should be exercised over the quality of work by paying students only when the work is well done. Here again, accuracy and not speed should be emphasized. Although some components of external evaluation of a student's work will be required for determining remuneration in this situation, the final goal should be for the child to learn to evaluate his own performance according to established criteria. As they move to higher levels within the work-study program, the children should move away from total dependence on others to dependence on themselves for evaluating the quality of achievement. The older retarded child should gain an appreciation for what constitutes acceptable and satisfactory work and not what he can get by with when someone is not keeping tabs on his performance. Some reward system, then, must become an integral part of this aspect of the program, not only because it replicates to some degree the actual work situation, but also because it helps to reinforce appropriate behavior.

Activities at this level of the work-study program will allow the teacher and work supervisor to collect meaningful and realistic data which subsequently can be used to gain a more precise estimate of the occupational expectations and apparent needs of each child. At this level when the students are actually working, their pattern of strengths and weaknesses will become obvious. As this profile is manifested, the teacher should restructure the classroom segments of the program in line with the weaknesses of each child and the requirements of the occupations with which they are or will be associated.

In-class activities with periodic out-of-school experiences in combination with extensive in-school work: This level of the work-study program allows the retarded to be gradually introduced into a new and less familiar work situation. The more cloistered environment characterizing their former situation will slowly move to the background, and the children now should be encouraged to use their skills and experiences in another type of occupational situation. It is significant, at this level, that they should still return to familiar territory for reorientation. This stable environment places them in a situation wherein the appropriateness of their behavior and that of others can be more accurately predicted. Moreover, in- and out-of-school experiences in concert with certain classroom activities provide them with an opportunity to test the reactions of themselves and others to situations arising during the out-of-school aspect of the program. When a youngster faces problems on the job, the in-school program component will provide him with a stable environment which allows the study of reasons for his behavior, or that of others, to certain situations.

The teacher should place each youngster in an out-of-school occupation which is closely related to his previous experience within the school building. The alternative placement opportunities should be studied so that some consistency is maintained between the in- and out-of-school experiences and job demands. For example, the youngsters might be employed in another school building as part of their out-of-school work.

The in-class activities characteristic of this stage of the program should focus on (1) helping the student maintain those previously developed skills and (2) rehabilitating or "beefing him up" in any areas in which certain deficiencies are exhibited. Continued emphasis should be given to using academic skills during the work experience period. A close relationship should be maintained between the child's academic skills and the occupational demands in order to strengthen this bond.

In-class activities with one-half day supervised out of school: At this stage of the program, the retarded should gradually move into a work situation which requires greater skills in independent living and personal responsibility. Each student should devote one-half day to a specific employment situation and return to the classroom at which time problems experienced on the job are considered and any needed remedial training is provided. At this stage, the retarded children must be exposed to a variety of occupational experiences and moved from one setting to another for at least one year's duration.

The responsibilities for supervision during this stage should be clearly delineated so that the employer and the work-study coordinator understand the limits of their responsibility. At no other time during the students' program will closer supervision and the complete analysis of strengths and weaknesses be as necessary and valuable. Likewise, an easy transition can be facilitated for the children from one relatively short-term work experience to another by the work-study coordinator identifying employment situations which are somewhat similar. A rational sequence should be identified which allows the students to move from one job to other jobs in a logical fashion without experiencing dramatic changes and alterations as they move. Factors requiring consideration in this sequencing include the job's manipulative expectations, level of intellectual ability required, type and number of possible social interactions to which the child will be exposed, academic qualifications required for success on each job, and the degree and types of responsibilities demanded of the retarded. The major point to be remembered is that the children move from one job to another in a fashion that requires some minimal change. As they move toward the final experiences at this stage of instruction, the characteristics and requirements of any final employment situations will no doubt differ substantially from expectations required during the students' early occupational activities.

The need for close coordination between the work-study supervisor and employers is obvious. One important dimension of this coordination must be a clear understanding and agreement by the employer of the objectives of the work-study program. Records should be maintained by the employer and work-study coordinator of each child's performance, areas of difficulty or potential difficulty, and indications of any additional experiences believed necessary to work in a satisfactory manner. The work-study coordinator should clearly identify for the employer any possible areas of difficulty for those students involved in a job. Likewise, the coordinator should continuously inform the employer about the student's activities and performance within the classroom environments.

As was true in the stage of instruction immediately preceding this, there is need for a systematic and intelligent reward system in all stages of the program. It must be recognized by all involved in the program, including the students, that they have been placed in the job situations for one-half day not primarily for purposes of supporting themselves or for making the money. This is to be viewed as part of a training program.

The pedagogical advantages in providing reinforcement and reward for desired behavior should be continued at this stage. The students should receive some type of financial remuneration for work accomplished during the period on the job. At the same time, accuracy of performance should be reinforced instead of speed and control maintained over the quality of the students' work. To this end, the coordinator and the employer might find it wise to reimburse the students according to the quality of their performance instead of on the basis of piecework or by the hour. The efficacy of this procedure requires study. In the absence of empirical support, teachers should not be hesitant to test innovative approaches as long as they are consistent with the program objectives and purposes.

Total out-of-school work experience, carefully supervised, leading eventually to placement: By the time the students have reached this stage of the work-study program, they should have systematically worked out any major weaknesses which might impede their success in occupational, social, and personal self-sufficiency. At this stage, it will no longer be necessary for the students to return to the classroom. They should have developed the basic skills required for total participation and integration into society.

The wide spectrum of experiences gained during the earlier stages of this work-study sequence will often result in students demonstrating an interest for being employed in a specific type of industry or employment situation. It should be recognized that some of the students may require transfer from one situation to another even during the course of their total out-of-school work experience. Along with the students, the work-study coordinator should analyze the various positions available and decide on the best situation. By using this approach, the retarded child will learn the practicalities of job analysis. This should aid the child to develop a keener awareness of his own abilities and weaknesses in relation to the expectations of various occupations.

It is the responsibility of the work-study coordinator to try to place each child in a permanent occupational situation. The division of vocational rehabilitation will be able to offer assistance during the stage of work placement. Full-time placement should not be attempted until the child reaches age eighteen or nineteen.

Follow-up: By the time a retarded child has been placed on a job, substantial investment has been made by the public schools and other cooperating agencies. This fact suggests the need for a careful evaluation and scrutiny of each child's performance after leaving school. A systematic follow-up of former students of the work-study program for one to three years after graduation should be undertaken to help those youngsters having difficulty as well as to introduce any needed modifications in the program sequence. Systematic assessments of job performance and integration into the community should be made. The retarded employee should be questioned and interviewed, the facts and attitudes of the employer studied in detail, and a remedial program immediately provided the employee if necessary. Ideally, then, the schools should be concerned about the total program effectiveness and provide any additional educational services required by the retarded employee. Adult education, then, constitutes a necessary part of the special-education program for the retarded.

The evaluation process

The need for consistent evaluation of the components of the work-study program has been stressed as central to the program's success. The coordinator must instruct employers of the students about techniques for evaluating those dimensions of significance encountered on the job. Moreover, evaluation is needed to identify potential employment situations and to determine the basic tasks and work components characteristic of each potential job situation.

Concerning the students, evaluation is necessary to identify significant weaknesses in those areas which require a certain level of achievement for successful employment; it is also necessary that each student's performance be measured against the specific goals at each stage of the work-study program. As the students satisfy the criteria at each level, they should proceed to the next stage of the program.

Evaluation of progress is conducted not only to adjust and modify a child's program, but also to provide students with feedback concerning their progress. It is important that focus not be placed on a child's weaknesses but that each student be rewarded for correct responses. Whenever one is made aware of his shortcomings, an opportunity to practice appropriate responses to the situation should be given. Likewise, it is important that the work-study coordinator inform employers of the desirability not to place undue emphasis on a child's weaknesses without demonstrating the correct and proper manner in which to perform. The situation requires some clinical sensitivity on the part of those working with the retarded. Errors should not be practiced. At the same time, the youngsters should not assume that their responses are satisfactory because they have not been alerted to their errors. Feedback from evaluations, therefore, needs to be provided to students.

Evaluation should effect some modification in the instructional program when patterns of weakness are exhibited consistently among children. It should be purposeful, the basic aim being to assess the degree to which the youngsters are able to satisfy the established program objectives. Suggestions for temporary or permanent revision of the work-study program will emanate from the data collected. The goals for each child will not necessarily be alike because of the variations which exist between the children.

A variety of techniques might be employed to check on the progress of students. If a child seems to be having difficulty in any of the academic areas, the employment of a selection of the evaluative techniques discussed in other sections of this book would be appropriate. If performance in social, personal, or occupational factors needs to be evaluated, the teacher may find checklists of various types helpful. These checklists, which do not necessarily require standardization, are primarily a means for determining certain general patterns of achievement. Kolstoe and Frey (1965), in the appendix of their book, have provided illustrations of several scales and checklists which work-study coordinators will find helpful in assessing the progress of students. Vocational rehabilitation has also developed evaluation forms of this nature.

The employers of work-study students should be required to cooperate in the evaluation process. Because of time limitations, they are frequently unable to schedule extensive conferences with either the employee or the work-study coordinator. The most parsimonious and practical means of gathering information from the employer about the work-study students is to provide him with a progress check sheet similar to those mentioned earlier.

Another factor requiring assessment is the attitudes of potential employers toward the retarded. Assessing the motives of the employer and his willingness to cooperate is a difficult problem. In most cases, the work-study coordinator will need to devote a great deal of time selling the school program to the various levels of management. The search for and identification of placement possibilities requires an enormous public relations effort and may involve other members of the community and local agencies to help locate job possibilities for students. The coordinator must not only sell the philosophy of the work-study program, he must sell the student as well. Employers should come to view the entire program in a positive fashion.

Additional concerns related to the work-study program

The program requires the services of a coordinator whose primary responsibilities involve locating potential employment situations, supervising students in their out-of-school vocational placement, and integrating the practical problems experienced by the students on the job with the in-class activities. The primary responsibility of the classroom instructor should be for all of the in-class activities and a portion of the in-school work program. Both of the instructors should coordinate their efforts closely and be responsible for consistently and systematically assessing the students under their direction.

The classroom in which these youngsters might be located should not differ significantly from a regular classroom in terms of the kind of equipment available. It might be advantageous to the program if the classroom were located in close proximity to an industrial arts laboratory and home economics classroom. This setting would provide closer coordination between the special-education instructor and other facets of the school program. This integration should occur in a realistic way and not be contrived.

The teacher can be of great personal assistance to the children and help maximize the possibility for their success at work by spending time helping the students be as attractive as possible. Much of the early instruction of the work-study program will deal with various practical ways for making themselves attractive to others. This means that attention should be given to grooming, cleanliness, personal relationships with others, the use of toilet articles, neat and appropriate dress, and other such factors. The judicious use of peer pressure may provide the stimulus for the younger mentally retarded youngsters understanding the value in attending to these personal and social considerations.

Active participation, reducing the newness of the various situations, and integrating past experiences with new problems and situations are important considerations for the success of the program.

The sequence of activities provided during the entire course of the program should consider these vital principles.

SELECTED REFERENCES

Beckman, A. S.: "Minimum Intelligence Levels for Several Occupations," *Personnel Journal,* vol. 9, 1930, pp. 309–313.

Bobroff, A.: "Economic Adjustment of 121 Adults, Formerly Students in Classes for Mental Retardates," *American Journal of Mental Deficiency,* vol. 60, 1956, pp. 525–535.

————: "A Survey of Social and Civic Participation of Adults Formerly in Classes for Mentally Retarded," *American Journal of Mental Deficiency,* vol. 61, 1956, pp. 127–133.

Collman, R. D. and Newlyn, D.: "Employment Success of Educationally Subnormal Ex-Pupils in England," *American Journal of Mental Deficiency,* vol. 60, 1956, pp. 733–743.

———— and ————: "Employment Success of Mentally Dull and Intellectually Normal Ex-Pupils in England," *American Journal of Mental Deficiency,* vol. 61, 1957, pp. 484–490.

Delp, H. A. and Lorenz, M.: "Follow-Up of 84 Public School Special-Class Pupils with IQ's Below 50," *American Journal of Mental Deficiency,* vol. 58, 1953, pp. 175–182.

DiMichael, S.: "Vocational Rehabilitation Works for the Mentally Retarded," *Personnel and Guidance Journal,* vol. 31, 1953, pp. 428–432.

Dinger, J. C.: "Post-School Adjustment of Former Educable Retarded Pupils," *Exceptional Children,* vol. 27, 1961, pp. 353–360.

Engel, A. M.: "Employment of the Mentally Retarded," *American Journal of Mental Deficiency,* vol. 57, 1952, pp. 243–267.

Goldberg, I. I.: "Coordination of Retardates' Experiences from School to Occupational Center," *American Journal of Mental Deficiency,* vol. 62, 1958, pp. 823–825.

Hitchcock, A. A.: "Vocational Training and Job Adjustment of the Mentally Deficient," *American Journal of Mental Deficiency,* vol. 59, 1954, pp. 100–106.

Kolstoe, O. P.: "An Examination of Some Characteristics Which Discriminate between Employed and Not-Employed Mentally Retarded Males," *American Journal of Mental Deficiency,* vol. 66, 1961, pp. 472–482.

———— and Frey, R. M.: *A High School Work-Study Program for Mentally Subnormal Students,* Southern Illinois University Press, Carbondale, Ill., 1965, pp. 95–96.

McCartney, L. D.: "Providing Occupational Readiness for Young Mentally Deficient Children of the Non-Familial Type," *American Journal of Mental Deficiency,* vol. 62, 1958, pp. 625–633.

Michael-Smith, H.: "A Study of the Personal Characteristics Desirable for the Vocational Success of the Mentally Deficient," *American Journal of Mental Deficiency,* vol. 55, 1950, pp. 139–143.

Peterson, L. and Smith, L. L.: "A Comparison of the Post-School Adjustment of Educable Mentally Retarded Adults with that of Adults of Normal Intelligence," *Exceptional Children,* vol. 26, 1960, pp. 404–408.

Porter, R. B. and Milazzo, T. C.: "A Comparison of Mentally Retarded Adults Who Attended a Special Class with Those Who Attended Regular School Classes," *Exceptional Children,* vol. 24, 1958, pp. 410–412.

adult education for the
mentally retarded and their parents

Educational programs for the adult mentally retarded and for parents of the retarded attending public schools have traditionally not been provided by the schools. Rehabilitation counselors have been most directly responsible for the adult retarded if they are registered, have been evaluated by the agency, are of the appropriate age, and reside in a community in which needed services are available. Unfortunately, in many instances, special-education teachers and coordinators fail to establish a close working relationship with vocational rehabilitation. This results in the retarded adults not being provided with professional advice, counsel, and other needed services. Parents of retarded children who are attending public schools are usually not incorporated in any of the existing programs unless they elect to join a parents' group, such as the National Association for Retarded Children, or are fortunate enough for their child to be taught by a teacher who is aware of the need to work with the parents as well as with the children.

The position taken here is that the schools must include adult education programs for former students who are retarded as well as for parents of all retarded children who are enrolled in the special program. This suggestion is admittedly idealistic when one considers the many other educational needs, such as extending school programs downward to include younger children, particularly those from lower socioeconomic communities. By attending to the needs of parents of former students, a complete program can be developed which will have impact on the participants and their families in terms of enhancing their potential stations in life. Moreover, the data gathered from this type of program will help to evaluate the efficacy of the activities, experiences, objectives, and rationale of the total special-education sequence provided retarded students. This longitudinal view of the special-education program provides the type of evaluative procedure needed to develop comprehensive educational services for the mentally retarded. The most commonly existing program structure, which dismisses the retarded at age eighteen never to see them again, not only lacks comprehensiveness and necessary follow-up but provides no basis or opportunity for testing the value of the student's earlier special-education experiences. Special education, therefore, must combine forces with vocational rehabilitation in each of these two important areas of adult education.

DIMENSIONS OF THE POSTSCHOOL PROGRAM

The objective of the immediate postschool program is one of helping former students with any particular difficulties they are encountering as members of the community. This aim, although broad in terms of the possible variety of problems the retarded individuals could experience, should deal with specific difficulties. In all aspects of this program, however, attempts should be made to have the retarded person generalize appropriate behavior related to a certain situation to all other areas of functioning in which such behavior would be equally appropriate. The degree to which the individual adjusts to his occupational situation and the extent of his satisfaction in personal and family development should constitute the two broad areas for emphasis in the adult education program for the mentally retarded. Before considering the specifics of each of these areas, the following points will help to focus more precisely on what might constitute the broad structure and intent of the postschool program.

1 When the students are placed on a job, they should understand that one condition of their employment is that they attend school one

evening each week in order to meet with either the work-study coordinator or a counselor trained in special education for the retarded. The length of time each student must continue attending these sessions should be variable and based totally on the mutual evaluation by the employer and the school representative. Factors considered before a retarded person is dismissed from the weekly sessions should include (1) the degree of success in the basic occupational expectations; (2) attitudes and values held by the student; (3) any specific weaknesses of an academic nature which deleteriously influence his performance on the job; (4) family difficulties; and (5) any personal, emotional, or social problems.

2 Each weekly session should be relatively unstructured in terms of content. This strategy will allow the instructor to capitalize on concerns and difficulties expressed by members of the group as well as by each individual's employer. Although unstructured, the sessions should be informative for the participants and viewed by them as being a valuable activity. Information dispensing, as well as formal and informal counseling and guidance, will constitute major segments of each session. As specific difficulties are identified, the instructor may wish to dramatize alternative ways of solving the problem by using role playing.

3 Each session should contain a relatively small number of participants with some group stability being maintained so that the participants will interact freely with other group members. Small groups are mandatory since many of the students' problems may be personal or specific to them although, no doubt, of general interest and importance to other members of the group. With large groups, it would be impossible for the instructor to adequately respond to the problems as they are presented, and the promise for wide group interaction would be minimized.

4 Although many of the problems and issues raised by the retarded employees and their employers may be real and legitimate, neither of these groups of people is trained to observe and assess the subtle factors which are frequently causative of difficulties. The instructor of the postschool program, although making use of information provided by others, should attempt to identify and focus on specific weaknesses exhibited by members of the class. This requires that the instructor be broadly trained and particularly sensitive to clues of diagnostic relevance.

5 The entire postschool program must become closely associated with the division of vocational rehabilitation and other community agencies in order to operate effectively. As specific weaknesses of an employee are identified by the instructor or employer, a decision should be made as to whether the program for rehabilitating the individual could be done most efficiently by the schools, vocational rehabilitation, or some other community agency such as mental

health, Crippled Children's Commission, or a legal advisory service. Although the schools have some responsibility for the postschool program, they and others should realize that effective integration of the retarded adult into the community will come about only after coordination has been effected among all the community services.

Follow-up of occupational adjustment

Specific characteristics of the follow-up components of the work-study program were discussed in the preceding chapter. The information gathered by the work-study coordinator when the work situation of the retarded employee is visited and observations by the employer should be discussed with the evening instructor and by the students in one of the early group sessions. Follow-up of the work-study program should be done for two reasons: first, to assist the public schools in revising or reorienting their program and, second, to evaluate the performance of each retarded individual and to provide any needed rehabilitative services. The latter point is probably the most important and suggests that a close collaborative relationship should exist between the work-study coordinator, the employer, and the evening instructor.

Social development, manipulative mastery, personal and emotional adequacy, and employee-employer relationships are areas which should receive attention in the postschool program. As information is gathered concerning how well the retarded adult performs in these areas, some judgment can be made regarding the necessity for any additional training. By the establishment of a close relationship with vocational rehabilitation, it will often be possible to schedule a series of short- and long-term training programs or relocate a retarded adult in a more restricted or sheltered occupational situation. It may not be possible to accurately diagnose the degree to which an individual will be able to become assimilated into a job during the course of the regular school program. When the more structured environment is removed, the retarded adult, no longer under the aegis of the work-study coordinator, may demonstrate significant weaknesses in behavior and management.

The type of data collected on the prospective employee during the course of the work-study program should continue to be gathered, although perhaps less formally, during the most immediate postschool period. These data will provide some general indication of the degree of employee growth and stability of performance over time. Recording segments of behavior periodically, but consistently, throughout the duration of the in- and out-of-school program has the potential for being helpful to the individual being studied and is also important to the total program structure as other students move through the various program components. Further, staff attrition requires objective, consistent, and systematic reporting so that communication among professionals at all levels and during various periods of time can be unambiguous and as parsimonious as possible.

Counseling the retarded adult

Irrespective of the type of educational situation with which the educable mentally retarded might have been previously associated, as adults they will probably blend into society. This in no way suggests that they will become community leaders or major contributors to the social order; instead, the aggressive and active participation of those members of the community who are more astute often camouflages any weaknesses which the retarded members might exhibit. To be sure, the schools should provide the retarded with experiences and activities which will allow them to move into the community on an independent and self-sufficient basis. The evidence indicates that as a group they will be able to do this irrespective of the type or caliber of their educational program.

The more crucial issue is how effectively the retarded will be able to manage their own affairs as adults. As much as possible must be done to help the retarded not find themselves in situations which require that they constantly solve a host of minor problems which have been precipitated by their ineffectiveness as problem solvers or by becoming associated with unscrupulous persons. If these little difficulties continue to occur, the retarded adult will become more deeply in debt, experiencing a host of problems—solutions for which are often not easily obvious to them. Eventually they will find themselves resorting to illegal or unethical behavior in an attempt to resolve these difficulties. Even after exposure to an outstanding social class program, the impact and significance of problems of adulthood are typically not felt. Because of youth and inexperience during the school years, problems of independent living as adults are not realistic facts of life. A postschool program, therefore, should help the retarded adult to sharpen his skills in solving the variety of personal and family problems which most will face.

Financial problems are among the most difficult problems for the retarded adult and have the greatest potential for causing severe difficulties. During the work-study program, and also during the intermediate school grades, educable children should have a complete exposure to a program of effective management of money. As students, however, they are not faced with the problems of feeding and clothing themselves, providing their own transportation to and from work, renting or purchasing a house, or judging when and under what circumstances a major item should be purchased. As adults, with money in their pockets, many will succumb to any number of a variety of pressures to spend their money foolishly. As students, most of the retarded will be able to repeat back to the teacher in a correct and appropriate manner all the advantages and disadvantages of installment buying. As adults, many of the retarded either will have forgotten or be unable to apply what they have previously learned about intelligently spending money. The weekly postschool sessions, then, should constantly consider problems related to the management of money. Although the retarded tend to marry partners with greater relative intellectual ability, it would be unwise to assume that clear thinking will always prevail when financial considerations are at stake.

Family planning should be another vital part of the postschool program. Most retarded adults are totally unaware of the many problems involved in marriage and in raising a family. Their impulsive nature will result in many of them marrying without considering all the ramifications of making such a decision. In addition, the postschool sessions should consider topics such as how to provide suitable housing, planning children and providing for their complete care, sharing responsibility between the husband and wife, and appropriate techniques for child rearing.

Educable children and adults should know of the large number of unscrupulous persons in our society who are interested in taking advantage of them and their families. The importance of the retarded realizing the seriousness of associating with people of this type cannot be overstated. The potential harm in dealing with such people should be made dramatic by using actual case material for instruction or by asking authority figures, such as the local police inspector, to visit with the students to discuss how to avoid these unprincipled people. The retarded should be aware of when they are being taken advantage of and what course of action to follow when they find themselves in this type of situation.

The postschool curriculum should also contain a program which centers around the worthy use of leisure time. They must be encouraged to make use of all their capabilities and engage in activities which foster good physical and mental health. Moreover, a stable, socially acceptable pattern of extracurricular behavior, which provides a means for relaxation and enjoyment, should be encouraged. Financial considerations related to these leisure time activities require explicit instructional attention. Examples of recreational activities which do not require heavy expenditure from the family budget should be described during the postschool program. The enjoyment of church groups or neighborhood activities should be emphasized.

The areas suggested as requiring special attention in the postschool program constitute only a sample of the types of concerns frequently manifested by the mentally retarded adult. It is impossible to predict all the potential areas of difficulty to be encountered by the retarded prior to the postschool years. Even if these factors could be identified, restrictions in time during the school program make it impossible for each to be considered in depth. Further, the unique situation of each mentally retarded person upon leaving the schools will result in problems which are specific to each individual and situation. To gain maximum advantage from a consistent and sequentially developed special program for the mentally retarded, small practical problems encountered on the job by each retarded person should be discussed before the difficulties become too large to handle, are generalized to other situations, or place the retarded in a relatively irreversible situation. The postschool program for the adult, in cooperation with programs offered by other agencies such as vocational rehabilitation, will offer the most ideal situation for them to learn how to appropriately solve practical problems faced every day.

Every aspect of the special-education program for the retarded is important and, in concert with other aspects of the program, provides the desired scope and sequence for them to develop into adequate citizens. Some educators would suggest that the preschool and the immediate postschool years are particularly crucial in the instructional program for the retarded. During the preschool years, the children learn to develop skills in those foundation areas on which academic skills are later based. During the immediate postschool years they have a chance to use the many skills developed during the school program in practical surroundings. The school should check on each child's effectiveness to apply those things learned earlier in their special program. Moreover, the retarded adult should be provided with remedial services when certain weaknesses are manifested.

ADULT EDUCATION FOR PARENTS OF THE MENTALLY RETARDED

Any comprehensive school program for the mentally retarded should include adult education for parents as an integral part of the total program structure. Although the children will spend most daylight contact hours in the public schools, the potentially deleterious influence that the uneducated or insensitive parent can have is often substantial enough to completely nullify the advantages of even the best special-education program. In considering the structure of an adult education program for parents of the retarded, the schools are faced with the need to deal with two somewhat unique and different populations, each of which requires a separate educational emphasis. On one hand, certain educable retarded children located in special classes have some type of organic dysfunction and are not basically the product of a deprived environment circumstance. These children typically represent families from better educated middle-class situations.

The second population represented in special classes for the retarded are those children who, because of severe environmental deprivation, have not had the full spectrum of experiences which would allow them to develop at an intellectual level commensurate with their chronological ages. Parents of these deprived children require a different orientation in an adult education program than those parents whose children represent some type of organic etiology. The nature of the concerns represented by each of these groups and recommendations for program emphasis will be considered in this section.

Parents from normal environments

Children who are retarded because of some type of neurological dysfunction which is not directly related to environmental deprivation typically present a perplexing problem to their parents. The situation is particularly difficult for those parents whose families are without a history of mental retardation. Because of some type of prenatal, perinatal, or postnatal difficulty, the child may have experienced minimal neurological damage which results in a certain degree of intellectual subnormality. Parents with this type of child are immediately placed in a new psychological situation wherein appropriate goals and paths by which these goals are reached are not well delineated. This situation results in wandering, vacillating, and trial-and-error behavior; parents in this situation often engage in clinic hopping. They are often unsure of the type of specialist whose advice they should seek, and their perplexity only increases when subsequent births produce intellectually normal siblings. Anxiety and tension surrounding the retarded child in this family are increased because of various intra- and extrafamily pressures brought to bear on the parents. Many individuals with whom they come in contact act as, and often are perceived as, experts. This results in the parents' becoming more tense about the situation and future of their child.

The special-education teacher is often the first professional concerned with behavior from whom parents with this type of child receive specific advice. The general practitioners and pediatricians, although frequently having had experience with intellectually subnormal children from a medical perspective, most often will not be aware of what should constitute an appropriate educational program for this type of retarded child. The special-education teacher, therefore, must be prepared to respond intelligently to the questions and concerns of the parents. One major educational thrust in this matter can be achieved by the schools including an adult educational program within the total structure of the special-education program.

Throughout the adult education sessions parents of the retarded must understand the teacher's willingness to help with everyday problems. The teacher must not be perceived by the parents as an expert in areas other than education. When the problems raised by parents exceed the professional training of the teacher, a referral should be made to experts in the areas of concern. Professionals representing these disciplines should be invited periodically to visit the class during the adult education program. Early in the parent education sessions, the problem of etiology or cause will come up. Parents must have the opportunity to freely discuss all the possibilities. Intelligent leadership by the teacher will help them arrive at the realization that the child's future should receive primary focus. It will be personally satisfying and advantageous for the parents to spend time discussing the range of possible reasons for their child being mentally retarded. Parents should be left with the belief that it is probably impossible for anyone to specify the cause of the condition and that any of a variety of difficulties could have resulted in the problem.

Each parent session should be informal. Parents should feel free to discuss any area of concern with other members of the group. The sessions should be such that the parents realize that their techniques used in handling their child are not being critically evaluated by others, including the group leader. Emphasis should be placed on the need for a coordinated effort between the home and the school. To this end, the school's objectives for each child should be clearly delineated and each parent informed of the present educational level and educational prognosis for his child.

Parents of the organically retarded typically have an unclear picture of the capabilities and future of their children. Many feel that their child will outgrow the intellectual slowness presently exhibited and eventually move into the regular class program. Other parents look for miracle cures, special diets, or unique kinds of therapy for habilitating their child. It is important that the parents gain a clear picture of the present status of their child and gain a reasonable perspective of the future for their child. This will take a long time to effect for many parents, and indeed, some will never arrive at a reasonable understanding on this matter. Before any reasonable interaction can occur between the home and school, the teacher must devote time and effort in helping parents place their understanding and expectations for the child in the proper perspective.

Early in the adult education program the translation of the school's program in terms of each child's situation should be thoroughly explained. Although this can be covered through planned lectures, it is recommended that the parents be allowed to observe demonstrations of various aspects of the school program. The atmosphere characteristic of a contrived demonstration should be avoided and a warm, realistic, and informal situation provided for parent observations. This technique provides parents with a more realistic picture of the dimensions of the school program and the strategies by which the aims are realized, and there is the added advantage of the parents' becoming more aware of the limitations of their own child's ability and level of achievement. The parents, thus, gain an appreciation of the special program and, at the same time, become aware of the techniques used by the teacher in handling each retarded child. Many of these same strategies are appropriate for use in the home.

Too much pressure on the mentally retarded to achieve is a common characteristic of the middle-class home. For reasons that may be related to lack of understanding or social pressures, parents, unknowingly, will often place their retarded youngster in an unreasonably stressful situation. For example, they may require the child to study or do homework beyond all reasonableness. This will result in the youngster becoming overly anxious in relating to the parents and others in the family. Moreover, the child will probably develop an attitude of disgust toward everything related to school activities. This situation is precipitated by well-meaning parents. The special-education teacher has the responsibility to clearly define the limits of what parents can reasonably expect of their child. If homework activities are recommended, parents must be given precise directions concerning the types of activities, the manner in which the activities are to be handled, and the amount of time the child is to devote to them. Characteristic of parents of all handicapped children is their desire to force the child into a position of being extended beyond the point of maximum effectiveness.

Middle-class parents of mentally retarded children are often hypersensitive to the social dimensions of the defect. For a variety of reasons, the parents will often be ambivalent toward their child. Attention during the parent counseling sessions must be given to all the emotional and social ramifications of the problem. This will involve the need for the sessions to be attended periodically by specialists such as a clinical psychologist, child psychiatrist, or psychiatric social worker.

If a mentally retarded child is to develop emotional stability and social assurance, and the parents to assume a healthy posture toward their child, the parents must attempt to understand their feelings toward the child before deliberating on other kinds of habilitative concerns. In addition to this, there is the need for all involved in the school program to assure parents that they are welcome to visit with any member of the professional team whenever the need arises in order to ask questions or express any concerns they might have. The school must communicate its willingness to assume leadership in the provision of an educational program which contains appropriate experiences leading to the retarded becoming successfully integrated into the community. In fact, the special educator should supply the means for coordinating efforts of various specialties. To illustrate this point, the special-education personnel should take leadership by relating their program with that offered by vocational rehabilitation and by constantly keeping the parents informed as to what is happening and what they can look forward to as the child's program progresses.

Parents whose children are environmentally deprived

An adult education program must also consider parents of those retarded children who have been reared in environmentally deprived areas. The type of focus for this program will probably differ from the emphasis placed on the adult program for parents of organically involved mentally retarded children. Parents of stimulus-deprived children will typically not be as eager to participate in the adult education programs as parents of organically involved children.

Working with families from lower socioeconomic situations presents a particularly difficult problem because their attitudes are inextricably associated with the poverty they have experienced and all that it entails. The initial thrust in any adult education program for these parents must be aimed at altering their attitudes toward their children as well as toward the total school program. These parents will not tolerate being preached to or badgered about the poor condition of their children and that they have incorrectly reared them. Each individual must realize the advantage of his participation in the adult education program and the benefits that could accrue to him and to his children. Indeed, perhaps the most difficult problem is the initial one of getting parents to attend the adult sessions. It may be necessary for the schools to make special provisions for these parents by conducting the sessions according to the best time in their schedule. If the educational program for the deprived retarded is to be effective, the schools must make some substantial effort to systematically work with these parents.

The first order of business in this program must be to assist them in realizing the advantages of working closely with the schools. Their attitudes toward the school program will change only after they can clearly see the personal advantages for cooperating. This must not be treated in a cavalier fashion; the instructor must understand that firmly entrenched attitudes which have been established over years because of constant frustration and an inability to provide for themselves and their families can be altered, at best, only very slightly and over an extended period of time. One strategy for helping the parents develop a positive view of the school's objectives is to provide some type of immediate and tangible evidence of the advantages in cooperating. Initially, then, the instructor should survey needs of the parents in an attempt to identify their most difficult problems and, in a forthright manner, make every attempt to assist them in resolving these difficulties. Eventually, as the parents gain greater experience with and confidence in the adult education program, their perception of the school's program in relation to their own retarded child will be altered. Although there is a need for focusing the initial thrust of the adult education program on changing attitudes of parents toward the schools, it should be recognized that dramatic changes in attitudes will be difficult to effect in relatively short periods of time.

Many parents living in lower socioeconomic circumstances are not aware of the aims of the special-education program for the mentally retarded. The most common view is that their child, because he is unable to perform in a regular class situation or because of a substantial behavior problem, has been placed in a situation wherein greater controls can be exercised by the schools. At the same time, many parents will believe that this new classroom situation is not designed to help their child develop skills for independent living. In short, parents from a deprived environment are usually unclear about the advantages of their child being located in a special-education situation and are often antagonistic toward this placement. Early in the adult program objectives and aims of the special-class program should be clearly discussed. Further, if the parents are to understand the practicalities of the situation, the instructor will need to describe what the school expects of each child and the specific instructional sequence planned for the students as they proceed through the special program. Throughout this session, the schools should help parents understand the variety of difficulties the children and teachers encounter in the day-to-day classroom situation and ways in which the parents can provide support at home so that the program objectives are more easily achieved. The advantage of a close relationship between the parents, their treatment of the child, and the activities and experiences of the school program should be emphasized.

Because of inordinately large families and the difficulties in social behavior frequently characteristic of children from lower socioeconomic situations, the instructor will find that these parents are interested in topics related to child rearing and techniques for dealing with personal and social difficulties. Problems in these areas are usually difficult for parents to fully understand or deal with in a healthy and socially acceptable manner. Because of their propinquity to the deprived environment, parents do not have a reasonable perspective and, therefore, judge the behavior of their children and themselves from a social reference point which differs from the middle socioeconomic strata. When everyone around you misbehaves, it is easy to lose sight of another reference point. The school program, therefore, must help these parents to understand some of the major factors related to healthy child-rearing practices, and instructors must suggest the range of activities and experiences in which parents can engage their children in the home to foster normal and healthy physical, social, and emotional development. Special attention should be given to the reactions of parents to the behavior of their children. Demonstrations, small group discussions, role playing, and films and other visual aids will help to make an impact on the parents.

Many parents from slum areas or pockets of poverty will exhibit a desperate need for information and counseling concerning family planning and occupational security. In most cases they will have inordinately large families and find themselves unable to adequately support the home. In a great number of the homes, the mother will be head of the household and often the only source of income. Other adults, often found living in these homes, will be indigent or handicapped and unable to contribute in any beneficial and tangible way. Welfare may be the only source of financial support; consequently, they will be unable to handle the continuous array of difficulties which arise.

The school's role should be one of providing these parents with information concerning those community services which will assist in resolving these difficulties. The school, obviously, cannot solve each of the many specific problems presented during the course of the parent program. A more reasonable approach is to inform parents of services provided by various agencies and to act as a liaison between the parents and these agencies. In this respect, therefore, the schools should both dispense appropriate information to parents and help to coordinate the various services relevant to each parent's situation.

Recent research has demonstrated the deleterious influence of poor nutrition on general physical and intellectual development. Adult education for parents of retarded children living in a deprived environment must provide detailed information concerning the dietary needs of these children. Clearly, it is important that this area be explored with parents in terms that are realistic. To present them with suggestions for properly feeding their young without considering the financial difficulties of this group will only serve to undermine the entire adult education program. A variety of alternative means for satisfying the basic nutritional requirements should be given and examples of ways to solve nutritional deficiencies actually demonstrated for the parents.

SELECTED REFERENCES

Albini, J. L. and Dinitz, S.: "Psychotherapy with Disturbed and Defective Children: An Evaluation of Changes in Behavior and Attitudes,"

American Journal of Mental Deficiency, vol. 69, 1965, pp. 560–567.

Auerbach, Aline B.: "Group Education for Parents of the Handicapped," *Children*, vol. 8, 1961, pp. 135–140.

Barber, T. M.: "Better Parent Education Means More Effective Public Relations," *American Journal of Mental Deficiency*, vol. 60, 1956, pp. 627–632.

Beck, Helen L.: "Counseling Parents of Retarded Children," *Children*, vol. 6, 1959, pp. 225–230.

Begab, M. J.: "Factors in Counseling Parents of Retarded Children," *American Journal of Mental Deficiency*, vol. 60, 1956, pp. 515–524.

Coleman, J. C.: "Group Therapy with Parents of Mentally Deficient Children," *American Journal of Mental Deficiency*, vol. 57, 1953, pp. 700–704.

Cotzin, M.: "Group Psychotherapy with Mentally Defective Problem Boys," *American Journal of Mental Deficiency*, vol. 53, 1948, pp. 268–283.

Dalton, J. and Epstein, H.: "Counseling Parents of Mildly Retarded Children," *Social Casework*, vol. 44, 1963, pp. 523–530.

French, A. C., Levbarg, M., and Michael-Smith, H.: "Parent Counseling as a Means of Improving the Performance of a Mentally Retarded Boy: A Case Study Presentation," *American Journal of Mental Deficiency*, vol. 58, 1952, pp. 13–20.

Goodman, L. and Rothman, R.: "The Development of a Group Counseling Program in a Clinic for Retarded Children," *American Journal of Mental Deficiency*, vol. 65, 1961, pp. 789–795.

Gordon, E. W. and Ullman, M.: "Reaction of Parents to Problems of Mental Retardation in Children," *American Journal of Mental Deficiency*, vol. 61, 1956, pp. 158–163.

Grebler, A. M.: "Parental Attitudes toward Mentally Retarded Children," *American Journal of Mental Deficiency*, vol. 56, 1952, pp. 475–483.

Hale, C. B.: "Parent Need for Education and Help with Family Problems," *California Journal of Education Research*, vol. 6, 1955, pp. 38–44.

Jensen, R. A.: "The Clinical Management of the Mentally Retarded Child and the Parents," *American Journal of Psychiatry*, vol. 106, 1950, pp. 830–833.

Kanner, L.: "Parents' Feelings about Retarded Children," *American Journal of Mental Deficiency*, vol. 57, 1953, pp. 375–383.

Kirk, S. A., Karnes, M. B., and Kirk, W. D.: *You and Your Retarded Child*, The Macmillan Company, New York, 1955.

Leichman, N. S.: *Parent Attitudes in Rearing Mentally Retarded Children*, California State Department of Education, Sacramento, Calif., 1962.

McDonald, E. T.: *Understand Those Feelings*, Stanwix House, Inc., Pittsburgh, 1962.

Mahoney, S. C.: "Observations Concerning Counseling with Parents of Mentally Retarded Children," *American Journal of Mental Deficiency*, , vol. 63, 1958, pp. 81–86.

Morris, E. F.: "Casework Training Needs for Counseling Parents of the

Retarded," *American Journal of Mental Deficiency*, vol. 59, 1955, pp. 510–516.

Mullen, F. A.: "The Teacher Works with the Parent of the Exceptional Child," *Education*, vol. 80, 1960, pp. 329–332.

Murray, M. A.: "Needs of Parents of Mentally Retarded Children," *American Journal of Mental Deficiency*, vol. 63, 1959, pp. 1078, 1088.

Peck, J. R. and Stephens, W. B.: "A Study of the Relationship between the Attitude and Behavior of Parents and that of their Mentally Defective Child," *American Journal of Mental Deficiency*, vol. 64, 1960, pp. 839–844.

Rankin, J. A.: "A Group Therapy Experiment with Mothers of Mentally Deficient Children," *American Journal of Mental Deficiency*, vol. 62, 1957, pp. 49–55.

Rheingold, H. L.: "Interpreting Mental Retardation to Parents," *Journal of Consulting Psychology*, vol. 9, 1945, pp. 142–148.

Roos, P.: "Psychological Counseling with Parents of Retarded Children," *Mental Retardation*, vol. 1, 1963, pp. 345–350.

Rose, J. A.: "Factors in the Development of Mentally Handicapped Children, Counseling Parents of Children with Mental Handicaps," *Proceedings of the 1958 Woods School Conference*, May 2–3, 1958.

Rosen, L.: "Selected Aspects in the Development of the Mother's Understanding of her Mentally Retarded Child," *American Journal of Mental Deficiency*, vol. 59, 1955, pp. 522–528.

Ross, A. O.: *The Exceptional Child in the Family: Helping Parents of Exceptional Children*, Grune and Stratton, Inc., New York, 1964.

Sarason, S. B.: "Individual Psychotherapy with Mentally Defective Individuals," *American Journal of Mental Deficiency*, vol. 56, 1952, pp. 803–805.

Scher, B.: "Help to Parents: An Integral Part of Service to the Retarded Child," *American Journal of Mental Deficiency*, vol. 60, 1955, pp. 169–175.

Sheimo, S. L.: "Problems in Helping Parents of Mentally Defective and Handicapped Children," *American Journal of Mental Deficiency*, vol. 56, 1951, pp. 42–47.

Stacey, C. L. and DeMartino, M. F. (eds.): *Counseling and Psychotherapy with the Mentally Retarded*, The Free Press of Glencoe, New York, 1957, pp. 615–851.

Sternlicht, M.: "Establishing an Initial Relationship in Group Psychotherapy with Delinquent Retarded Male Adolescents," *American Journal of Mental Deficiency*, vol. 69, 1964, pp. 39–41.

Thorne, R. C.: "Counseling and Psychotherapy with Mental Defectives," *American Journal of Mental Deficiency*, vol. 52, 1948, pp. 263–271.

Tizard, J. and Grad, J. C.: *The Mentally Handicapped and Their Families*, Oxford University Press, Inc., New York, 1961.

Watson, E. H.: "Counseling Parents of Mentally Deficient Children," *Pediatrics*, vol. 22, 1958, pp. 401–408.

Weingold, J. T.: "Parents Counseling Other Parents," *Children Limited,* vol. 12, 1963, p. 2.

———— and Hormuth, R. P.: "Group Guidance of Mentally Retarded Children," *Journal of Clinical Psychology,* vol. 9, 1953, pp. 118–124.

Wiest, G.: "Psychotherapy with the Mentally Retarded," *American Journal of Mental Deficiency,* vol. 59, 1955, pp. 640–644.

Yepsen, L.: "Counseling the Mentally Retarded," *American Journal of Mental Deficiency,* vol. 57, 1952, pp. 205–213.

Zwerling, I.: "The Initial Counseling of Parents with Mentally Retarded Children," *Journal of Pediatrics,* vol. 44, 1954, pp. 469–479.

chapter twelve

elements of organization
and administration

In each chapter, the need for efficiency in the special-education program has been stressed. In a general sense, this can be fostered by properly sequencing material, providing a flexible program designed to satisfy each student and allow the teacher to move quickly into areas of particular relevance to each student's educational profile, and systematically articulating with other segments of the community which are able to offer various services to the retarded. The matter of fitting each segment of instruction into the total special-education program, in a fashion not to be antagonistic to other sections of the program and at the same time totally consistent with the overall objectives, should be of daily concern to the teacher. Use should be made of the different in- and out-of-school resources available to the teacher.

Teaching effectiveness can be increased in each classroom

263

when the teacher considers certain elements of organization and management on a day-to-day basis. This chapter will discuss certain predominant issues which, although specific to each classroom, will determine the degree to which instruction will be efficient and effective.

CONSIDERATIONS WITHIN CLASSROOM UNITS

Daily lesson plans

Because the retarded learn slowly and show such small increments of growth in achievement, there is a natural tendency for teachers of these children to be less diligent in developing daily lesson plans than teachers of other children. Planning lessons each day is especially necessary for teachers of the retarded. The objectives and aims of a specific classroom program, as well as the total special-education sequence, will be difficult to effect properly and efficiently without the consistent planning and coordination among activities and experiences. Moreover, the inefficient learning of the retarded suggests that the teacher needs to structure the type of environment which will provide the most propitious situation for learning.

Each segment of the daily lesson plan should contain clear and explicitly stated objectives. These objectives should be of the short-term variety and well within the students' range of accomplishment by the end of each instructional unit. These intermediate objectives should be consistent with the objectives of other units employed during the same day. Further, they must be in harmony with the broader objectives of the week, month, and semester. Each activity and experience in the lesson plan must fit into the total program scheme and *be a part of* and *not apart from* what is occurring in other classrooms.

As the students proceed through the special program, the objectives associated with each daily lesson plan should eventually allow the children to achieve the broad special-program objectives. If one or more of the special-education teachers is unaware or unclear about the program goals and decides to develop class objectives which are incompatible with these larger program aims, the retarded students will find some difficulty in relating past experiences to present activities as well as developing adequate skills at the more advanced levels of instruction. Even in the daily lesson plan, therefore, the teacher must be cognizant of the need for integration between classroom programs.

The daily lesson plan in each subject area should encompass conceptual and task commonalities existing in other subject areas. It will be helpful for the students to learn how to relate concepts in one area to correlated factors in other subjects. Common threads existing among daily units should be explicitly pointed out to the students.

No characteristic is more important in the daily lesson plan than the logical sequencing of ideas and tasks. The presentation of material and the participation elements within each lesson unit should move from simple to more complex and from concrete activities to abstractions. The beginning of each lesson should first focus on general foundation concepts and gradually elaborate and build on this basic underpinning by presenting more specific facts related to the topic being considered. This notion has theoretical support and, if properly implemented, will exert substantial influence in making learning efficient and effective. The theoretical need for sequencing instruction was discussed in a general way in Chapter 2 and more specifically in Chapter 5 in which the idea was presented that perceptual-motor development is a necessary requirement for subsequent learning.

After stating specific objectives for the day, the teacher should introduce a sequence into each daily lesson plan by analyzing the components of the material to be presented and the tasks which will lead to the objectives being accomplished. Outlining the presentation will help the teacher identify and order the instructional segments. Such an outline will (1) explicitly identify the major components contained in the lesson and the strategies most appropriate for teaching the material, (2) provide a check on the logical sequential presentation of the components contained in the lesson, (3) help evaluate the degree to which the daily lessons meet the objectives for the day, week, or for longer periods of time, (4) reduce wandering and ad-lib behavior on the part of the teacher, (5) control emphasis being placed on irrelevant or less important material, and (6) provide a clear means for checking on the manner in which all the units of the entire program relate to each other.

The intent of outlining and sequencing a lesson plan is not to emphasize rigidity in methods of presentation or in the course of study. Rather, the purpose is to encourage the special-class teacher to focus on those procedures which will be most productive in teaching the children. Moreover, this technique will help to reduce random instructional behavior by the teacher as well as control the presentation of material of tangential value which only minimally or in no way focuses on the basic special-education objectives. The use of an outline, therefore, helps to keep the teacher on a relatively planned path, establishes certain goals for each day, and reduces the possibility of the teacher succumbing to a discussion of irrelevant concerns. At the same time a daily lesson plan is recommended, clinical sensitivity to important diagnostic clues suggestive of the need for some alteration of the modes of presentation or in content will be required of the teacher. Such latitude is necessary in order to pursue any specific areas which in the teacher's judgment are indicative of particular student weakness.

Principles of learning which were reviewed earlier should be incorporated into all aspects of the daily lesson plan. Using these principles will help the day's objectives to be met in an efficacious way. Since the instructional mode may need to be varied frequently, the teacher should make use of audio-visual aids whenever an instructional advantage is obvious.

Grouping

One of the most time-honored means for individualizing instruction has been to separate a class into smaller units which within themselves are relatively homogeneous in one or more characteristics. Level of achievement has been the criterion most often used for selecting groups. The children's performance is related to that of their fellow students in any of a number of possible subject areas. Because of the wide variation that typically exists within and between children, stability of the class groups between subject-matter areas rarely occurs. For example, a child might be located in the top group in arithmetic but in a much lower reading group. Other criteria are used only infrequently in determining groups; however, when used, chronological age and interest level are typically chosen.

From the perspective of clinical teaching, using achievement level as the sole criterion for grouping children is insufficient. It was suggested previously that two or more children achieving at the same level, having the same chronological age and intellectual ability, could be experiencing difficulty in a certain area, such as reading, for reasons which are completely different. To illustrate, a child could be underachieving in reading because of visualization difficulties; another child who achieves at the same level could be experiencing problems because of auditory difficulties. If the criterion of achievement alone is used for grouping these children, they would probably be placed in the same reading group. A more complete evaluation would lead to the conclusion that the most appropriate teaching strategy for each student to better learn how to read should in no way be similar. In fact, the evidence suggests that one child should have an auditory emphasis and the other student a visually oriented program.

Grouping for instruction requires that the teacher demonstrate clinical awareness of each child's pattern of strengths and weaknesses by frequently surveying the performance of students on important dimensions. Those schools without comprehensive psychological services must be satisfied with using informal estimates in place of the more preferred formal measures. In those systems with adequate school psychological services, a more precise identification of relevant instructional factors will provide greater assurance in identifying classroom groups.

Any scheme for grouping should consider the processes, or techniques, which children use to learn. Each of us tends to employ a preferred strategy for learning. The intellectually normal most often are equally adept in using various modes for learning, irrespective of the particular technique preferred by the teacher. Educable mentally retarded children are more inclined toward using nonverbal strategies and the visual channel for learning than a more verbal or auditory approach. As children develop these preferences and styles, the teacher should know of these patterns and group students accordingly. Placing an auditorially oriented child with a group of visually oriented students will result in a reduction in the level of performance of the child preferring the auditory approach as well as result in increased confusion for the entire group. In grouping, therefore, each child's profile and the manner of presentation which will work best for each youngster should be considered. Using this combination approach in grouping will realistically individualize instruction on those dimensions most crucial for effecting efficient learning. Imprecise criteria for grouping, such as achievement, could be more damaging than no grouping at all, should a child be placed with other students who are taught and learn best with an approach which is incompatible with his own style.

Instructional groups in classes for the retarded should not exceed two or three. Teaching will be less efficient when more than three groups are used in a subject area. Some heterogeneity will certainly exist within groups; however, this situation is preferred to the logical alternative of increasing the number of groups. The teacher must recognize that grouping should be very flexible in terms of the length of time each group is to be maintained. Intact groups should be used only until the intended purpose for establishing the groups is satisfied. Indeed, their makeup may change quite frequently according to the degree to which instruction with a particular group results in the remediation of weaknesses of the group members. A clear rationale should be developed for forming an instructional group; as these reasons are satisfied, the groups should be dissolved or altered accordingly.

There is an obvious instructional advantage in grouping children. This advantage will be lost if the criteria used for determining the group's constituents are viewed as unimportant or are vague. Grouping is employed so that children with similar problems can be exposed to the most appropriate method possible based on their unique characteristics and not solely on achievement.

Using psychological reports

The assessment of an educable mentally retarded child by a skilled school psychologist has the potential for being the single most significant determinant of the direction of a retarded child's educational program. This type of comprehensive analysis of the relevant educational and psychological attributes and weaknesses should form the basis for methods and curriculum. This type of assessment depends on (1) the training and experience of the school psychologist and his awareness of important diagnostic clues, (2) the ability of the school psychologist to translate diagnostic findings into practical educational considerations, (3) the time available to the psychologist for administering the necessary evaluative procedures appropriate to each situation, and (4) the opportunity the psychologist has to consistently reevaluate each special-class child at least every three years.

For a variety of reasons, this optimum situation is more the exception than the rule; school systems are often unable to hire or locate competent school psychologists who are also skilled educational diagnosticians. The alternative most frequently employed is for the schools to hire someone with limited experience to test large groups of children in order to satisfy state or local regulations concerning the placement of retarded children in special classes. All that is legally required in many locations is that the children be individually tested and if found to meet the stated criteria, placed in a special classroom.

This procedure illustrates the wide difference separating the phenomenon of testing from clinical assessment. *Testing* is the quantitative evaluation of any dimension; whereas *assessment* requires clinical insight and involves both qualitative and quantitative procedures. To be educationally meaningful to the classroom teacher, testing is not enough; assessment is also necessary. It is of little educational advantage for the classroom teacher to know only that students have scored at a certain IQ level on an intelligence test. This information, at best, provides only some general indication of the approximate rate at which the children will learn. It does not tell the teacher where to start a child in reading and arithmetic, nor does it provide a description of any idiosyncratic patterns which might be highly relevant and suggest possible tactics for facilitating learning. Faced with incomplete data on children, the special-education teacher must employ informal strategies for identifying the profiles of children in order to judge the direction a special program should take.

All evaluative procedures should lead to practical educational planning for the classrooms. The primary reason for assessment is to check on past procedures and to provide a rationale for informed reorientation of the program. The school psychologist is obligated to interpret and translate the results of the evaluations in a practical way for teachers. The instruments selected by the examiner should be wisely chosen and lead to data which are precise, parsimonious, and pertinent. The following psychological report on Charles Zap illustrates an assessment which has practical value for the classroom teacher.

PSYCHOLOGICAL REPORT ON CHARLES ZAP

NAME: Charles Zap   ELIGIBLE: Yes

AGE: 15-4   SCHOOL: Hart School

BIRTH DATE: 11-18-44   GRADE: Fifth

REASON FOR REFERRAL: Charles was referred for a psychological examination to determine his eligibility for placement in a special class for educable mentally handicapped. He came to this community from Reddington in January, spent a few weeks in the Burwell schools, a few weeks in the Salem schools, and was soon spotted by teachers as being retarded in learning ability. He is a passive, obedient, and cooperative boy. His teacher feels that he is industrious, that he uses initiative in trying to learn, and that he perseveres on a task. He gets along well with his schoolmates, but when necessary has recently learned to stand up for himself instead of calling for help.

HEALTH AND SCHOOL HISTORY: Charles's schooling was delayed because he was sickly as a baby. He had frequent colds, rheumatism, and a limp. He entered first grade at the age of eight. He repeated several grades, changed schools several times, and now at the age of fifteen is unable to do fifth-grade work. His mother feels that Charles was slower developing than most of her other children.

FAMILY BACKGROUND: Charles ("Buddy") is the middle of seven children. The three oldest children and the boy two years younger than Charles are still in Reddington with the oldest daughter who is married. Charles and the two youngest children (nine and eleven) live with the mother and her new husband in Salem. Charles has always been a "mama's boy" and preferred to come with his mother rather than stay in Reddington with the other, older children. The new father seems to be interested in the children. The mother says he is "crazy about them" and is home every night. The mother seems warm and friendly, though substantially limited in vocabulary. She does housework but is home every day after 2:30.

PRESENT TEST RESULTS:

3-15-60	Wechsler Intelligence Scale for Children	IQ 62
	Verbal Scale	IQ 67
	Performance Scale	IQ 64
	Wide Range Achievement Test	
	Reading Grade	1.7
	Spelling Grade	3.1
	Arithmetic Grade	5.0
	Gray Oral Paragraphs	Below 1.4

COMMENTS: Charles appears to be a stable, well-oriented boy who recognizes his inabilities but is not overly concerned by failure. He is easy going, works slowly, and in many instances was satisfied with incomplete responses. On one of the other puzzles he asked the examiner, "Can you put it together?" On the other hand he is quite cooperative and willing to put forth considerable effort if he understands the goal.

On the WISC he showed a wide range of abilities on the various subtests, scoring at a seven-year level on several tests (Similarities, Picture Arrangement, Block Design, and Object Assembly) but above two years on Comprehension, Arithmetic, and Picture Completion, doing particularly well on the latter.

Educationally, he shows marked discrepancies. In reading he is practically a non-reader, although he knows a few sight words and utilizes initial sounds a little bit in guessing at words. He needs to be taught a more adequate method of deciphering new words and in continuing to learn some sight words. He is presently working on the Dolch picture word cards. In arithmetic, Charles works very carefully, accurately, and scores at a beginning fifth-grade level in arithmetic computation.

SUMMARY AND CONCLUSIONS: Charles is a mentally handicapped boy of fifteen who seems to be emotionally stable, very cooperative, and willing to work. He is in need of some individual help in remedial reading. He is working well in the mechanics of arithmetic, at a high fourth- or low fifth-grade level.

RECOMMENDATIONS:

1 Charles is eligible for placement in a special class for educable mentally handicapped children.

2 He is in need of some consistent help in learning to read, and especially needs some help in understanding phonics as a means of learning to work out new words. This should be taught in a systematic, consistent manner.

3 Goals should be clearly defined and kept within his ability to achieve. He will gain considerable satisfaction from accomplishing well-defined goals.

4 Since Charles is approaching the age when he may want to hold some kind of a job, it would be well for him to have some understanding of the nature and requirements of certain types of work activities and some of the qualities which go into making a good worker. His industriousness and stable personality should make it possible for him to develop into a good worker.

Using other available services

Because of the many associated problems characteristic of the mentally retarded, the teacher will find it necessary to call on specialists from other fields for purposes of evaluation and consultation. The schools will not be able to provide the comprehensive array of special services required, and, therefore, arrangements should be made to use private and community services, in addition to those available within the school system.

Many of the retarded will require medical and paramedical services. The incidence of other types of handicaps is high among this group. Since many of their problems are of a medical nature, the classroom teacher should consult with each child's physician in order to be aware of and know how to handle all possible contingencies. The retarded children from deprived settings will often need to be referred to clinics for a variety of problems since their parents are most often unable to handle their medical needs.

Speech, social work, psychiatry, family counseling, and community mental health services may be needed by the retarded. As specialists on their educational problems, teachers should insist that all necessary ancillary services be provided for the retarded and their families. The school administration should be kept informed concerning the unique needs of each child. The teacher has the responsibility for making recommendations to the administration whenever appropriate.

Maintaining records

To establish continuity between classes, and to allow for day-to-day and week-by-week checks on each child's progress, special-education personnel must develop standard procedures for maintaining records. This will require specific delineation of the essential components of instruction in terms of the short- and long-term program objectives. This task should be given first order priority and developed around the instructional units in each subject area at every classroom level. For example, the scope of the program for the primary-level classes in reading should be identified and the specific components of the content to be covered during that period broken down and appropriately sequenced. This should be followed by the development of a checklist which will allow the teacher at every level to indicate the progress of students as each youngster proceeds through the sequentially ordered program. When the child moves to the intermediate level, the teacher at that level can immediately ascertain where the child is achieving, any areas of unusual strength or weakness to be considered during the course of instruction, any preferred method of instruction which has been especially successful in the past, and what has previously been taught the child.

Systematizing procedures for record keeping helps teachers to know where emphasis should be placed in teaching each child. Moreover, it gives a clear indication of the scope and sequence of instruction in each classroom and in terms of the total special program. As children move through various phases of the program, consistent and periodic checks should be made to determine their progress. This effort is of particular value because of the integration between levels it effects. Further, this effort is of diagnostic value because it provides a basis for supplementing and revising the program structure according to those data collected on the special-education students. Although anecdotal data are of value, the pressures of the classroom program do not give the teacher enough time to adequately sample and record the behavior of each child. Emphasis, therefore, should be placed on obtaining as much objective information as possible through the use of formal and informal procedures.

Grading procedures

Procedures for grading the retarded have been and still are of general concern to parents, children, teachers, and administrators. The major problem is whether the retarded children should be graded in the same manner as other children in the public schools. The retarded students and their parents are usually more inclined to favor a grading system similar to that employed in the regular classrooms. This position is taken because of their frequent association with the normal children. Other possible reasons for holding this belief are the parents' greater familiarity with standard grading procedures, their wish to make comparisons with other children in the same school program, and their frequent feeling that perhaps an error in placement has been made by the schools.

Employing the typical grading system is attractive to administrators because it reduces for them the possibility of being placed in a position of recommending that the retarded children receive the same type of diploma as the intellectually normal students. Teachers of the retarded often find themselves caught in a dissonant situation with the intense opinion of the parents, children, and school administration expressed on one hand and, on the other, the relative meaninglessness derived by grading the retarded students in the same way as the normal. Further complicating the picture is the decision that teachers must make as to whether a child should be graded in terms of progress made during a specific period of time or in comparison with other class members. The research is unclear on these matters, and, therefore, the schools must base their decision about grading on a logical and commonsense basis.

Because of the confusion surrounding the use of the traditional grading system with the retarded, and to allow for clear communication to their parents, writing letters to parents about their child's performance and progress has the best potential for making student evaluation most meaningful and effective. The content of these letters should summarize the teacher's observations as recorded on the daily or weekly checklists used for record keeping. This method will allow teachers to point out specifically those areas in which each child is weak and strong. Moreover, it will give some indication of the nature the educational program will take in subsequent periods.

The teacher will want to meet with parents frequently in order to get their personal observations of their child's progress. This information will aid in the formulation of the classroom program. The retarded youngsters should be informed of their own progress in school. The older children can be interviewed by the teacher, and, in some cases, the parents might be present. For the younger children, the content of letters to the parents can be summarized and reported to the youngsters by using "S" for satisfactory, "N" for needs improvement, and "U" for unsatisfactory.

Classroom experimentation

Advancement of knowledge within a profession is based in a large measure on the insights and observations of those directly involved in the work. For example, in repairing certain types of birth deformities, such as the cleft palate condition, plastic surgeons have contributed to an increase in scientific awareness of possible techniques for repairing this deformity to effect functional and cosmetic excellence. Although most surgeons are aware of these technical advancements, variation still exists in terms of the final excellence of repairs. Many professionals believe that technical knowledge must be combined with artistic sensitivity to effect an optimum performance in any area in which human change is involved. This analogy holds true in teaching the mentally retarded. Libraries are filled with reports of studies outlining the learning characteristics of the mentally retarded. Each of these studies has some bearing on teaching and learning; however, effective learning can occur only after the material has been translated and made available to the teacher for implementation in the classroom. The point is that the acceptance of a new technique will not necessarily occur because the value of the technique has been demonstrated.

By virtue of having to deal with the practical problems of instructing mentally retarded children, the teacher is in an excellent position to test, through informal experimentation, any techniques or procedures which seem to have potential merit. Many of the best leads for tightly controlled investigations emanate from the experiences of classroom teachers. The special educator's laboratory is the classroom, and, although the academicians have an important contribution to make in research, the awareness of classroom practicalities by teachers is of great value. Schools should encourage special-education teachers to conduct small pilot studies. For example, teachers could offer great service to the field by experimenting with and evaluating new instructional techniques and media. As teachers become familiar with the capabilities of their children and the scope of the material to be covered, they will feel more free to develop and evaluate innovative practices.

CONSIDERATIONS BETWEEN CLASSROOM UNITS

The need for clear organization between each classroom unit and levels of instruction within the total special-education program has been emphasized earlier. An outstanding teacher at any one level of the program will exert only minimal long-term influence on students if the program lacks integration and articulation among other units. Implicit in this notion is the need for schools to develop classroom units from preschool through the postschool level. To begin a special program for retarded children at the junior- or senior-high-school level, without the earlier grades wherein students have the opportunity to proceed through a sequential program, will generally be unsuccessful. Even under the most desirable conditions, this type of school program will result in a "crash program" and, at best, will help the retarded to meet and solve problems within society in only a rote and not in a conceptual manner. This structure is antagonistic to the basic theme and philosophy of effective program development for the retarded in the schools. Students should be given opportunities to conceptually develop all the basic skills required for independent living. This goal will be met only after coordination and collaboration have occurred among all levels of the school program.

Special classes or special schools

School systems must decide whether to locate the retarded in special classes or special schools. Educators must weigh the advantages and disadvantages of each of these administrative plans before deciding on this question. Special schools have the obvious advantage of providing centralization of all ancillary services needed by the retarded. Specialists such as speech therapists, public health nurses, psychiatric social workers, and school psychologists can be located within the special school and supply all the services required by students in that school. In addition, coordination among the classroom units at the various levels is easier to effect when the staff is centralized. Communication will be facilitated by this propinquity. Although these advantages are noteworthy, there are certain disadvantages in locating children in special schools. One substantial problem of the special-school plan is the transportation of children to the school from great distances. Moreover, special schools are typically not designed exclusively for the educable mentally retarded but usually contain other types of handicapped children with various degrees of involvement.

To place the retarded in special classes within a regular school rules out centralizing all the ancillary services necessary for these children. The difficulty in integrating various units of the program is increased. Transportation problems are reduced because many of the retarded youngsters would be located in special classes in a school within their own community. The greatest advantage of the special-class plan is that the educable child has an opportunity to associate with intellectually normal children. If they are to learn how to live effectively within the community, the retarded should have many opportunities to be integrated with the normal. When the retarded are placed in a special school with only other handicapped children, their situation is so atypical that realistic experiences leading to the development of self-sufficiency cannot be provided. The decision concerning placement is a difficult one; however, it should be kept in mind that integration between special-education units and the provision of ancillary services can be effected easier than the alternatives of attempting to find opportunities for the retarded in special schools to be integrated with their normal peers. In all fairness, however, it should be pointed out that there is little or no conclusive research evidence to support the advantage of using any single administrative plan over other alternatives.

Itinerant services

Rural communities have a particular need to provide the expertise of itinerant specialists to those teachers of the retarded who lack formal preparation and experience. A large urban center has specialists of this type readily available and, in addition, often has consultants in specific subject areas such as in reading, arithmetic, counseling, and technical and vocational education. Rural communities are typically not so fortunate. The use of mobile units offers the most reasonable approach for providing such services to teachers in rural schools. This technique has proved successful in several sections of the country in which special diagnostic and remedial services are needed by children who have unique learning problems.

Each mobile unit would have a certain present schedule for traveling to various sections of a county or state. All equipment and personnel required for offering these services would travel with the unit and provide comprehensive diagnostic and remedial consulting services to the appropriate school personnel. The coordination of this effort should emanate from the state or county department of public instruction and have the cooperation and collaboration of other state and county agencies. Plenty of time must be provided at each stop to answer questions of teachers, administrators, and parents concerning the children who have been examined by members of the unit. Systematic records should be kept by the unit secretary and specific recommendations reported back to principals of schools in those areas visited by the unit. Periodic reevaluation of each child should be required in order for the system to operate effectively.

In-service training

The rapid advancement of research and training with the retarded has not made it possible for teachers to keep up with innovations and trends in this field. The time devoted to the day-to-day planning and activities within the special class does not leave the teacher with much time for engaging in professional affairs such as attending professional meetings, reading professional journals, or registering for extension courses at a local university or college. To remedy this situation, school systems must provide special-education teachers with a chance to become familiar with new practices and procedures which may be of value in teaching retarded youngsters. In-service training programs and workshops provide an excellent opportunity for new ideas to be discussed and tested. Teachers will benefit most from those in-service programs which are devoted to a translation and synthesis of results from those studies in psychology and education which have direct implications for education of the retarded. To implement this procedure, school systems should give some thought to including educational psychologists on their staffs. This specialist would have the responsibility for interpreting research for teachers and translating findings into practical classroom application. Academicians have not provided this necessary service to schools. The lag that exists between evidence and practice in programs for the re-tarded makes all the more imperative the need for including this type of professional person on the school staff.

Coordination among the various levels of instruction for the retarded can be facilitated by regularly scheduled in-service meetings. During these sessions, teachers should have an opportunity to realistically coordinate their efforts. Although these meetings are valuable, more time should be made available for teachers to meet on an extended basis to consider program revision, program emphasis, and other matters related to the coordination and sequencing of instruction. Many teachers feel that a week-long workshop, either at the end of the school year or at the beginning of the subsequent school year, provides an excellent opportunity to study such matters. Workshops are valuable, although they require intensive planning so that time is not wasted during the sessions.

index

index

Ability level, of association, 68–69, 73, 110–111
  diagnosing, 37–41
  language, 110–111
  mental age and, 37–38
  number, 16
  performance and, 33–34
  productive-thinking, 47
  reasoning, 16
  receptive, 85–86, 110
  spatial, 16
  verbal, 16
  word fluency, 16
Academy of Science (France), 8
Accuracy, stressing, 59
Achievement, 38–40
  indicator of, 38
  school grade analysis, 39–40
Addition of numbers, computational errors in, 173–174
  identifying weaknesses in, 172–173
  informal testing for, 169
  simple, 184–186
  use of zero in, 185–186
Adult education, 242, 247–259
  for mentally retarded, 247–253
    counseling, 251–253
    occupational adjustment follow-up, 250–251
    postschool program, 248–253
  for parents, 247–248, 253–259
    environmentally deprived, 257–259
    from normal environments, 254–257
Anderson, P. S., 123, 157
Arithmetic program, 163–196
  assessing readiness, 166–171
  basic objectives of, 164–165

Arithmetic program, borrowing and carrying numbers, 187–191
  diagnosis of deficits, 171–174
  establishing level, 167–171
  estimating potential, 166
  evaluating skills, 165–166
  number concepts, associating with numerals, 182–183
    classification, 176–177
    conservation, 179–180
    correspondence, 177–179
    ordering, 180–181
    reversibility, 179–180
  teaching procedures, 174–196
    addition, 184–186
    division, 191–194
    fractions, 194–195
    place value, 187–191
    measurement, 195–196
    multiplication, 191–194
    subtraction, 186–187
  tests, achievement, 167–171
    identifying weaknesses, 172–173
    readiness, 166
Arizona Articulation Proficiency Scale, The, 100
Arthur Point Scale of Performance Tests, 81
Association ability, instruction guidelines, 68–69, 88–89
  language, 110–111
  receptive capabilities and, 73
Attention, factors increasing or decreasing, 67–68
  lack of, 55
  for reading readiness, 135
Auditory discrimination, 93–94
  in reading, 148–153
  readiness, 134

Auditory discrimination, sequence for teaching, 149–153

Babbling sounds, 97, 98
Bangs, J. E., 99
Banta, T. J., 45
Barnett, C., 42
Bateman, B. D., 109
Baumeister, A., 42, 46
Beedle, R., 46
Behavior, from frustration, 208
    social awareness and, 209–211
Behavior modification, 211–224
    defined, 211
Bender-Gestalt Test, 81
Bennett, E. L., 21
Benoit, E. P., 26
Bensberg, G. J., 46, 164
Benton, A. L., 79
Bereiter, C., 164, 175
Betts, E. A., 137, 149
Binet, Alfred, 15–16
Binet Scale, 15–16
Birch, J. W., 93
Blackhurst, A. E., 215
Blake, K., 42
Bond, G. L., 141
Boredom, 58
Boston University Speech Sound Discrimination Picture Test, 100
Brace Scale of Motor Ability, 82
Brueckner Diagnostic Arithmetic Tests, 172
Bryant, P. E., 46
Burns, P. C., 164

California Arithmetic Tests, 167
California Reading Tests, 136
California Test of Mental Maturity, 131
Cantor, G. N., 44, 46
Capobianco, R. J., 164

Cardinal numbers, concept of, 183
Cartwright, G. P., 124–125
Christensen, P. R., 16
Churchill, E. M., 175
Clark Picture Inventory Test, 100
Clarke, A. D. B., 164
Clarke, A. M., 164
Classification of numbers, 176–177
Classroom counseling, 220–223
Cleland, E. J., 141–142
Coghill, G. E., 17
Cognitive development, 14–30
    dimensions of intelligence, 14–17
        early approaches to, 15–16
        structure of, 16–17
    environment and, 17–23
        manipulation, 21–23
        genetic interaction, 17–20
    Hebb's theory, 23–28
        implications of, 27–28
        intelligence defined, 25–26
        mental retardation, 28
        perception of events, 23–25
Communication development, 92–125
    language, 108–121
        activities for, 120–121
        assessing difficulties, 112–114
        association, 110–111
        automatic-sequential aspects of, 111–112
        expressive components of, 111
        procedures for, 114–121
        retarded characteristics, 109–112
        tests, 112–114
    speech, 93–108
        assessment of difficulties, 100–103
        auditory discrimination, 93–94

Communication development,
    speech, correcting
        difficulties, 103–108
    defective sounds and, 107
    ear training, 106–107
    effective models for, 94–95
    environment and, 95–96, 103
    exercising of articulators,
        106
    feedback system, 94
    mechanisms responsible for,
        95–96
    monitoring system, 94
    retarded characteristics, 96–
        100
    stabilizing new sounds, 107–
        108
    stages of, 96
    techniques for improving,
        104–108
    written word, 121–125
        expression, 124–125
        handwriting skill, 121–123
        spelling, 123–124
Comprehension, reading, 159
Conservation of numbers, 179–
    180
Coordinated Scale of Attainments
    in Arithmetic, 167
Correspondence of number con-
    cepts, 177–179
Costello, H. M., 164
Counseling, postschool program,
    251–253
    for social development, 220–
        223
Cruickshank, W. M., 163
Cuisenaire rods, 177, 179, 181,
    183
Cureton, T. K., 201
Cureton Physical Fitness Test, 82

Denny, M. R., 79–80
Deno, Dina A., 143
Deoxyribonucleic acid (DNA), 20

Descoeudres, Alice, 9
Developmental Reading Tests, 136
Diagnostic Arithmetic Tests, 172
Diagnostic Chart for Fundamental
    Processes in Arithmetic, 173
Diagnostic Tests in Arithmetic
    Fundamentals, 173
Diagnostic Tests and Self-Helps in
    Arithmetic, 173
Diamond, M. C., 21
Dickerson, D. J., 44
Differential Language Facility
    Test, 113
Discrimination, auditory, 93–94,
    134, 148–153
    in learning process, 43–44, 55
        instruction guidelines, 64–65
    letter, 143–148
    visual, 134, 143
Distance, measuring of, 196
Division of numbers, 191–194
    computational errors in, 173–
        174
    identifying weaknesses, 172–
        173
    informal testing for, 170
    long-division approach, 193–
        194
Dobzhansky, T., 17
Doll, Eugene E., 8
Doren Diagnostic Reading Tests
    of Word Recognition Skills,
    140
Duncan, John, 9
Dunn, L. M., 164
Dye, H. B., 22

Easy Steps in Arithmetic Test,
    173
Echolalia, 98
Edmiston Motor Capacity Test,
    82
Education, of mentally retarded,
    1–12
    adult, 247–253

Education, of mentally retarded,
    contemporary trends, 9–10
  educators and, 7–10
  extent of professional in-
    volvement, 2–4
  first attempts at, 7–8
  parents of, 247–248, 253–
    259
  research efforts, 4–7
  teacher preparation, 11–12
  Montessori method, 9
  program planning, in areas of
    weakness, 61–70
  instruction guidelines, 54–
    61
  objectives, 52–54
  primary methodological con-
    cerns, 50–70
  scope and sequence, 51–52
Educational Policies Commission,
    52
Ellis, N. R., 42, 44–46
Embedded Figures Test, 81
Emotional development, 203–209
  factors relevant to, 204
  teaching methods, 211–224
Employment, 215, 226–246
  pragmatic considerations, 226–
    230
  preparation for, 225–245
  work-study program, 230–246
Engelmann, S., 164, 175
Environment, adult education pro-
    gram and, 254–259
  cognitive development and, 17–
    23
  manipulation, 21–23
  speech disturbances from, 95–
    96, 103
Essential Arithmetic Tests, 173
Exercises, 57
  physical fitness, 201
  reading, 141
Expression of ideas, 69–70, 74
  language, 108–121
  motor, 118

Expression of ideas, vocal, 74, 118

Faculty theory of intelligence, 15
Family planning, 252
Feedback system, 57, 74
  speech development, 94
First words, child's, 97–98
Forgus, Ronald H., 71
Fouracre, M. H., 164
Fractions (number), 194–195
  emphasis in, 195
Frey, R. M., 236, 237, 243
Frustration, behavior resulting
    from, 208
  reducing, 209

Gallagher, J. J., 33, 71
Gates Basic Reading Tests, 136
Gates-McKippop Reading Diagnos-
    tic Tests, 139
Gates Primary Reading Tests, 136
Genetics, environment and, 17–20
Gibson, E. J., 143
Gilbert, Thomas R., 59
Girardeau, F. L., 44
Glovsky, L., 94
Goda, S., 94
Goddard, H. H., 17–18
Goertzen, S. M., 99, 109
Goldstein, H., 45, 200
Gottesman, I., 17
Grading system, 272–273
  as analysis of achievement, 39–
    40
Gray Oral Reading Tests, 139
Gregg, A. E., 200
Group instruction, 266–267
Group Intelligence Tests, 131
Guilford, J. P., 47
  structure of intellect model,
    16–17

Handbook of Speech Pathology
    (ed. Travis), 102

Handwriting, capital letters, 123
  competitive situations in, 122
  developing, 121–123
Harrington, M., 200
Harrison, S., 109
Headrick, M., 42
Hebb, D. O., 20, 78–79, 177
  theory of mental development,
    23–28
    implications of, 27–28
    intelligence defined, 25–26
    mental retardation, 28
    overlearning on, 59
    perception of events, 23–25
    perceptual-motor, 76–79
    on retention characteristics,
      42
Hebb-Williams Intelligence Test,
  20
Heber, Rick, 200, 203
Hegge, T., 60
Heinemann, S. H., 59
Hermelin, O., 41
Hetherington, E. M., 45
Hicks, L., 143
Himelstein, P., 8
Hood, H. B., 175
Hottel, J. V., 44
House, B., 42, 44
Hunt, J. McV., 78
Hunton, V., 143

Illinois Test of Psycholinguistic
  Abilities, 40, 109, 111, 112,
  133 ,166
Incidental learning, 45
  instruction guidelines, 65–66
Individual differences, assessing,
  32–47
  diagnosing strengths and weak-
    nesses, 37–41
  inter-individual variability, 34–
    36
  intra-individual variability, 36–
    37

Individual differences, learning
  characteristics, 41–47
  movement toward emphasizing
    in, 15
  rationale for concern about, 33–
    34
Inhibition, reducing of, 59–60
Initial learning, instruction guidelines, 66–67
  practice and, 66
Inskeep, Annie L., 9
Instruction, arithmetic, 163–196
  assessing readiness, 166–
    171
  basic objectives, 164–165
  borrowing and carrying num-
    bers, 187–191
  diagnosis of deficits, 171–
    174
  establishing level for, 167–
    171
  estimating potential for, 166
  evaluating skills, 165–166
  procedures, 174–196
  tests, 166–173
guidelines, in areas of weak-
    ness, 61–70
  developing perceptual-motor
    skills, 84–90
reading, 128–160
  approaches to, 153–154
  auditory discrimination, 148–
    160
  basic objectives of, 130
  comprehension, 159–160
  diagnosing deficits, 138–142
  evaluating skills, 130–142
  letter discrimination, 143–
    148
  sight vocabulary, 152–153
  stages in, 154–157
  word analysis, 156–159
  word-attack skills, 152–153
(See also Communication development; program planning)

Intelligence, assessing tests for, 28–30
  dimensions of, 14–17
  environment and, 17–23
    manipulation, 21–23
  genetic interaction, 17–20
  Hebb's theory of, 23–28
  tests, assessing, 28–30
    determining deviation, 34–36
    limitations, 28–29
    the mean, 34
Inter-individual variability, 34–36
Internal monitoring system, 74
Intra-individual variability, 36–37
Iowa Silent Reading Tests, 136
Iscoe, I., 44
Itard, Jean-Marc-Gaspard, 7–8, 85

Jensen, A., 42
Johnson, G. O., 42, 175, 215
Johnson, M. S., 137

Kallikak, Martin, 17–18
Karlin, I. W., 99
Karp, Etta E., 149
Kass, C., 45
Kephart, N. C., 75–76, 83, 84, 89–90
Kettner, N. W., 16
Kirk, S. A., 22, 32, 40, 52, 60, 99, 157, 175, 215
Kirk, W., 60
Kodman, F., 93
Kolstoe, O. P., 236, 237, 243
Krasner, L., 211
Krech, D., 21
Kress, R. A., 137
Kvaraceus, W. C., 200

Language development, 108–121
  activities for, 120–121
  assessing difficulties, 112–114
  association, 110–111

Language development, automa-tic-sequential aspects of, 111–112
  expressive components of, 111
  procedures for, 114–121
  retarded characteristics, 109–112
  tests, 112–114
Learning process, 41–47
  in areas of weakness, 61–70
  assessment of, 80–84
  association ability, 68–69
  attention spans, 67–68
  discrimination, 43–44, 55, 64–65
  emphasizing success in, 56–57
  exercises, 57
  expression of ideas, 69–70
  Hebbian relationships, 76–79
  hypothesized hierarchy for, 76–77
  impeding, 57
  incidental, 45, 65–66
  initial, 66–67
  instruction guidelines, 54–70, 84–90
    association ability, 68–69
    developing perceptual motor skills, 84–90
    expression of ideas, 69–70
  long-term retention, 41–43
  minimizing change, 60
  motivation, 55–56
  overlearning, 58–59
  perceptual-motor development, 71–90
    association, 88–89
    receptive ability, 85–88
    in responding, 89–90
  practice periods, 57–58, 66
  primary methodological con-cerns, 50–70
  productive thinking, 47
  rationale for emphasizing, 74–76
  reaction time, 45–46

Leaning process, readiness, 54–55
  reducing inhibition, 59–60
  research disagreements in, 79–80
  sequence of, 72–74
  short-term retention, 41–43
  stressing accuracy, 59
  transfer, 46
  using child's strengths, 60–61
Learning set, 44–45
  defined, 44
  notions of transfer and, 46
Lee-Clark Fundamentals Survey Tests, 167
Lee-Clark Reading Readiness Test, 133, 166
Lehtinen, L. E., 122
Letter discrimination, 143–148
Lincoln-Oseretsky Motor Development Scale, 82
Lipman, R. S., 79, 80
Long-term memory retention, 41–43
  instruction guidelines, 63–64
Lorge-Thorndike Intelligence Test, 131
Los Angeles Diagnostic Tests, 172
Lovell, K., 175
Lucito, L., 33

McCarthy, J. J., 40, 109, 110
McCullough Word Analysis Tests, 140
McGee, R. K., 143
McKay, E., 46
McMenemy, R. A., 157, 160
Malpass, L. F., 79
Mandler, G., 59
Mannix, J. B., 175
Marianne Frostig Developmental Test of Visual Perception, 81
Matthews, J., 93, 99
Measurement (mathematical), 195–196

Meier, G. W., 143
Memory retention, 16, 41–43
  instruction guidelines, 61–64
Mental age, calculating, 37–38
Mental health development, 203–209
  factors relevant to, 204
Mentally retarded, adult education for, 247–253
  barriers of, 207–208
  development of, areas of communication, 92–125
    arithmetic program, 163–196
    cognitive, 14–30
    perceptual-motor, 71–90
    personal skill, 199–224
    primary methodological concerns in, 50–70
    reading program, 128–160
    social skill, 199–224
  education of, 1–12
    adult, 247–253
    contemporary trends, 9–10
    educators and, 7–10
    extent of professional involvement, 2–4
    first attempts at, 7–8
    parents of, 247–248, 253–259
    research efforts, 4–7
    teacher preparation, 11–12
  employment preparation, 225–245
  goals of, 205–207
  Hebbian explanation for, 26–28
  needs of, 205–207
  research, 4–7
  role of Federal government in, 1–2
Merrill-Palmer Scale of Mental Tests, 81
Metropolitan Achievement Test, 38, 136, 167
Minimal-change principle, 60
Money, measuring, 195

Monitoring system, 57
  speech development, 94
Montessori, Maria, 8, 9, 85
Montessori schools, 9
Moore Eye-Hand Coordination and
    Color-Matching Test, 81
Mueller, M. W., 109
Multiplication of numbers, 191–
    194
  computational errors in, 173–
    174
  identifying weaknesses, 172–
    173
  informal testing for, 169–170
  two-place, 192
Myklebust, H. R., 109

National Association for Retarded
    Children, 247
National Plan to Combat Mental
    Retardation, 2
Newland, T. E., 28
Number concepts, 175–183
  ability, 16
  associating with numerals,
    182–183
  classification, 176–177
  conservation, 179–180
  correspondence of, 177–179
  of ordering, 180–181
  reversibility, 179–180
Nutrition, control of, 202
  physical fitness and, 259

O'Connor, N., 41
Orlando, R., 44
Orton, K. D., 46
Osgood, C. E., 112
Otis Quick-Scoring Mental Ability
    Test, 131
Otto, W., 157, 160
Overlearning, 58–59
  defined, 58

Parson's Language Sample Test,
    113
Peabody Picture Vocabulary Test,
    113, 131
Peins, M., 109
Perceptual Forms Test, 81
Perceptual-motor development,
    71–90, 201
  assessment of, 80–84
  disagreements in, 79–80
  Hebbian relationships, 76–79
  hypothesized hierarchy for, 76–
    77
  rationale for emphasizing, 74–
    76
  research disagreements in, 79–
    80
  sequence of, 72–74
  teaching guidelines, 84–90
    association, 88–89
    receptive ability, 85–88
    in responding, 89–90
Personal attractiveness, 201–203,
    234
Personal skill development, 199–
    224, 228
  emotional growth, 203–209
  mental health, 203–209
  personal attractiveness, 201–
    203
  physical health, 201–203
  social awareness, 203–211
  teaching methods, 211–224
    classroom counseling, 220–
    223
    miscellaneous, 223–224
    sociodrama, 214–220
Phenotype, defined, 17
Phenylketonuria, 19
Physical fitness, exercises, 201
  nutritional considerations, 202,
    259
Physical health, 201–203
Piaget, J., 78–79, 143, 164, 172,
    175–177
Pick, H. C., 143

Pick, H. L., 143
Place value of numbers, 187–191
  use of zero in, 188
Porteus Maze Test, 81
Postman, L., 59
Poucher, G. E., 200
Practice periods, 57–58
  initial learning and, 66
President's Panel on Mental Retardation, 1–2
Pre-Tests of Vision, Hearing, and Motor Coordination, 81
Proactive inhibition, 59–60
Productive-thinking programs, 47
Program planning, administration of, 263–277
  available services, 271
  classroom experimentation, 273–274
  daily lesson, 264–269
  grading system, 272–273
  group instruction, 266–267
  psychological reports, 268–271
  record keeping, 271–272
  adult education, 247–259
    for mentally retarded, 247–253
    parents, 247–248, 253–259
  in areas of weakness, 61–70
  instruction guidelines, 54–61
  objectives, 52–54
    checklist, 53
  organization, 263–277
    between classroom units, 274–277
    within classroom units, 264–274
    in-service training, 276–277
    itinerant services, 275–276
    special class or special school, 275
  primary methodological concerns, 50–70
  scope and sequence, 51–52
Progressive Matrices Test, 81

Pryer, M., 42
Psychological reports, 268–271
Punishment, 212
Purdue Perceptual-Motor Survey, The (Roach and Kephart), 133, 166
  dimensions evaluated by, 83–84

Radler, D. H., 89–90
Rail-Walking Test, 82
Rainy, D., 46
Reaction time, 45–46
Reading program, activity disinterest and, 55–56
  approaches to, 153–154
  assessing levels of readiness, 132–133
  auditory discrimination, 148–153
  basic objectives of, 130
  comprehension, 159–160
  diagnosing deficits, 138–142
  estimating potential, 131–132
  evaluating skills, 130–142
  exercises, 141
  instruction, 128–160
    establishing level for, 133–138
  letter discrimination, 143–148
  sight vocabulary, 152–153
  stages in, 154–157
  tests, 131–133
    achievement, 136
    diagnostic, 139–140
  visual discrimination in, 143
  word analysis, 156–159
  word-attack skills, 152–153
Readings on the Exceptional Child (eds. Trapp and Himelstein), 8
Reasoning ability, 16
Receptive ability, 85–86, 110
Record keeping, 271–272
Reflexive sounds, infant's, 97

Retroactive inhibition, 59–60
Reversibility of numbers, 179–180
Ribonucleic acid (RNA), 20
Rigrodsky, S., 94
Roach, E. G., 84
Rohwer, W., 42
Role playing (see Sociodrama)
Rose, J., 42
Rosenzweig, M. R., 21
Roswell-Chall Diagnostic Reading
   Test of Work Analysis Skills,
   140
Rouse, S. T., 47
Rudel, R. G., 44
Russell, David H., 149
Russell, Elizabeth F., 149

Schlanger, B. B., 94
Scholastic Reading Readiness
   Test, 133
Séguin, Édouard, 8–9, 85
Shirley, Mary M., 17
Short-term memory retention, 41–
   43
   instruction guidelines, 61–63
Sight vocabulary, 152–153
Silent Reading Diagnostic Tests,
   140
Skeels, H. M., 22
Skinner, B. F., 112
Skodak, M., 22
Sloan, W., 44, 46
Smith, J. O., 109
Smith, Nila Banton, 149
Smith, T., 42, 46
Social skills development, 199–
   224, 228
   counseling for, 220–223
   emotional growth, 203–209
   mental health, 203–209
   personal attractiveness, 201–
      203
   physical health, 201–203
   social awareness, 203–211
      specific focus in, 210–211

Social skills development, teach-
      ing methods, 211–224
   classroom counseling, 220–
      223
   miscellaneous, 223–224
Sociodrama, 214–220, 228, 235
   beginning, 216–217
   delineating the roles, 215–216
   diagnostic value, 217–218
   identifying the problem, 215–
      216
   postdramatization discussion,
      217
   process of, 215
   with the retarded, 218–220
Spache, G. D., 157
Spache Diagnostic Reading
   Scales, 139
Spatial ability, 16
Spearman, C., 15
Speech Articulation Test for Young
   Children, 100
Speech correctionists, 103–104
Speech development, 93–108
   assessment of difficulties, 100–
      103
   auditory discrimination, 93–94
   defective sounds and, 107
   difficulties, 100–108
      correcting, 103–108
   ear training, 106–107
   effective models for, 94–95
   environment and, 95–96, 103
   exercising of articulators, 106
   feedback system, 94
   mechanisms responsible for,
      95–96
   monitoring system, 94
   retarded characteristics, 96–
      100
   stabilizing new sounds, 107–
      108
   stages of, 96
   techniques for improving, 104–
      108
Speech Diagnostic Chart Test, 100

Spelling, approach to reading, 153
  developing skills in, 123–
    124
Spiral Aftereffect Test, 81
Spivack, G., 79
Spontaneous flexibility, 16
Spradlin, J. E., 44, 99, 109
Standard Reading Test, The, 133
Stanford Achievement Test, 38,
    136, 167
Stanford-Binet Intelligence Scale,
    15, 16, 131
  assessing, 30
  deaf children and, 35
  mean intelligence quotient for,
    34
Stephens, W. B., 172
Stevenson, H. W., 44, 45
Strang, R., 141, 142
Strauss, A. A., 122, 164
Strauss Syndrome, 110, 111
Strazzula, M., 99
Structure of Intellect Model, 16–
    17
Subtraction of numbers, computa-
    tional errors in, 173–174
  identifying weaknesses, 172–
    173
  informal testing for, 169
  simple, 186–187
  use of zero in, 186
Swartz, J. D., 45

Teachers, hostility toward, 204
  preparation of, 11–12
Templin-Darley Screening and Di-
    agnostic Tests of Articula-
    tion, 100
Tension, 207–209
  reducing, 209
  releasing, 204–205
Terman, Lewis Madison, 15
Tests, arithmetic, 166, 169–170,
    172–173
  intelligence, 28–30, 34–36

Tests, language development,
    112–114
  reading, 131–133, 136, 139–
    140
  speech difficulty, 100
  (See also specific tests)
Thurstone, L. L., 15–16
Tight, T. J., 143
Time, measuring of, 195–196
Tinker, M. A., 141
Tisdall, W. J., 47
Trainor, Robin, 148
Transfer, learning sets and, 46
Trapp, E. P., 8
Travis, Lee Edward, 102

Ullmann, L. P., 211
University of Illinois Physical Fit-
    ness Research Center, 201
Unusual Uses Test, 16

Van Riper, C., 96, 100, 103
Verbal ability, 16
Victor (wild boy of Averyon), 7, 8
Visual discrimination in reading,
    134, 143
Volume, measurement of, 196
Vrguhart, D., 46

Walk, R. D., 143
Wallin, J. E. W., 200
Watson Reading-Readiness Test,
    133
Wechsler Intelligence Scale for
    Children (WISC), 16, 33, 131
  assessing, 30
  mean intelligence quotient for,
    34
Weidner-Fensch Speech Screen-
    ing Test, 100
Weight, measurement of, 196
Wellman, B. L., 22
Wepman, Joseph, 148, 152

Werner, H., 164
Wetherell, J., 109
Wide Range Achievement Test, 38, 136, 167
Wiseman, D. E., 114
Woodward, M., 164
Word fluency ability, 16
Work-study program, 229, 230–246
  basis for successful, 230–233
  coordinating, 244–245
  evaluation of progress, 242–244
  occupational placement factors, 235–236
  personal factors, 234–235

Work-study program, preliminary classroom experiences, 233
  relationship between study and work, 236–242
  teaching considerations, 233–246
Written communication development, 121–125
  expression, 124–125
  handwriting skill, 121–123
  spelling, 123–124

Zaporozhets, A. V., 143
Zeaman, D., 42, 44